£2 -50

Masters of Cricket

MASTERS OF CRICKET

FROM TRUMPER TO MAY

JACK FINGLETON

Introduction by David Frith

THE PAVILION LIBRARY

First published in Great Britain in 1958

Copyright © The Estate of Jack Fingleton 1958/1990
Introduction copyright © David Frith 1990

First published in the Pavilion Library in 1990 by
PAVILION BOOKS LIMITED
196 Shaftesbury Avenue
London WC2H 8JL

Series Editor: Steve Dobell

A CIP catalogue record for this book
is available from the British Library

ISBN 1 85145 496 9 Hbk
ISBN 1 85145 457 8 Pbk

Printed and bound in Great Britain by
Biddles Limited, Guildford

INTRODUCTION

I miss Jack Fingleton. We were mates as only two fellows who'd had a squabble could be. He was already my favourite cricket-writer (sharing with Cardus, at least) when I first tagged on to his coat-tails during the 1968 Australian tour of England. He tolerated a ceaseless string of questions about Test matches and Sheffield Shield matches and identities of long ago, giving detailed and patient answers, soaked richly in opinion and vibrant with authority. He exuded the toughness and resilience necessary in all Test opening batsmen – particularly when ill-health afflicted him in the early 1970s – as well as the sensitivity essential in writers of touch. That sensitivity, displayed in his fine recall and his word-power, was sometimes transformed into tetchiness. It was as if the ex-cricketer needed, purely for stimulation, someone to come at him, fast-bowler fashion, all the time, so that he could duck or hook or even take a masochistic blow on the shoulder. It often seemed that every conversation was high debate. At his best he scored verbal hundreds at will. At other times he turned innocent comment into suspected innuendo.

I fell foul of him in writing of his role in Harold Larwood's emigration to Australia. Jack felt that the word 'mischievous' put him professionally in a bad light. It was as if I'd bowled a sustained barrage of bouncers at him, and he'd decided not to speak to me between overs – or ever again for that matter. He used another as an intermediary in airing his grievance and demanding reparation. Through that third person I managed to establish that I had meant no harm and that he had surely deliberately misinterpreted my meaning. After several volleys of letters, some of which made publication, the matter was laid to rest . . . and he hardly spoke to me on the next Australian tour.

But, thank goodness, the thaw came, and before his marvellous life came to an end in 1981 he had even agreed to write for me – a summary of the 1980 Centenary Test match for *Wisden Cricket Monthly* and a piece for the Lord's Taverners' souvenir dinner programme. As ever, each and every line was worth reading. He was weakened by illness, but the fire still glowed – dare one say it? – mischievously.

Our reconciliation came about in a strange way. Standing as umpire in an England v Australia Press game at Harrogate (which was also graced by Kerry Packer's presence as a player) in 1977, Jack decided to tease Ian Chappell, a man of not dissimilar nature. Fingo no-balled 'Chappelli', called 'wide', warned him for running on the pitch, and threatened to report him for bad language – *all off one ball!* I was standing at mid-on, amused but minding my own business, when Fingo turned to me and winked. Elsewhere in that match, in one of my life's golden hours, I batted with Chappell – and almost managed to keep up with him. The upshot was that, next morning, in the Headingley press-box, Fingo looked across, caught my eye, and said in a generously loud voice, 'Ah, Cover-Drive Frith!'

Perhaps the secret, in part, of Jack Fingleton's appealing style was the teasing argumentativeness about him, a quality he shared with his old pal and team-mate Bill O'Reilly. There was a total absence of blandness. Because of this, Fingo was so good on the air too. When broadcasting for the BBC he became, if anything, even more Australian. The vowels and the growls rendered the radio-set a rubbery, animated thing. He once listened patiently to the scorer reiterating to the nation how J. H. W. Fingleton had been dismissed without scoring in either innings of the 1932-33 ('Bodyline') Test at Adelaide. When Jack regained the strike he not only balanced the matter somewhat by alluding to the 83 he had made in the preceding Test, but asked the scorer how many Test centuries he had scored. (Fingleton had made five, five more than the scorer.) That closed the discussion on 'pairs'.

On another occasion the same wretched chap was talking about England's required run-rate for victory on the final afternoon: 'We need 4.75 per over.' Jack was heard to sniff, the perfect sound-effect for what followed from one who was unquestionably a patriot, but equally worthily a professional – and therefore objective – critic of international cricket. 'Weeeee?' he intoned in an ever-upward rumble. 'WEEEEE? Who's *WEEEE?*' His co-broadcaster cleared his throat and whispered 'England'.

In *Masters of Cricket*, written by Jack Fingleton while at the peak of his career in authorship, there are some favourite chapters. The mighty but now elderly and deaf Warren Bardsley comes close to having himself thrown out of the public gallery in Canberra's Parliament House as his loud remarks, addressed to friend and political journalist Fingleton, carry down to the debating floor. The pages that follow bring old 'Bards' alive and demonstrate what a superlative left-hander he was, though, of course, his name hardly springs commonly to the lips of today's cognoscenti.

So much of this material is enhanced by the personal acquaintance of the writer with his subject. As with Bardsley, much of the insight into S. F. Barnes and Armstrong and Herbie Collins, Kippax, Ponsford and the legendary Macartney comes from an understanding of what kind of men they were and from the standpoint of one who was a top-class player himself – for which there is no substitute. Not that he was unaware of his own reputation for dourness. As with Bill Lawry of a later generation, Fingleton could laugh (though with tinges of pride) at his own defensive reputation.

He tells with relish, in the Armstrong chapter, how R. G. Menzies' lament over that famous Fingleton 'pair' met with a two-word response from the 'Big Ship': 'Can't bat.'

Elsewhere, of course, you will taste the wry, defiant brand of Fingletonism. He refers to Hobbs and Rhodes's record stand of 221 at Cape Town in 1910, and then asterisks a footnote to the effect that 'W. A. Brown and another Australian toppled this record in Cape Town in 1936.' Oh yes, he was proud of his achievements. And why shouldn't he have been? That 1936 Test match saw Fingo make the first of a string of four consecutive Test centuries. How many of you have made four Test centuries in a row, he might archly have asked if he felt ruffled by something any of us might have said.

The tramdriver's son who fought his way to the top of two tall trees – cricket and journalism – was very much his own man, perpetually struck by the wonder of it all: that from such ordinary beginnings he became a world-famous performer (even though he constantly bemoaned the plight of one who 'didn't bat with Bradman; you *ran for him!*'); and that he moved among prime ministers and princes. In cricket, too, he moved among Masters, past and present, the evidence of which glows in this book.

Jack Fingleton was stimulating company. And now so are his books, his legacy. His spirit will surely not object if I turn round Churchill's words of tribute to F. E. Smith and apply them to Fingo, who 'banked his treasure in the hearts of his friends, and they will cherish his memory until their time is come.'

Guildford, 1989   David Frith

JACK FINGLETON

MASTERS OF CRICKET
From Trumper to May

With a foreword by
The Right Hon. R. G. Menzies, C.H., P.C., M.P.
Prime Minister of Australia

To Jacquelyn May Ann

CONTENTS

CONTENTS

FOREWORD

By The Right Honourable R. G. Menzies, Prime Minister of Australia

The greatest charm of cricket is that it gathers into its family circle the clever and the dull, the expert and the incompetent, the famous and the obscure. They are united by family affection. And that common affection levels out their differences, produces an astonishing democracy of expression, and enables the twelfth man in the junior country school team to exchange ideas, sometimes quite dogmatic, with the Test Match opener.

These are necessary remarks for they explain why the famous cricketer Jack Fingleton honours me with his friendship and listens with assumed but generous interest, or tolerance, to my reminiscences (which are harmless) and my theories (which are astonishing).

Fingleton's guilty secret, of course, is that he is a journalist. He lives at Canberra, attends my Press conferences, and puts awkward questions to me with a slightly quizzical air. In short, we are in our daily lives occupational enemies; because politician and newspaper-man are competitors in the moulding of public opinion.

When the Press conference is over he starts to leave with the others. But every now and then he turns back, by request, and we have ten glorious minutes on cricket. He was, as the cricket world knows, the famous No. 1 for Australia for a long time. In the cricket team of a small Australian country school I was No. 11 in batting but rose higher in bowling, being No. 10, and preferred to the wicket-keeper. But I talk to my friend Fingleton about the great game as if I were his equal. This phenomenon is due partly to a natural and cultivated impudence in my nature; partly to a benevolent gentility which, thanks to television, is growing upon Jack with the ripening years; and partly to the fact, to which I have referred, that enthusiasm for cricket and cricketers is not the monopoly of the skilled.

Our conversations would astonish the scientifically minded. For example, he said to me one day: 'Do you think it possible for a bowler literally to make pace off the pitch?' R. G. M.: 'Of course. I remember that in my days as a juvenile batsman all bowlers who ever bowled to me made frightful pace off the pitch; I can swear to it; I shall never forget it; and anyhow what about F. R. Foster and M. W. Tate?'

Jack laughed tolerantly and waited. I therefore continued, saying: 'I suppose that literally a ball which has struck the turf cannot thereafter *increase* its momentum. But if, for example, it is bowled with a lot of top spin or skids from a wet surface it will lose *less* momentum than was *expected* and will therefore appear to have gained speed. The effect is psychological. The batsman is surprised, and the ball gets past his bat.'

Jack was very impressed by this reasoning and has frequently promised me to devote a chapter to it in his next book. But he has never done it; no doubt for good reason. So, as you see, I am sneaking it in for myself. It is my literary 'wrong 'un.' It is my one great contribution, if not to the science of cricket at least to the arguments about it.

Cricket books were once a rarity. They now come by the score. But apart from the old masters of a bygone era whose essays still retain a flavour of their own, great writing, literature, about cricket remains rare. I still think that Neville Cardus at his best was and is the supreme stylist. But, of course, he and C. E. Montague and Howard Spring did not labour in vain under C. P. Scott of the *Manchester Guardian*. Of the others, I can readily name a dozen whose books I can re-read on winter nights with undimmed pleasure. There are others again, of humble or borrowed talents, who keep the records straight. But there are not more than a handful who, like Jack Fingleton, combine a clear and 'nervous' English style, neither barren nor over-decorated, with an intimate perception of the techniques and subtleties of the game, how it looks and feels out in the middle; its moves and counter-moves; so that each recorded contest comes to life in the mind's eye.

I am sure that this book, like its predecessors from the same pen, will have a great and deserved success.

Introduction

This book is an attempt, in a way, to do some sort of justice to players of other days.

The current player doesn't lack attention or publicity. The ration of books after a Test series could be said, perhaps, to run to about two books per player, so that cricket readers are left in no doubt whether their favourite player takes one or two lumps of sugar in his tea, and whether he puts on his right or left pad first. Additionally, modern Test players seem to be as adept with a pen as the bat. Eight of England's 1956 team at the Oval were also authors!

Players of other days were apparently not so gifted, and this book represents, in the main, an attempt to recall some of their names and some of the great deeds of the past. The sub-title 'From Trumper to May' seems inclusive, but, of course, it cannot be at all. The field is too wide to cover in a single book and there are many whom I played with and against—Hammond, Tate, Compton, McCabe, Oldfield, O'Reilly, and others—who merit much more attention than I have given them here. However, I have written of them in other books, and particularly of Sir Donald Bradman, upon whom I based *Brightly Fades the Don*, my story of his last tour of England.

A Sydney reviewer once took me to task because, in my

book on the 1953 tour of England, I gave Alan Kippax only a few paragraphs. Kippax, of course, was not on the 1953 tour of England. He last toured there in 1934 and I had written of him fully (having played much cricket with him) in an earlier book. But the writer who would please reviewers —especially those who sign only with initials—can be likened to the old man with his son and the donkey.

I don't think the name of Trumper will die in cricket. A. H. Chisholm, the renowned Australian ornithologist and a former newspaper editor of mine, was kind enough to run his eagle eye over the manuscript of this book, and he told me of an occasion when he was posting material back to me from a Sydney post-office. It was one of those single-attendant offices. Mr. Chisholm handed in the envelope and the elderly attendant happened to see my name on it. 'Is he writing any more cricket books?' asked the attendant. 'You have in your hand now,' said Mr. Chisholm, 'some material by Jack Fingleton dealing with Victor Trumper.' Where-upon, said Mr. Chisholm, the eyes of the elderly one lit up and (while the queue for attention grew ever longer) he arranged his varied postal paraphernalia to depict a cricket field and then began to demonstrate how Trumper would tear it to bits.

No, I don't think Vic Trumper's name will fade. Nor will that of Hobbs or Barnes or Macartney. Only a few years ago, when England and Australia met in a Rugby League Test at Sydney, a very old man wandered into the crowded bar of the Members' Stand and began to polish the plaque to Trumper while the football was in progress. It was one of Trumper's anniversaries.

I have to thank the Australian Prime Minister, Mr. Menzies, for a very gracious and generous foreword. As he has indicated, we meet often but in a different field—a field on which he plays a superb defensive bat when in a particular mood. No journalistic off-break or googly has a chance of getting past his defence. His name appears often in these pages, which is not to be wondered at because I have a very high opinion of his cricket acumen and knowledge, and I find his opinions very refreshing—and to the point. One thing, however. One of us has convinced the other because I, too, believe a ball *can* make pace off the pitch! His foreword does me much more credit than I did him when he chose me as captain of his first Prime Minister's Eleven in Canberra. In that match, against the West Indies, I managed the minimum —first ball!

Two Englishmen, Sir Jack Hobbs and Sidney Barnes, have been most helpful to me and that assistance, from two great men of the game, is much appreciated. H. L. Collins, too, gave me generously of his time and his vast store of knowledge. The editor of the London *Sunday Times* allowed me to reprint 'Farewell to Cricket.' My thanks to them all.

J. H. F.

Canberra, April, 1958.

One

___

NEVER ANOTHER LIKE VICTOR

On June 28, 1915, Victor Trumper died at Sydney in his thirty-eighth year. His funeral caused the streets of the city to be blocked and he was carried to his grave by eleven Australian cricketers. In London, in the midst of World War I and all its momentous happenings, the event was featured on newspaper posters, as, for example, 'Death of a Great Cricketer.'

Men said then—and some in both Australia and England still say it—'There will never be another like Vic Trumper.'

I never saw Trumper bat; I was only a few years old when he died. But so often have I listened to stories of him, so often have I seen a new light come into the eyes of people at the mention of his name, so much have I read of him, that I am prepared to believe that nobody, before or since, ever achieved the standards of batsmanship set by Trumper. Sir Pelham Warner, Warren Bardsley, Vernon Ransford and others saw all the great moderns and near-moderns—Bradman, Ponsford, Hobbs, Hammond, Hutton, Compton, McCabe and the like—yet there was more than loyalty to their own generation when they cast their minds back over the years and said, 'There will never be another like Vic.'

Many players, it is true, made more runs; but runs can never be accepted as the true indication of a player's greatness. A fighting innings of thirty or so under difficult conditions is lost in cold statistics, yet its merits may far outweigh many staid (and unnecessary) centuries that are recorded for all time. The longer I live, I am pleased to say, the less nationalistic I become. The outcome of a match is interesting but not, on the scales of time, of any great moment. What *IS* important is whether a particular contest gives to posterity a challenge that is accepted and won, or yields in classical technique an innings or a bowling effort that makes the game richer, so that the devotee can say years afterwards, with joy in his voice, 'I saw that performance.'

Trumper went to bat one day against Victoria in Sydney on a wet pitch. The first ball from Jack Saunders (a terror on such pitches) beat him completely. Saunders' eyes lit up. His fellow-Victorians grinned in anticipation. Trumper smiled broadly. 'Why, Jack,' he called down the pitch, 'what a thing to do to an old friend. Well, it's either you or me for it.'

And then, by dazzling footwork and miraculous stroke-play, Trumper hit a century in 60 minutes.

At the beginning of 1904, in Melbourne, Trumper faced up to Rhodes and Hirst on a wet pitch. These Yorkshiremen were two of the greatest left-handed bowlers of all time and a wet Melbourne pitch was known as the worst in the world, with balls from a good length lifting quickly around the chin.

Trumper was first in and last out, for 74, in a total of 122. Hopkins made 18 and Duff 10. Noble, Syd Gregory, Trumble and Armstrong made 9 between them!

That innings caused Charles Fry, in one of his unpredictable moments, to rise suddenly from a reverie during a dinner in London and say: 'Gentlemen, charge your glasses. I give you the toast of the world's greatest batsman. Drink to Victor Trumper, first man in, last man out, on a bad pitch and against Hirst and Rhodes.'

Fry knew the full value of such an innings on such a pitch and against two skilled left-handers. His short and unexpected speech brought down the house.

No less interesting is the fact that Mrs. Fry (who may or may not have had some knowledge of cricket) shared her famous husband's admiration of Trumper. My information on this point comes from the Sydney *Bulletin* of the period. It appears that Mrs. Fry declared in a London periodical that Vic Trumper was an artist and that some day someone would paint his portrait and have it hung in a National Gallery. 'He will be,' the lady said, 'dressed in white, with his splendid neck bared to the wind, standing on short green grass against a blue sky; he will be waiting for the ball, the orchestra to strike up.'

Given this stimulus, the Australian poet, Victor Daley (who wrote topical verse under the name of 'Creeve Roe') broke into rhyme in the *Bulletin*. Here are examples from his seven verses entitled 'Trumper':

> Ho Statesmen, Patriots, Bards make way!
> Your fame has sunk to zero:
> For Victor Trumper is today
> Our one Australian hero.

> High purpose glitters in his eye,
> He scorns the filthy dollar;
> His splendid neck, says Mrs. Fry,
> Is innocent of collar. . . .

> Is there not, haply, in the land
> Some native-born Murillo
> To paint, in colours rich and grand,
> This Wielder of the Willow?

> Nay, rather let a statue be
> Erected his renown to,
> That future citizens might see
> The gods their sires bowed down to.

Evoe Trumper! As for me
It all ends with the moral
That fame grows on the Willow Tree
And no more on the laurel.

My formative days in cricket were spent in the Sydney suburb of Waverley. We adjoined Paddington, the club of Trumper and Noble, but we yielded to no Sydney club in the proud possession of internationals and other first-class players. Carter, all the twentieth-century Gregorys, Kippax, Hendry, Collins, Frank O'Keefe (one of our very best batsmen who, denied opportunities, went to Victoria, hit two centuries in a game against New South Wales, and then went to the Lancashire League, there dying soon afterwards) and many other proficient players figured with Waverley and established the high standards of the district. One of the great sources of the club's strength was that cricket, and talk of it, flowed through the life of the district. All the internationals I have mentioned showed themselves on the local oval at practice during the week and played there in the club games on Saturday afternoons.

Saturday evenings and Sunday mornings were given over to post-mortems. We had four grade sides and promising youngsters, if unable to make grade, were fitted in with the Veterans team where they played under the leadership of men such as Syd Gregory, Australian captain, and Tom Howard, treasurer of the 1934 team to England.

The returning warriors, coming from their games in distant suburbs, would meticulously report in at Bondi Junction on Saturday evenings and at Waverley Park on Sunday mornings—unless, of course, dire personal disaster induced them to go to ground for a week. At those rendezvous both players and critics gathered and form and happenings were first reported and then dissected and judged. It was a hard and discerning school of criticism. Those no longer able to play were in their element as they passed solemn judgment upon some 'shyster' or 'grubber'—Waverley terms for the lowly cricketer. Few merited the accolade of a 'great' performance. Even 'good' was seldom used. In the main, ranking varied from 'fair' to 'quite good.'

These critics—some lovely characters among them—knew their cricket. When they had disposed of the present they drifted, fondly, to the hallowed ground of the past, and always, I found, the day's reminiscences ended on Victor Trumper.

As I walked home I used to wonder how one cricketer could so capture the imagination above all others; and the imagination, moreover, of men so steeped in the game that they were the severest of critics. Yet even years after Trumper's death they spoke wistfully of him and would brook no interlopers. Nor criticism. Trumper was unique in that nobody ever criticised him as a cricketer or as a man. In England, in Australia, in South Africa, listening to men who knew and played against him, I never at any time heard a derogatory word said against Trumper. That could not be said of any other cricketer of any generation.

A mark of a great man is the power of making lasting impressions upon people he meets. Winston Churchill once wrote of F. E. Smith, the first Earl of Birkenhead: 'Some men when they die after busy, toilsome, successful lives leave a great stock of scrip and securities, of acres or factories or the goodwill of large undertakings. F. E. banked his treasure in the hearts of his friends, and they will cherish his memory until their time is come.'

That could also have been written of Trumper. He left no stock or securities. He was a singularly unsuccessful business man. He ran a sporting goods firm in the city of

Sydney but he was too generous with his gifts to accumulate money. Once, on the morning of a Test, he was working in his shop and allowed time to elude him. He hurried into his coat, took down a new bat from the rack, caught a taxi to the Sydney Cricket Ground—and made 185 not out!

It has been said that this was the most brilliant and versatile innings ever played by the Master. The match was the famous one in which R. E. Foster, the Englishman, hit a brilliant 287 in his first Test and Clem Hill was concerned in the most tumultuous run-out in the history of Test cricket—but I tell those stories elsewhere in this book.

An admirer of Trumper came into his shop after the match and asked whether he could buy a bat Trumper had used.

Yes, he was told. There was the bat used in the recent Test. The admirer's eyes sparkled. How much would it be?

'Well,' said the impractical Victor, 'it was a 45s. bat but it is now second-hand. You can have it for a pound.'

What a difference, this, from a modern I know who swapped a bat with which he had made a record for one of the most fabulous cars seen on a roadway (but that is another story that doesn't belong here).

Another tale of Trumper—there are dozens—was told me by Vernon Ransford, his comrade in many Australian Elevens.

The Australians were dressing at Melbourne for a Test, against Sherwell's South Africans, when there came a knock at the door. Was Mr. Trumper available?

Trumper went to the door and found a young man, a complete stranger, holding a bat. He was anxious to begin in the bat-making business. This was one of his bats and he wondered whether Mr. Trumper would use it in the Test.

This usage of material is one of the niceties of 'amateur' sport. A successful player is retained to use the material of a

certain sports outfitter. Not only, by his play, is he expected
to bring glory and advertisement to the firm's goods, but he
must also be well practised in presenting the name on his
equipment whenever his photograph is being taken. Thus,
when you see a triumphant winner of Wimbledon in a
photograph, you have a fair chance of seeing also the name
of the racquet used as the hero pushes it to the front. Strictly
speaking, of course, amateurs are not allowed to associate
their names with sporting goods—and knowing editors
now sometimes help them to observe the proprieties by
blacking-out the name in the printed photograph!

That angle on sport was not developed in Trumper's day.
He would have had in his bag several bats that suited him in
weight and balance but, nevertheless, he didn't hesitate about
accepting the young applicant's gruesome-looking bat. It
weighed almost 3 lb. 6 oz. and it staggered his team-mates.

'Surely,' one of them said, 'you won't use that blunderbuss,
Vic?'

'He's only a young chap and he's starting out in business,'
replied Trumper. 'If I can get a few runs with this it might
help him.'

He made 87 (probably wearying of lifting it!), inscribed it
on the back with a hearty recommendation, and gave it back
to the delighted young man.

Hanson Carter, the great wicket-keeper, was my first
club captain. 'You must never,' he once sternly told me,
'compare Hobbs, Bradman or anybody else with Trumper.
If you want to try and classify the great batsmen in the game,
put Victor Trumper way up there—on his own—and then
you can begin to talk about the rest.'

So, too, with Charlie Macartney, upon whose shoulders
the mantle of Trumper was supposed to have descended. He
revelled in talking of the things Trumper did. So did Rans-

ford. I sat with him in his office a few years ago when he was secretary of the Melbourne Cricket Ground and he went into rhapsodies regarding the dismally wet season in England in 1902 when Trumper made 2,570 runs.

'If Vic had been greedy, it could have been 4,000,' said Ransford. 'His highest score, despite all the centuries he scored, was only 128. He could, obviously, have turned many of those centuries into double ones had he wished. But he was too generous. He looked around for some deserving character, a youngster maybe, or some player down on his luck, and unostentatiously gave him his wicket. That was Vic.'

Wisden's wrote of Trumper and that tour: 'Trumper stood alone. He put everybody else into the shade. No one, not even Ranjitsinhji has been at once so brilliant and so consistent since Dr. W. G. Grace was at his best.'

The English bosie bowler, Bosanquet, clean bowled Trumper with the first bosie he sent down to him. 'Plum' Warner describes it:

'It was in Sydney in 1903. Trumper and Duff had gone in first and in 35 minutes had scored 72 runs by batting, every stroke of which I remember vividly to this day. Bosanquet went on to bowl and his first ball pitched a good length just outside the off-stump. Trumper thought it was a leg-break and proceeded to cut it late, as he hoped, for four, but it came back and down went his off-stump. Subsequently, he used to "murder" Bosanquet but it is worth recording that the first "googly" ever bowled in Australia bowled out the man who, in spite of all the fine deeds of Don Bradman, many Australians regard as the finest batsman their country has ever produced.

It is very doubtful if there has ever been a greater batsman and his wonderful deeds would have been even greater but for indifferent health, which, in the end, cut short his life.

No one ever played so naturally, and he was as modest as he was magnificent. To this day in Australia, he is regarded as the highest ideal of batsmanship. He was, I think, the most fascinating batsman I have seen. He had grace, ease, style and power and a quickness of foot both in jumping out and in getting back to a ball that can surely never be surpassed.

He had every known stroke and one or two of his own. When set on a good wicket it seemed impossible to place a field for him. He was somewhat slightly built, but his sense of timing was so perfect that he hit the ball with tremendous power. Most bowlers are agreed that he was the most difficult batsman to keep quiet. I have heard a great bowler remark, "I could, in the ordinary way, keep most people from scoring quickly, but I always felt rather helpless against Trumper, for he was so quick, and he had so many strokes." His brilliant batting stirred cricketing England. His unrivalled skill and resource will never be forgotten. No cricketer was ever more popular, and he deserved it, for he preserved the modesty of true greatness and was the beau-ideal of a cricketer.'

On one occasion, after batting brilliantly at Kennington Oval, Trumper 'ducked' an official dinner at night. The fact was, simply, that he didn't want to be talking 'shop' among cricketers and receiving plaudits. He was duly fined for missing an official engagement!

The South Africans had a quick introduction to Trumper. An Australian team called at the Union on the way home from England, where Trumper had had a most successful tour.

There were opinions that Trumper wouldn't find the matting pitches of South Africa too easy and money changed hands to say that, in the few matches played there, Trumper wouldn't make a century. He hit a double-century in his very first game on the mat!

The South Africans in Australia in 1910-11 were mesmerised by his skill. This was the team with all the bosie bowlers, but Trumper cut, hooked and drove at will. He had a fascinating stroke against a fast yorker. He lifted his back foot, jabbed down on the ball with his bat at an angle and it streaked away to the square-leg boundary. Somewhat naturally, they called it the dog-stroke.

He teased Percy Sherwell, the Springbok captain. When a fieldsman was shifted, Trumper deliberately hit the next ball where that man had been. He was a consummate master at placement. Later, somebody commiserated with Sherwell at having his captaincy, his bowlers and his fieldsmen torn to tatters while Trumper made 214; whereupon the Springbok said, 'Ah, don't talk about it. We have seen batting today.'

Neville Cardus, the Trumper of cricket writing, once wrote, 'The art of Trumper is like the art in a bird's flight, an ˙rt that knows not how wonderful it is. Batting was for him a superb dissipation, a spontaneous spreading of fine feathers.'

How unfortunate it is that Trumper slightly preceded the movie-camera age!

Posterity has the chance of seeing all the moderns in action, as it has of hearing all the great singing voices. Mr. Menzies, our Prime Minister, has a thrilling film of Don Bradman—there are a number of copies of the same film in existence—and to see Bradman on the screen is to realise again, instantly, his great stature as a batsman. The speed of his footwork, the flay of his bat, the manner in which he 'smelt' the ball, so over the ball was his head—all this has been caught and kept for the years to come and, in the evidence of the film, there can be no possible disputation over Bradman's status in the game.

With Trumper it is different. All we have, so far as I know, are the several photographic 'stills' of him at the beginning of an off-drive and at the finish and, also, of his stance at the crease. But these do portray his art. The two of him playing the off-drive are technically perfect in every detail—his feet, his shoulders, his head, his back swing, his follow-through with the proper transfer of weight and then, finally, the full, flowing arc of the bat. His stance is perfection.

Those who saw and knew Trumper used to say that Macartney, Jackson and Kippax were reminiscent of him; but that even when they were at their greatest they served only to rekindle memories of the Great Man. He was, obviously, supreme on the field; and a man of kind and generous nature, of consideration for his fellow-man, off the field. He embodied, to those who knew him, all that was good and noble in cricket and life.

'Where would you like your field placed?' 'Plum' Warner, as captain, once asked George Hirst. And Hirst replied, 'It doesn't much matter, sir, where we put 'em. Victor will still do as 'e likes.'

The evidence, then, would seem to be conclusive. Many of Trumper's greatest innings were played in the full face of adversity, the true test of worth. He rose to heights on wet wickets where others tumbled to earth. Although some half a dozen or so players down the years could be regarded as really great, Trumper, as Carter said, merits a niche of his own. He brought to the game an artistry, a talent, and an inherent modesty not manifested by any other cricketer. In short, he possessed all the graces.

Two

ENGLAND'S GREATEST BATSMAN

Melbourne	1911-12	126 not out
Adelaide	1911-12	187
Melbourne	1911-12	178
Lords	1912	107
Melbourne	1920-21	122
Adelaide	1920-21	123
Melbourne	1924-25	154
Adelaide	1924-25	119
Sydney	1924-25	115
Lords	1926	119
The Oval	1926	100
Melbourne	1928-29	142

That is the Test story, in centuries, of John Berry Hobbs—now Sir Jack—against Australia. Twelve centuries, more than those of any other Englishman, against the Great Enemy!

Those centuries, of course, tell only part of the story of the man who, as Australian Test players agree, was the best batsman ever produced by England. You don't judge a cricketer by centuries alone. Quite often such a score is not nearly as valuable to a side as a 40 or 50 made in difficult circumstances—that is, when the strain is on with every pressing minute a test of temperament and resource. And Jack Hobbs was at his very best when the fight was toughest. One other important point: from his first Test match in Melbourne on January 1, 1908, to his last at his home Oval in Kennington, Surrey, in 1930, Jack Hobbs always opened the innings. He got no easy runs, after the sting was taken out of the bowling. He did his own de-stinging.

Furthermore, that long list of centuries could well have been half as long again. In his first Test innings Hobbs almost made a century. He had scored 83 in three hours of correct batsmanship when Cotter clean-bowled him. He later scored 72 in the same series in Sydney. He made a brilliant 62 not out —scoring twice as fast as the redoubtable C. B. Fry—to push England home to a ten wickets win against Australia in a low-scoring game on a horrible pitch at Birmingham in 1909. In 1926 he scored 88 at Leeds, 74 in the next Test at Old Trafford, 74 at Adelaide in 1929, 65 in his last Test innings in Australia at Melbourne, and 78 and 74 at Nottingham in 1930.

It is readily seen, therefore, that Hobbs, given just a little luck, could have added another half dozen or more centuries to his list against Australia.

He played in 41 Tests against Australia and had 71 innings for 3,636 runs at an average of 54·23. He played in 18 Tests against South Africa with 29 innings for 1,562 runs at an average of 60·07. He had only two Tests against the West Indies, for 212 runs at an average of 106.

In all Test cricket, then, with his average not buttressed by games against India, Pakistan and New Zealand, he made 5,410 runs at an average of 56·94. His record number of first-class centuries is 197. He made 61,221 first-class runs at an average of 50·63. Although figures indicate the greatness of Hobbs they don't convey the grandeur of his batting, his faultless technique, and the manner in which he captivated those who could recognise and analyse style. Australians who played against him over the years believe cricket never produced a more correct batsman than Hobbs.

From 1907 to 1930 Hobbs batted against this imposing list of Australian bowlers: Saunders, Noble, Armstrong, Macartney, Cotter, Laver, Whitty, Hordern, Minnett, Kelleway, Gregory, McDonald, Mailey, Arthur Richardson, Grimmett, Ironmonger, Oxenham, Blackie, Wall, Hornibrook, McCabe, Fairfax and a'Beckett.

In that list there is every conceivable type of bowler—fast right and fast left, medium spinners and swervers, bosie, leg-breakers and off-breakers, cutters, seamers and top-spinners—men who bowled with a plan behind every ball or men who just relied upon their natural ability. And they were, too, players who had shrewd captains such as Noble, Clem Hill, Sid Gregory, Armstrong, Collins, Ryder and Woodfull to set fields to the best purpose.

Hobbs took them all in his century-making stride. In fact, he was 'strung up' only in the final days of his career when Bill Bowes, with a bowling intent not in keeping with his nature, gave the master a dose of bodyline on his native pitch at the Oval. Hobbs remonstrated at the wicket against such intimidatory tactics (they were severely condemned in the Press next day by Sir Pelham Warner) and, knowing that something alien to the spirit of cricket had entered it, he began to pack his cricket gear for good. He played Test cricket until he was 48; he played for Surrey until he was 52.

During tours of England, I used to think fondly of Hobbs, Tom Hayward and Ranjitsinhji as I walked on various mornings across Parker's Piece to the Cambridge ground. It was on the Piece that Hobbs and Hayward first played cricket and it was there, too, that the Indian prince first began to reveal his genius to England.

Parker's Piece is a delightful stretch of green parkland but I felt unhappy there one morning in 1948 when I saw a fast bowler producing the most outrageous bumpers from a good length. Sorrowing for the well-being of the courageous batsmen who stood up to such bowling, on such a 'pitch,' I hurried into Fenner's, there to watch the less-terrifying bumpers of Lindwall and Miller.

However, the Piece must have had much to do with the correct moulding of Hobbs's technique. Provided a young batsman has inherent ability there is no better place to build a solid defence than on a turf that scoots, jumps and imparts abnormal break to the ball. Given too much of it a batsman could form bad habits, such as drawing away from the ball, but the correct amount at a formative time leads to a sharpening of the eyesight, quick footwork and deft wielding of the bat. Such an experience leads the youngster to notable deeds when he finds himself on better, truer pitches.

Hobbs has acknowledged his debt to Tom Hayward in his early days—Hayward introduced him to Surrey—but it is well to note Hobbs's claim that he never had an hour's coaching in his life. He was a self-made cricketer—observing, thinking and executing for himself.

He didn't copy Hayward's stance at the wickets, although there was a similarity. Hobbs improved on Hayward's stance, which was decidedly two-eyed, with the left foot pointing almost straight up the pitch, the two shoulders round and the face practically full on to the bowler. Hobbs, like Denis Compton, had his face, and thus his right shoulder, a little fuller to the bowler than most top-ranking batsmen and herein, as with Compton, could have been the secret of his remarkable prowess in playing on-side strokes. I think that *was* the case, although, and in this consideration I include Compton again, Hobbs could not have played the cover-drive and the square-drive—both forward—had his body not been admirably positioned to allow of the correct back-swing. Such strokes are immediately denied the 'two-eyed' stancer because he can't swing back *through* his body.

Hobbs was one of the twelve children of a groundsman at Jesus College, Cambridge. His own first job was as grounds-man at Bedford school, where he also did some net-bowling against the schoolboys. His life was thus inseparable from cricket but he had an early set-back when he was recom-mended to the Essex County Club and found not good enough! Essex turned him down.

Then he tried with Surrey, was immediately accepted and in his second match scored a glorious 155 against Essex. Every run must have given him a special pleasure and, know-ing that their club had spurned him, the Essex players must have had some galling thoughts at the end of that game—and forever afterwards through Hobbs's great career.

Fittingly enough, for he was years afterwards to displace the Great Man as a scorer of centuries, Hobbs played his first game for Surrey against the Gentlemen of England, captained by Dr. W. G. Grace. The game of cricket was to know no greater stealer of a run than Hobbs and, facing up to Grace, he should have got off the mark with a quick single.

Hobbs, very nervous against Grace, played several balls and then played one a few yards up the pitch. He quickly sensed there was a run to be 'stolen' but just as he began his run the quavery voice of the Doctor came down the pitch: 'Thank you, youngster, just tap it back here and save my poor old legs!'

And Hobbs, suitably impressed by the Old Man, who was

a terror to the game's newcomers, tapped the ball back to him. He made 18 in the first innings and 88 in the second.

Hobbs played for Surrey against Darling's great Australian side of 1905. He batted beautifully against Cotter, then at his fastest, and had reached 94 when a thrilling throw-in by Clem Hill from the Kennington Oval boundary hit the stumps and ran him out. It was a compliment Hobbs often returned to the Australians. Perhaps the greatest cover-point ever— quick in anticipation, swift to the ball and unerring in his under-the-shoulder return—he had 15 run-outs on his second tour of Australia in 1912.

No cover-point can ever be considered great unless he has deft, twinkling footwork. As the ball speeds towards him, cover-point must be on the way in to meet it, for a split second thus gained could bring the run-out and, moreover, he should so position his movements in to the ball that he is, immediately, ready to receive the ball and throw it to the desired end with one action. A champion cover-point must possess an additional sense. He must sense what the batsmen are doing, for his own eyes never leave the ball. He must, too, be a 'fox,' yielding a single here and there to snare the batsman into a feeling of safety and, when his chance comes, cover-point must be able to hit the stumps from side-on nine times out of ten. Jack Hobbs had the lot—all the tricks.

Hobbs's Test career against Australia was preceded by disappointment. A. O. Jones brought the English side to Australia in 1907 with Hobbs making his first trip. Jones became ill on the eve of the First Test in Sydney and Hobbs seemed certain to get the position. But the selectors did an odd thing, although it was to prove most successful. George Gunn, of Nottinghamshire, had travelled with the team on a health trip and he was asked to play, instead of Hobbs.

Hobbs was not only bitterly disappointed; he thought he had been badly treated, even though Gunn proved the hero of the game, scoring 119 and 74 in a masterly manner in his first Test. Anyway, Hobbs almost equalled the century feat with 83 in the following Test in Melbourne. Gunn headed the Test averages of the tour, 462 at an average of 51·33, and Hobbs was second with 302 runs at 43·14. Together, Gunn and Hobbs put on 134 in the final Test in Sydney. It was a partnership, according to those who saw it, which hasn't been excelled, for classical batsmanship, by any other two Englishmen in Australia.

Hobbs went home to make a 'duck' in his first Test innings against the Australians in England. The Birmingham pitch then was helpful to bowlers. Blythe and Hirst ran through Australia for the meagre total of 74. Hobbs opened for England but Macartney, with the new ball, had him quickly l.b.w. Macartney also bowled MacLaren for five and Fry for a 'duck.' But in the second innings Hobbs made a brilliant 62 not out, top score for the match—and England won by ten wickets. His stroke play was classical, so much so that Englishmen described it as the best since Vic Trumper's performances of 1902.

That was a time of outstanding batting strength in English cricket. There were so many men of brilliance knocking at the Test door that those inside could barely afford to fail. Yet, with his own place by no means assured, Hobbs was responsible at Leeds for what the Australians thought was a remarkable gesture.

The captain, M. A. Noble told the story thus:

'Hobbs forced a ball off his back foot between short-leg and mid-on. In doing so he knocked off one of the bails. Believing that it was done in the act of making the stroke we appealed for hit wicket, but the umpire gave him not out on the ground that he had completed the stroke before his foot touched the stump.

'Two or three balls later Hobbs made a weak attempt to play a straight one and was bowled. My impression was then —and still is—that Hobbs believed himself legally to be out and deliberately allowed himself to be bowled. It is a most difficult thing to allow yourself to be bowled without betraying the fact to the bowler or someone fielding near the wicket. It was a match of small scores and the loss then of a player of Hobbs's ability probably had a determining influence upon our success in that game.'

Another Australian captain who spoke in warm terms of Hobbs's outstanding sportsmanship was H. L. Collins. In the chapter on Collins I write of how Hobbs gave himself out at Kennington Oval against the Australians after the umpire had said not out. Few Test cricketers down the years have done that. Most accept an umpire's blunder when it is their way on the principle that they are sometimes given out when they are not and, indeed, some of the moderns stay when an obvious catch has been made in the hope, unworthy as it is, that the umpire will make a mistake!

As I have said, Hobbs's greatness as a batsman lay not only in the fact that he got many runs with incredible consistency but also in the manner in which he made them. He was perfect in the execution of every stroke. His footwork was a model for all players and his style was irreproachable. He was always attractive to watch—a neat, compact figure, faultlessly attired in flannels—whether he was moving along at a fast rate or was on the defensive.

I asked him once which innings he considered the best he had played in Australia.

'Well,' he replied, 'it's a long time since I retired from first-class cricket, twenty-three years, and it was five years earlier that I last played in Australia. Memory grows dim. Quite naturally, I suppose, on being asked which was my best innings I try to recall which was the best of the nine Test centuries I scored in your country. There was that one in 1912 when I made 178 and along with Wilfred Rhodes put on 323 for the first wicket. England won the rubber by winning that match.

'Then there was the 122 in the second Test at Melbourne in 1921, made for the most part on a rain-damaged wicket: but we lost that match. Both of those innings gave me a lot of pleasure because I felt that I had played pretty well—if I may, with modesty, say so.'

I put it to him that an achievement that will never be forgotten in Australia was the 49 he made in England's second innings of the third Test in Melbourne of the 1928-29 tour.

'Yes,' he agreed, 'perhaps it would be wise to select that innings as England won the match against all the odds. You would be surprised at the number of Aussies who mention that match when they call to see me in Fleet Street. Just the same as folk here speak about the fifth Test at the Oval in 1926—another "sticky".' (Hobbs made a brilliant 100 on this later occasion, England winning back the Ashes.)

He continued· 'I well remember waiting in Melbourne for the wicket to dry so that we could continue the match. Australia still had two wickets to fall. I can recall very well how our friends came to the pavilion to commiserate with us, saying what a pity it was the rain came. We thought so too. We considered we didn't have a chance of getting the runs. That old campaigner Hughie Trumble, then secretary of the Melbourne Cricket Club, told us in all seriousness that 70 would be a good score in our second innings. Well, as you know, we chased 332 and eventually won by three wickets. Our success caused quite a stir at home. I remember that a

London newspaper cabled out £100 each to Herbert Sutcliffe and myself.'

It was the opening partnership of 105 between Hobbs and Sutcliffe that enabled England to win that match. Not only was it rich in runs but it defied the Australian attack on one of the worst wickets known in Melbourne. Considering the difficulties, that opening partnership would possibly rank as the most outstanding one in Test history.

The wicket was bad all day, going through different phases. Thirty points of rain had fallen and the English innings began in gentle sunshine, increasing in intensity and drying the pitch in patches so that there were spots off which the ball kicked disconcertingly. It was at its most dangerous period from lunch to the tea interval.

The Australians had no fast bowler in this match, the opening bowlers, Hendry and a'Beckett, being no more than medium-pace, but there was an abundance of varied spin in Oxenham (medium off-breaks), Grimmett (leg-breaks) and Blackie (slow to slow-medium off-breaks).

On such a pitch against such spinners, the English task should have been an impossible one but, right from the beginning, the two great opening batsmen dominated the pitch and the Australians.

For over after over, Blackie bowled around the wicket with a packed leg-side field, but by superb dead-bat play and adept pad-play, together with the most astute judgment in not playing at the ball when it wasn't necessary, Hobbs and Sutcliffe went on for one hour, then two hours and finally came to tea with the score 0-78—Hobbs 36 and Sutcliffe 32. The whole members' stand rose to them in acclamation.

In effect, the leg-theory tactics of the Australians played into the hands of two such proficient batsmen. Ryder, fast-medium, often hit the body but never seemed likely to hit the

stumps. Both batsmen were black and blue on the body—
Hobbs was once hit on the head by Ryder—but they never
flinched, even though the sharply rising balls yielded many
byes off Oldfield's body. Indeed, one ball from Oxenham
rose so sharply off a length that it cleared Oldfield's head (the
keeper was standing up to the stumps) for two byes. Three
successive balls from Oxenham particularly revealed the
conditions—one rose high and went from Oldfield's gloves
to first slip, the next hit Sutcliffe on the shoulder and the next
went for a bye off Oldfield's shoulder.

While Hendry was bowling, Richardson, Blackie, Ryder,
Bradman and a'Beckett formed a complete circle of under
ten yards diameter around the batsman from silly-point to
forward short-leg.

The two Englishmen on that day demoralised the Australian bowling, the fielding and the captaincy of Ryder. They
gave their usual superb lesson of running between the
wickets. One never let the other down. This was exemplified
time after time in their calling and acceptance, many of the
runs, of a seemingly dangerous nature at the beginning, being
completed at a walk. Once, Hobbs walked out of his crease
several yards before Blackie bowled and placed him to the
on for two.

The century came in 133 minutes. Just before this the old
field-marshal, Hobbs, using the stratagem of signalling for a
bat, sent a message to Chapman in the pavilion to change his
batting order, sending Jardine in next before Hammond.

It was a shrewd piece of advice. Hobbs went l.b.w. to
Blackie at 49, but at stumps England were 1-171—Sutcliffe 83
and Jardine 18. There were 13 byes in that total. Commenting on this in England, Strudwick said: 'A wet wicket in
Melbourne is about the worst of its kind, especially for the
wicket-keeper. The ball does all sorts of funny things.'

In short, the old firm of Hobbs and Sutcliffe, making their eighth opening stand of a century against the Australians, out-generalled and out-played Ryder and his men. The next day, with three wickets falling for 14 after the match was all but won, England took the honours by three wickets. Sutcliffe played perhaps his greatest innings, 6½ hours for 135—but undoubtedly it was that opening stand that won the match.

Hobbs found his first great opening partner for England in Wilfred Rhodes and it was fitting that another Yorkshire-man, Sutcliffe, should have been his second. Hobbs and Rhodes made a record 221 for the first wicket against South Africa in Cape Town in 1910*: and in Melbourne in 1912 they put on 323 against Australia. This still stands as a record for Tests.

Hobbs was at his best in Melbourne, as his records show. In 1926, after Australia had hit up a record first innings tally of 600, one London newspaper announced on its placard: 'Australia 600: Come on Hobbs!' With Sutcliffe, Hobbs batted all the next day, the opening being worth 283. The same newspaper said on its placard next day: 'Thank you Hobbs!'

I am glad to know Jack Hobbs and to have seen him bat though, incidentally, my feelings as a youngster at Sydney were mixed one day when I saw Oldfield catch him on the leg-side off Gregory for none—a catch off a leg-glance, the greatest wicket-keeping catch and shrewdest example of co-operation between bowler and keeper that I have ever seen.

Good to have seen Jack Hobbs bat? Why, much better than that, I once opened an innings with him. He had retired

* W. A. Brown and another Australian toppled this record in Cape Town in 1936.

two years from Test cricket and was in Australia on a writing assignment. We both played for the Press against the Australian Navy at Rushcutters Bay, Sydney, and I knew no prouder moment in cricket than when I walked through the gate to open the innings with the Master. I recall very clearly the neat manner in which he tapped a ball off the very first delivery and we finished the run at a walk, so superbly had he placed the single.

On December 16, 1957, Sir Jack celebrated his seventy-fifth birthday in London, being entertained at a no-speeches lunch in a London tavern organised by the Master's club—for he was, indeed, the Master. At the lunch were Sir Pelham (Plum) Warner, George Gunn, who kept Hobbs out of that First Test in Sydney fifty years before, 'Tich' Freeman, George Geary, Patsy Hendren, Jack Crawford, Peter May and others who delighted in the presence of the Master—still erect and well, his eyes full of good humour and love of his fellow man.

In tours of England one of my greatest pleasures is to see Sir Jack of a Test Saturday in the various Press boxes. His notes on the game appear in a Sunday newspaper so that a Saturday is his sole appearance with us, but it is a joy to see him, to greet him and have a few words. Like his stroke-making, there is nothing uppish about Sir Jack. He is everybody's friend, and I think he appreciates that as much as his great string of records and figures.

'Figures,' an admirer once wrote of Hobbs, 'can convey no idea of the Master, of his full-blooded hooking when he was young, of his driving on light, swift feet, of his peerless square-cut, of his leaning leg-glance, of the natural growth of his talents to a quite regal control and superiority.'

There was all that and success, too, as I have stressed, when the fight was hardest, when the pitch was cranky. Somebody once aptly observed that it was Hobbs who took the description 'unplayable' out of the category of pitches.

Recently Douglas Jardine, who saw many great batsmen at close quarters, was asked to name the greatest. He didn't hesitate. 'Hobbs,' said Jardine, 'is number one every time. He was so good on bad pitches.' The interviewer interposed another name. Jardine looked out the window—and refused to answer.

Three

THE STORY OF WARREN BARDSLEY

The last time I sat and spoke with Warren Bardsley I did so
with some trepidation and much listening. For several good
reasons one usually did the listening when 'Bards' was about,
but on this final occasion (he died soon afterwards) he was
holding forth in the Visitors' Gallery of Parliament House,
Canberra. And Speaker Archie Cameron, a likeable man but
a very stern one, cast more than one look in our direction.

Some debate was in progress and from the Press Gallery
I had seen Warren and his wife come into the House. I slipped
down to join them because I was very fond of Bardsley.
'A good speaker, this bloke,' said Bardsley in a loud whisper.
Speaker Cameron turned towards us. Years before at Liverpool, England, Bardsley had been 'pinked' (as he termed it)
by a fellow Australian and one-time Test mate, Ted Mc-
Donald. This hit on the head had left him somewhat deaf
and, like most others similarly afflicted, he was apt to raise
his voice in conversation.

Speaker Cameron was no sporting man. Not long before
he had, somewhat churlishly, forbidden the loan of Parlia-
mentary cups and saucers for the Prime Minister's match
against the West Indians at Manuka Oval and, of course, he
would not have known Bardsley. Moreover, the same
Archie Cameron had ordered the removal of a photograph

of Phar Lap from the barber's room at Parliament House, an action that shocked horse-loving Australians to whom Phar Lap was the Bradman of racing.

But Warren saw not the Speaker and was not deterred from commenting on one of the debaters. 'This bloke's on a good length, Jack,' he said in a loud whisper. 'Who's he?' I had visions of the Serjeant-at-Arms presenting us with the Speaker's compliments and asking us to continue our conversation in the lobbies but, instead, there came a note from the Prime Minister inviting Warren to his rooms. The Prime Minister knew Bardsley and, like me, was fond of him, and especially of his stories.

At the present time, in these days of hustle, it would be difficult, I think, to have a recurrence of Bardsley's record as a cricketer; yet in the story is an indication of the long and often tortuous path that must be trod if a cricketer of modest beginnings is to reach the heights—as Bardsley certainly did.

Bardsley was not a man of brilliance. He came into first-class cricket when Victor Trumper was shedding his genius over the cricketing fields of Australia and, naturally, inspiring large numbers of youngsters. All wanted to be Trumpers. Bardsley, on his part, soon realised that he could never be a Trumper. But he also realised that he could, by hard work, become a first-class tradesman.

Even as a youth, Bardsley had both feet firmly on the pitch. He analysed his assets and put Trumper beyond his aspirations. The parks and the ovals of Sydney in the early days of this century were strewn with the stumps of ambitious young fellows who, in attempting to emulate Trumper, paid the penalty of trying to achieve the impossible.

Sensibly, Bardsley decided that he would get out of cricket only what he was prepared to put into it. There could be no short cuts. His early policy, and indeed the policy he was still following at his career's end, was hard work, plus close thought that deepened into concentration. Thus he became one of the best left-handed batsmen in Australia's history.

He toured England for the first time in 1909, becoming the first player ever to make a century in both innings of a Test; and he toured England for the last time in 1926, laying another stone of immortality for himself by batting through the whole of Australia's first innings of the Lord's Test, making 193 out of 383.

Only a purist in orthodoxy could endure and succeed (as Jack Hobbs also did) over so long and so vital a period. It was a period which saw the discovery of the bosie, the exploitation of short, fast bowling on the leg-stump, the acute leg-side field placing (Fred Root of Worcestershire), and the perfection of swing bowling.

Every now and then cricket will throw up a freak who lasts only as long as the keen edge of his eyesight. I once played with a rich character in Waverley named Hughie Davidson who, for a short period, kept wickets for New South Wales with distinction. Davidson was also an interstate hockey player and, so far as the seasons were concerned, all he changed was his clothes. In batting, he would advance his front foot up the pitch, stoop low, and play murderous hockey sweeps to leg. These shots were as remarkable and as full-blooded as the others they drew from the bowler; but their raffish success decreased as Davidson's years increased.

Bardsley prospered so long because he was correct in everything he did. He stood at the crease as upright as a guardsman. Most opening batsmen like to think they can change course for a swinger by holding the bat low on the handle, but Bardsley held his bat exceedingly high. His right hand disdained a batting glove. His flicks with the bat, while awaiting the ball, were meticulously straight back. He never allowed any waverings or hysterical flutterings out towards point. This backswing, perhaps the first essential towards success, was always a model for the young. Back and down and always along the line of flight of the ball.

Appropriately, Bardsley was born in Nevertire, north of the Macquarie River in what was, in a sense, the Never-Never of New South Wales. He was named after the nearby town of Warren and his cricket career began when the family transferred to Sydney because his father had become headmaster of a school in a suburb known as Forest Lodge.

The elder Bardsley had a deep, old-fashioned love of cricket, and he saw in Warren a means of achieving a more personal link with the game than he himself had ever known. He must have been a shrewd man. He didn't fuss over Warren, driving him to the game, but merely provided the implements and the opportunities. Like the good schoolmaster he undoubtedly was, he had, too, eyes for others, and his period at Forest Lodge coincided with the youthful rise of Cotter, Kelleway and Oldfield, all Test men. Another Bardsley, Ray, was to play for New South Wales so that with Warren too it could be said that no other Australian headmaster—or possibly English—gave so many riches to the cricketing world as did Bardsley senior.

'Tibby' Cotter was killed at Gallipoli in 1915. He was one of the greatest of fast bowlers and Bardsley always retained the vivid picture of his knocking the middle stumps of Hobbs and Fry out of the ground at Leeds in the Test of 1909.

Cotter was the terror of the school playground. The lads played on an asphalt pitch during recess and Bardsley was one of the very few who showed an interest in batting when Cotter was bowling. The bounce off the asphalt was high and there were always broken palings in the fence at the rear all the time Cotter was at school. Bardsley declared that once, in a school game, they had to put six long-stops to Tibby.

'As I saw Tibby breaking stumps, breaking fingers and breaking ribs,' Bardsley once told me, 'I never stopped giving thanks that I was always on his side and never against him.'

Cricket was not only a summer game for those lads. They also played during the winter, and in that period Bardsley rose every morning to do physical exercises—he wanted a strong body and supple wrists. Exercises done, he would go to a park to join Cotter, Kelleway, Oldfield and others in an hour's cricket before breakfast. If there happened to be a game in a paddock as Bardsley was coming home from school, it wasn't long before he had wheedled himself into that as well.

Giving thought to improving his stamina and footwork, he took up boxing. He even took up ju-jitsu. To strengthen his wrists further he squeezed a tennis-ball on the way to and from school. These were the incidentals. Of prime importance, as he came to young manhood, was the time he spent at the nets. All told, he once reasoned, he spent quite a few years of his life at cricket nets.

'My aim,' he once told me, 'was to have eyesight and footwork in perfect working order and co-ordination by the time I got into the middle. If you have to find these things in the middle you have no right to be there. You must be in perfect physical shape and form long before that. You have to work for these things very early in the piece.'

A famous pianist, Warren once pointed out, never achieved the top without years of solid grind and daily practice. Thus, as a pianist worked at his instrument, so Bardsley worked with a bat.

This complete addiction to work at the nets was a feature of Bardsley's generation and, I think, mine too.

I once met an official of the New South Wales Cricket Association who had managed a side on what we call our southern tour. This was a modern side, travelling by air, and he was staggered at the little interest his charges took in net practice at Adelaide and Melbourne. They seemed, he said, to have no sooner left the dressing-room for the nets than they were back again.

He contrasted that attitude with a New South Wales side he knew in Bardsley's time, when travel was by train and the journey to Adelaide was broken in Melbourne for a few hours. The players asked the manager to get all the cricket bags down to the Melbourne nets so that they could occupy the spare hours there. Then, on the day before the game against South Australia in Adelaide, the players spent both the morning and the afternoon at the nets.

In case it should be thought that the New South Wales players of the period of which I write stood more in need of practice, let me name them: Collins, Bardsley, Macartney, Kippax, Andrews, Taylor, Kelleway, Gregory, Hendry, Oldfield and Mailey—every one a Test player of distinction. These were the men who hustled their manager—and it was a hustle—to get their bags off the train for a few hours at the Melbourne nets.

I am sufficiently modern, I hope, not to be over-critical of our present day cricketers but I do think they have grown away from net-play. Some, indeed, want to get more out of the game than they are prepared to put into it. I can't say whether it is a matter of disposition, or of too many tours, or of too much air-travel; but I do know that I admired Bardsley when he told me of the attention he gave to detail. He left nothing to chance.

When Bardsley went to England for the first time in 1909, he would rise early on the first day of a match and go down to the ground before breakfast. He did this because he wanted to feel that he knew the ground when he walked out to bat.

He used to tell of the surprise he got on the opening day of the 1909 tour. He walked on to the Trent Bridge field before breakfast and couldn't see a pitch anywhere. He asked the groundsman, 'Where's your pitch for today's game?' The groundsman staggered him by replying, 'I'll pick one out in a minute and go to work on it.'

That story gave me the impression that Bardsley thought present-day players were molly-coddled by well-prepared pitches (he would not have thought so on a few occasions in England in 1956!), and I had too an idea that his disdain for records might have come in the mellowness of his retirement. Certainly he himself had a pretty voracious appetite for runs as he was climbing the ladder.

His first three innings in 1909 yielded 63, 76 and 63 not out —a splendid start for a man of 24 years on his first trip—but he wasn't satisfied. He wanted a three-figure score and, when it came against Essex it was sorely needed. He opened with Hartigan. Two wickets were down for eight when Ransford, another young left-hander having his first trip, joined Bardsley. In three hours and twenty minutes these two young men added 355, and in a way that clearly suggested that two more left-handed scourges had come to flay English bowlers where Hill and Darling had left off.

Ransford went for 174 and Bardsley flopped on the ground and gave himself over to pleasant thoughts as Trumper walked down the pavilion steps.

'Let me see,' mused Bardsley. 'I'm nearly two hundred now. There's almost another three hours to stumps. With a bit of luck I should be about four hundred by tonight.'

That spot of reasoning—worthy of the latter day Bradman —was soon jolted into nothingness.

He moved safely past two hundred and at 217 pushed one out to the covers and called to Trumper, 'Come one.' Off sprinted Bardsley but when he got half way he saw that Trumper hadn't left his crease. Bardsley was run out by the proverbial mile. He was still brooding over why Trumper had left him high and dry when Victor returned to the pavilion after making 74 in sixty minutes.

In a hurt voice Bardsley said: 'That was a bad show, Vic. There was an easy single in it and it was my call and everything. Why did you leave me stranded?'

'Now look here, Warren,' said Trumper. 'You had made over two hundred. How many more did you want to make? There are, you know, a few others in this side who like an innings.'

Bardsley said he learnt the lesson and ever afterwards felt contempt for batsmen who went on and on after runs when the soul had gone out of the game and runs were of no account.

He ran into more trouble at Glasgow. The batting order took a sharp about-turn with Bardsley batting No. 10 and Armstrong No. 11. Bardsley hit a century and then a note was brought to him from the captain Noble. All it said was: 'Get out!' So Bardsley did as he was told—he hit a high catch intentionally and walked off.

'What the dickens did you do that for?' exploded Armstrong. 'Don't you think I'd like a bit of a hit too?'

Bardsley showed him the note. That brought him further trouble in the pavilion. 'When I send you a note,' said Noble, 'it is obviously meant for you and not to be made public property!' Which moves one to wonder what Noble and his ilk would have thought of many modern players who have private notes, talks and the like made public property in print almost before a tour has finished!

There were times when Bardsley thought there was more trouble for him in the pavilion than in the middle.

On another occasion he was batting with Noble and had just reached his century with a boundary. As he walked back past Noble he looked at his skipper, expecting words of commendation. Instead, Noble merely looked at him and said, 'Well, and how many sixes are you going to hit now?'

Bardsley took the hint and was swallowed up by the pavilion in no time.

Noble was known as a captain who brooked no nonsense. He ran his side as a unit, not for individuals, and those who played with him would not have had it any other way. Bardsley once told me he thought there was much less selfishness in cricket in his day than in mine. I remained noncommital (not necessarily disagreeing) and he went on to tell me the story of Sammy Carter and Trumper. They were watching Trumper from the pavilion and he moved to 95.

'Whoever is next had better get his things together,' called out Carter. 'Vic won't be long now.'

That meant that Trumper would get *himself* out as soon as he reached the century. All this, from the basic spirit of the game, is commendable. A criticism in England against the Australians of 1948 was that they regarded every match as a Test; they never relented. On the other hand, a criticism against the Australians of 1909 was that they were not 'stern' enough. You can't please everybody!

After that first trip to England it was written of Bardsley: 'Of all the men new to England, none made so big an impression. More orthodox in method than many of Australia's greatest batsmen, his was always a terribly difficult wicket to get, so accurate was his footwork, so beautifully straight his bat, whether in back or forward play. But Bardsley was always full of strokes, a beautiful cutter, and wonderfully skilful at forcing and "running" the ball to leg; above all he had the temperament for playing long innings in big cricket.'

That was written of Bardsley at the start of his career: it could well have been written of him, also, at the finish, for he changed his technique over the years by not even a flourish. His last great Test innings was in 1926 when he scored 193 not out at Lord's, and that on a pitch that was dry at one end and wet at the other, calling for a different batting technique at either end. A hose had been left running overnight.

Some of our legislators had tart tongues where Bardsley was concerned. Still giving everything he had, he was plugging along for his club in the late 1920s when I began playing with Waverley. Everything he did in the middle was a lesson for the young player and yet, I recall, the up-and-coming were warned against him. He was, they said, a sour old Test player—one to be avoided. (Maybe they say the same of me today!)

Bardsley had high cricketing standards. He spoke out of the left side of his mouth with a gruff voice that belied the inner man but, like many another, he could not be bothered any longer with the game when he felt pin-prickings. This is one reason why many of the rich heritages of the past have not been handed down in Australian cricket. Unlike English cricket, which gathers the old gaffers to the game with links of affection and respect, Australian cricket too often puts off the old name for the new, and the average old-timer, after the first twinge of regret, is not greatly put out over it. If he feels that he isn't wanted he simply finds a niche in another game and in other company, and thus becomes lost to cricket for ever.

Bardsley was once so highly regarded that he was made

sole selector for New South Wales. He staked his reputation by choosing a young doctor, H. V. Hordern, just returned from studies in the United States. The Australian selectors followed Bardsley's lead and Hordern took 5-85 and 7-90 in his first Test against England, and that against a side including Hobbs, George Gunn, Rhodes, Mead, Hearne, Foster, Woolley and Douglas. Hordern thus equalled the record of the Kent bowler, F. Martin, who took twelve wickets in his first and only Test. I must learn, some day, what happened to Martin, because even after such a burst he was not chosen for the next Test at Manchester.

Hordern, whose nickname was 'Ranji,' (possibly because he was so swarthy), was a slow bowler, expert in the bosie, and he took 32 wickets in that series at an average of 24. Because of the demands of his profession and the war he never again played for Australia. The point is, however, that Bardsley must be given high marks for so quickly recognising his merit.

Now, it has to be admitted that some old cricketers are thorough bores. You find them at most grounds, always eager to revive the past at the expense of the present. Bardsley was certainly not one of these. He dipped often into the past, but always in a fond manner. I never found him sour or embittered.

I saw him once when Morris, another left-hander and an outstanding cricketer for any generation, was having a sad run of outs.

'I can almost cry when I see Morris failing,' said Bardsley. 'He's one of the very best cricketers. All his Test centuries shout that. But he's fallen into the horrible habit of playing the ball on the move. He's shuffling now as he plays. He's lost grip of himself. I could put him right in five minutes. Doesn't anybody tell him these things?'

I couldn't answer that. A wise maxim in Australian cricket is never to give personal advice unless it is sought.

Bardsley, like all the others, adored Trumper; but only a little way behind was Cotter.

'By cripes,' he once exclaimed, 'Tibby was a real corker. Strong, big. Never got tired. He broke more stumps than any other fast bowler I knew. We were always running out of stumps down at Wentworth Park. Tibby loved to break stumps and he loved to "pink" a batsman. Every fast bowler does. Gregory, McDonald, Larwood—the whole ruddy lot of 'em. Just as soon hit a batsman as the stumps. And no harm in that either, I suppose.

'We were playing North Sydney one day and Tibby was in great form. Knocking stumps over in all directions. In came Stud White and first ball Tibby smashed Stud's fingers against the handle of the bat. A sickening crunch. They took Stud off to hospital. Never forget Tibby's remark. "Well," he said, wiping his hands, "that's one of the —— out of the way." About an hour later Stud came back to bat again with his fingers heavily bandaged. Very brave man, Stud. Tibby took one look at him and snorted, "Give me that ball. I'll break the ——'s neck this time." Tibby reckoned that when he "pinked" a batsman he should remain "pinked".'

Bardsley, as I remarked earlier, was himself 'pinked' in Liverpool, England. He tried to hook a short one from McDonald, when the latter was playing for Lancashire, and received a hit on the ear. Another inch or two and it would have hit his temple and, possibly, he might have rested for all time in English soil—as was the fate of McDonald himself.

Bardsley had a delightful quirk in conversation. Whenever I induced him to tell me of his best innings he would always start by saying, 'Well, to cut a long story short.' I have no doubt that many a bowler, after looking at his broad bat for many hours, would have liked him to cut his innings short.

Which was his greatest feat in Test cricket? He himself favoured the time—as well he might—when in 1909 he got a century in each innings of the Oval Test. Tests, then, were only of three days' duration, and S. F. Barnes was at his peak.

'Some people believed Barnes to be the best bowler in the world,' said Bardsley. Not, you will notice, that Bardsley said this himself. He modestly put it on to other people, as if he, himself, had some doubt in the matter.

He liked to recall, too, the occasion in 1926 when he played through the innings at Lord's for 193. He was congratulated on that feat by Dr. H. V. Evatt, then a rising young barrister.

Bardsley's acknowledgment was typical. 'I'd swop it for one of your degrees,' he told Evatt.

'Well,' said Evatt, 'give me the 93. You keep the 100 and the not out and you can have any degrees I've got!'

Once, in a manner that I hoped was disarming, I said to Warren, 'What about F. R. Foster?'

I perceived, even years afterwards, a slight wince. That English left-hander had been a blight on Bardsley's early career—very much as Bedser was with Morris. Foster came to Australia in 1910-11 and, swinging the ball late across Bardsley's body (left-handed opening batsmen rarely get this ball, a common one to a right-hander), he clean bowled him four times in the Tests. Bardsley was dropped from the fifth and final one, but in his preceding innings, so they said, he merely dropped into the dressing-room on his way back from the middle, took Bill Whitty, our left-handed bowler, and led him to the nets at the back where he had him bowl almost unceasingly to him. It was said that Bardsley in that season wore Whitty more into the ground than did the English batsmen, but it was indicative of how Bardsley set out to overcome his problems. Not that he did with Foster.

Bardsley played with or against many of the richest characters in the game. He told me how he once faced up to a 'pair' against George Hirst.

Hirst had sent his stumps flying for nil in the first innings and Warren said he didn't feel very happy about things as he faced the same bowler in the second innings. But, to his great surprise, Hirst threw up a full-toss, which Bardsley tucked away for three.

'As I finished at Hirst's end,' said Bardsley, 'I smiled at him and said "Thanks." I thought that he had presented me, a young player, with a full-toss to get me off the "pair." But Hirst glared at me. "Doon't thank me," he said, "bloody ball slipped!" And then he clean bowled me again, for three.'

Like all his fellows, Bardsley idolised Vic Trumper. In Melbourne once, when Trumper was captain of New South Wales, there were loud cheers from the Victorian room when their skipper won the toss. He sent New South Wales in on a Melbourne glue-pot, as bad a pitch as cricket knows.

Trumper said to Bardsley, 'Come on, Curly, put them on. You and I are for it. Stay there half an hour and I'll always remember you.'

Bardsley continued the tale: 'Well, to cut a long story short, we were still there at lunch-time. Vic was 50 and I was 70. The South Africans were here for a Test series and saw that game. One of them said later, "If you can do that on a glue-pot, what will you do against us on a good pitch?" '

In England in 1921, when Australia won three Tests and drew the other two, no fewer than 29 men played for England in the series. They played 14 bowlers and never once, according to Bardsley, played G. M. Louden, of Essex, the best bowler in England.

The story goes that plenty of duck-shoving went on when Bardsley and Collins batted against Louden. Bardsley would try to give Collins the strike; Collins, in turn, would try and manoeuvre the other into it. All the Australians were agreed that Louden was the best bowler they met in England in that year.

Why didn't England pick him for the Tests?

'Well,' said Bardsley, 'all we did was tell the truth. We told everybody that Louden was England's best bowler. They thought we were leg-pulling and just didn't pick him!'*

One could go on and on about Bardsley but I must remind myself to cut a long story reasonably short. The last time I saw him was when a cold, wintry wind was blowing in off the Pacific and we were burying in the cemetery upon the Waverley cliffs the remains of Dr. Rowley Pope—friend, adviser and medical comforter to every Australian team to England for many, many years. Many famous Australian cricketers were grouped around the graveside and as the ceremony concluded I asked Warren what were his thoughts.

'I was just thinking what a great bloke old Doc was,' said Bardsley. 'I was thinking of him and then I just happened to see So-and-so across there and I thought, "Poor old So-and-so. By cripes, he's looking old." And then I thought, well, I suppose some of them are looking at me and saying, "Poor old Bards. By cripes, he's looking old!" That's just the trouble. We are all just poor old So-and-so's.'

But not really. You couldn't pity men with memories as rich and as happy as Bardsley. Yarning with him was one of the most pleasant experiences I have known in cricket.

* I told this story on B.B.C. Television in England in 1956 when somebody asked whether it was true that Australians tried to play certain individuals into a Test team against them. I offered it as proof that we were much too simple for such a cunning device! Later that summer, when I was playing in a village game at Amersham, Louden came and introduced himself to me. I barely had time for more than a few words with him. English summers speed too fast.

Perhaps it was because we had so much in common—the feelings of a Test opener as he waits for the first ball.

In Test matches, Bardsley made 1,487 runs against England at an average of 33; 982 against South Africa at 61; and in Australia's Sheffield Shield games he made 4,171 at 60. These would be outstanding figures in any era, and the fact that they were made when the ball was red and the bowlers and fieldsmen were on their toes makes them (to me, at least) all the rosier.

Four

THE GREAT BOWLING OF
SYD BARNES

Write the name of S. F. Barnes, of Staffordshire, England, and set against it this bowling analysis: 11 overs, 7 maidens, 6 runs, 5 wickets. There you have the finest piece of bowling ever seen in Test cricket, for it was performed on a true pitch at Melbourne and the wickets were those of Bardsley, Kelleway, Hill, Armstrong and Minnett.

I first saw Barnes in London in April, 1953, at a Cricket Writers' Dinner at the Skinners' Hall. He had turned 80 years a few days before, yet he was a proud and erect figure as he stood up with Jack Hobbs (70), and Ian Craig (17), to take wine with the chairman, Charles Bray. Barnes signed his autograph in copper-plate writing, his hand as steady as his bowling was reputed to be. Soon after that he turned out in a Testimonial match in which the sides were captained by Walter Robins and Bill Edrich, and before the game began Barnes said to his captain, Robins, 'You had better give me an old ball. I might run through the other side with a new one and spoil your match!'

Barnes was to bowl the opening over of that match. He felt so well after the one over that he promptly bowled another. That at 80!

I met him again later in the tour at Stoke, and we had just

settled down to a good old cricketers' 'yarn' when an official came up and said that our Prime Minister, Mr. Menzies, was anxious to see him. I am still in the process of forgiving the Prime Minister!

There was a mix-up over the 1901 English side to Australia. The M.C.C. could not get a satisfactory side together and passed the job over to Archie MacLaren with their blessing. Yorkshire made the task no easier by withholding Hirst and Rhodes, and MacLaren, as a brave and knowledgeable man should often do, backed his own judgment—he did so by plucking Barnes out of the Lancashire League. Barnes had played a few games for Warwickshire as a fast bowler, but he was a spinner when MacLaren spotted and selected him.

Barnes had played only two Tests in Australia when he was being acclaimed as the finest hard-wicket bowler England had sent abroad. A few years later M. A. Noble singled him out as the world's finest bowler, and to this day Sir Pelham Warner plumps for him as the greatest bowler he has ever seen.

Barnes's first Test wicket was that of Victor Trumper; he caught and bowled him for two in Sydney. Also, he clean-bowled Clem Hill in the same innings. Barnes took 5-65 in that innings (he got only 1-74 in the second), but in the next Test, at Melbourne, his name was being spoken everywhere because he took 6-42 and 7-121 (he got Trumper and Hill in both innings). Melbourne was to be his best Test ground.

Misfortune hit him hard in the next Test at Adelaide. He suffered a knee injury, withdrew from the match, and didn't play in another Test until the July one at Sheffield in 1902. He took there 6-49 in the first innings and 1-50: yet, un-accountably, he wasn't chosen in the immortal next Test at Old Trafford, which Australia won by three runs. Barnes didn't play against Australia again in England until 1909, and he missed another trip to Australia.

It is interesting that Noble should have placed Barnes on a pedestal for, in fact, Barnes learnt a lot about swing bowling from Noble. Barnes began, as most bowlers do, as a fast bowler, but he soon learned that there was more to the business than sheer speed. He experimented with finger-spin, both off and leg, and it was as a medium-paced spinner that he was singled out for the Australian tour by MacLaren. Barnes possessed a very shrewd and deductive cricket brain. He closely watched the other leading bowlers of that day and quickly applied some of their technique to his own bowling.

Monty Noble, in particular, captivated him. Here was an off-spinner of the old and original school (very similar to the latter-day Jim Laker) who possessed all the variations of the art. Noble would gain tricks of flight by delivering the ball at various heights—gaining this by dipping or straightening his right leg at the moment of release—and he had an out-curve as distinct from the ordinary off-break. If a breeze came in from fine-leg, Noble was in his element as he curved, floated, and dropped the ball with side-spin and over-spin. He brought to the cricket field much of the technique of the baseball pitcher.

I don't know whether modern Test bowlers have a union in which they swop the tricks of the trade—I think not—but Syd Barnes found that Noble lived up to his name, for the great Australian all-rounder and captain gave him many tips on bowling.

Barnes not only wanted off-breaks and leg-breaks from the pitch. He wanted movement in the air as well, and in England he studied the great English left-hander, George Hirst. The normal swing of a right-hand bowler to a right-hand batsman with the new ball is from leg to off. Similarly, a left-hand bowler will swing in from off to leg—as Hirst did.

Barnes practised with his leg-break allied to a certain body action at the moment of delivery and, hey presto! he found movement in the air similar to Hirst's natural swing.

But observe these important differences in the technique of Barnes and let me illustrate them by referring to Maurice Tate, one of the greatest of all bowlers. Tate was a glorious mover of the new ball, mostly from the leg and with tremendous whip off the pitch. His swing (as distinct from swerve, which comes from spin) was gained by holding the ball in the normal fashion with the line of stitches facing the batsman. This swing comes late in the ball's flight, and the ball, off the pitch, continues on in the direction of the swing—that is, towards the slips. A nightmare of a ball, too!

When Barnes swung in the air from the leg, by spin, the ball turned back from the off. When he swung in from the off, with his leg-break action, the ball gripped the pitch with its spin and turned from the leg. In the case of Hirst—and Alec Bedser, with his in-swing, being a right-hander—the ball, on hitting the pitch, continues out towards the leg-slips. Thus Barnes's swerves broke from the pitch in directions different from the normal swings.

'At the time I was able to bowl these,' Barnes recently told me by letter, 'I thought I was at a disadvantage in having to spin the ball when I could see bowlers doing the same by simply placing the ball in their hand and letting go; but I soon learned that the advantage was with me because by spinning the ball, if the wicket would take spin, the ball would come back against the swing. . . . I may say I did not bowl a ball but that I had to spin, and that is, to my way of thinking, the reason for what success I attained.'

In Barnes's first Test innings against Australia, Charlie

Macartney was at the bowler's end when Barnes clean-bowled Trumper. 'The ball was fast on the leg stump,' said Macartney, 'but just before it pitched it swung suddenly to the off. Then it pitched, broke back, and took Vic's leg-stump. It was the sort of ball a man might see if he was dreaming or drunk.'

Those who have played against Barnes—unfortunately, there are now not many left—have told me that he was accurate and kept a perfect length. He had variations of pace and flight and could regulate the spot at which his swing became effective. He could also regulate the amount of break. Moreover, he used the width of the crease, first over the stumps, then from halfway, and then from the edge.

'But I never bowled all out at the stumps,' he maintained. 'I liked to study the batsman and then bowl at his strokes. I intended him to make a stroke and then I tried to beat it. I tried to make the batsman move. It is amazing how often a batsman will make a mistake if you induce him to use his feet.'

I asked him about that December morning of 1911. 'Naturally, I was very pleased,' he said, 'but I did not consider it the highlight of my career, for I knew that it was possible to bowl well with little or no result. On the other hand, one could bowl not nearly so well and reap quite a harvest of wickets—you know as well as I do that there is a very small margin between success and failure.'

And then, after a pause: 'Still, I think I did bowl well that day.'

Of course he did. I looked up the files.

They had bands at Test matches in those days—they did in Sydney right up to 1931 when the Springbok captain, Jock Cameron, asked the band not to play as he could not concentrate while the music was in the air.

The band in Melbourne was playing comic-opera tunes as the Englishmen were led out by Johnny Douglas. The early morning was dull and close and around eleven o'clock there were a few drops of rain. The weather looked like developing into a thunderstorm. But Clem Hill, winning the toss, feared neither the light nor the moisture-laden atmosphere—lending swing to a new ball—nor even the pitch. 'Bad luck, Johnny,' he said to Douglas, 'we'll bat.'

There was a slight mist as the umpires walked out. Bardsley had been put through a pretty rigorous physical test and had been pronounced fit, although, after a battering from Foster in Sydney, he was well strapped up as he walked out with Kelleway to open the innings.

Kelleway was very wary in playing the first over from Foster. Then Barnes prepared to bowl to Bardsley. Barnes, in collaboration with Douglsa, took a long time to settle his field. He was most pernickety in this matter.

At last he was satisfied and over came the first ball. It was on a good length and Bardsley shaped at it very cautiously. He missed, and it hit him on the leg and went into his stumps—an in-swinger that would have had the Australian l.b.w. had it not bowled him.

Another left-hander, Hill, was next, and he took a single from the first ball, a fact to be noted because it was a long time before another run was scored from Barnes.

Hill faced up to Barnes again for his next over, and a torrid one it was. There was an immediate and loud appeal for l.b.w. but it was rejected, and Hill, defending desperately, saw the over through.

Kelleway faced Barnes for his next over. He missed completely an in-swinger on his leg stump that straightened up and he was out l.b.w. Australia: 2 for 5.

In came Armstrong and he saw Hill in all manner of

trouble. Barnes gave him one that was an off-break to him, and followed with an in-swinger. Then came one a little wider, going away, which Hill allowed to pass. The final ball of the over pitched on Hill's leg stump and hit the top of the off-stump. Australia: 3 for 8.

As captain, Hill had put Trumper lower on the list so that he could bat with the sheen gone from the ball. But Trumper came now with the ball still almost new. Meanwhile, spectators were busy recalling an earlier tour by Warner's team when Australia batted in Sydney on a perfect pitch under a thundery sky, and Hill, Trumper and Duff were out for 12, leaving Noble and Armstrong to stop the collapse. This time, as Trumper walked out in the tense atmosphere, a great cheer went up. Trumper would succeed where the others had failed!

Armstrong drove Foster for three and then faced Barnes. Immediate exit! He snicked his first ball and Smith caught him behind.

Four Australian wickets were gone for eight, and of that very modest figure only a single run had been scored from Barnes. He had taken four wickets for one run! Test cricket had not seen the like of this before.

Ransford, on his home ground, now joined Trumper, and the latter brought a relieved cheer, like a clap of thunder, as he brilliantly back-cut Foster. The ball went like a streak, incidentally hitting Douglas on the shins, and the batsmen ran two. Rain began to fall now and the players came off after 45 minutes of play.

They were back again 15 minutes later. Barnes bowled a maiden to Ransford, feverishly defensive. Then in the next over, from Foster, Trumper made two delicious late cuts to the rails. It looked like another maiden over from Barnes to Ransford, but the left-hander got Barnes away to leg for a single off the last ball. It had been an hour since the previous and only run had been taken from Barnes.

Barnes didn't seem himself in his next over. He bowled a full toss that went high over Ransford's head for four byes. At the end of the over he spoke to Douglas. Barnes had been ill during the preceding week and there was a doubt whether he would play. He told Douglas that he couldn't see the other end. Everything seemed to be going round and round.

So, to the great relief of the Melbourne crowd—and also of the batsmen at the wickets—Barnes left the field. He didn't return until after lunch.

The Australian players, on their way from the dressing-room to lunch in another pavilion, had to run the gauntlet of many an anxious inquiry from the spectators. What was wrong? Was something amiss with the wicket? To all inquiries the humbled Australians gave the one reply, 'Barnes!'

Foster knocked Trumper's stumps back after lunch, and then Barnes took the ball again. Australia: 5 for 33.

Minnett, a notable performer in the preceding Test at Sydney, came next and promptly snicked Barnes to third slip. He was dropped. But after scoring two, he skied Barnes to cover, where Jack Hobbs was waiting. Six down for 38, and Barnes had the remarkable bowling figures cited in the first paragraph of this chapter—11 overs, 7 maidens, 6 runs, 5 wickets.

Barnes got no more wickets in that innings. He finished with 5-44 off 23 overs. Actually, he should have had another wicket when Hordern spooned one up in front, a catch that could have been taken by any one of five men but for the fact that each one left it to the other fellow. He might, too, have had the last man, Whitty. All the players, including Whitty, himself, thought he had been clean bowled. Indeed,

67

the usual procession to the pavilion had begun when Umpire Crockett, who was at square leg, held that the ball had come back from the keeper's pads and called out 'No, no!' The other umpire then gave Whitty not out, and 35 more runs were added to the score.

Ransford was Australia's best batsman; he played coolly and intelligently for 43. Hordern, after his let-off, got 49 not out, Carter a cheeky 29, and Whitty and Cotter 14 each.

The day provided many other incidents. With the score 8-125 Barnes came on to relieve Hearne. Very carefully, Barnes motioned his fieldsmen this way and that, upon which a portion of the crowd in the Outer began to hoot him for not 'getting on with it.'

Barnes resented the hooting. He threw down the ball and stood with his arms folded. While a few still hooted, members and others cheered. 'It was,' wrote a Sydney critic, 'a most unwarranted display against a man who had bowled magnificently. It evidenced, too a most partisan spirit. It was confined to a hostile section in the shilling stand, and such unfair treatment undoubtedly interfered with Barnes's bowling. In his next over there was a similar outbreak by the hoodlums, but the occupants of the members' reserve cheered him and the noisy element was quickly quelled by the counter-demonstration.'

'During the tea interval,' the Sydney critic added, 'the demonstration against Barnes was universally condemned, and it was suggested that the Victorian authorities should at once follow the example of the New South Wales Association and announce that they would prosecute offenders for unruly or riotous behaviour. After the interval, when Barnes bowled again, the crowd was perfectly quiet, a couple of policemen being in the middle of the noisy section. But it was the worst demonstration of partisanship seen on the ground.'

Spectators cheered Barnes all the way to the pavilion when the innings ended. It was said of Barnes then that he was too reserved, too stern, to be popular with his fellows, but I imagine that he, like the latter-day O'Reilly, looked upon all batsmen as his natural enemies. Not for him frivolities on the field or the happy exchange of pleasantries. He meant business from the first ball, and never more than on that Melbourne morning of December 30, 1911.

It was perhaps the most historic morning in Test history. England won finally by eight wickets, Hearne and Hobbs getting centuries and F. R. Foster 6-91 in the second innings. Some said the Foster-Barnes partnership was the greatest bowling one ever.

Now, in his eighties, Barnes is courteous, gentle and gracious. He is as straight in figure as on that Melbourne morning, a splendid specimen of physical fitness, and his mind is alert and discerning. He pays tribute to the modern bowler, if not many modern bowling methods, and I like very much this expression of opinion, one which the world of officialdom must listen to some day: 'The l.b.w. rule, as it is now, has done much harm to cricket. It has shut out the lovely off-side strokes. There is too much defensive bowling outside the leg stump to leg fields and too much playing by the batsmen off the back foot. If you are going to get wickets, you must attack the batsman. If you are going to get runs, you must attack the bowler. That is the game of cricket. One must attack the other, and every bowler should welcome it when a batsman shows a desire to step into him. It is then, if he uses his head, that a bowler has most chance. But that l.b.w. rule—no! It has done too much harm already.'

Well said Syd Barnes. And, I may add, the world of cricket wishes you well for your century, not out, in 1973.

AUSTRALIA *v.* ENGLAND

At Melbourne, December 30, 1911; January 1, 2 and 3, 1912
England won by 8 wickets

Australia—

C. Kelleway, lbw, b Barnes	2	— c Gunn, b Foster	13
W. Bardsley, b Barnes	0	— run out	16
C. Hill (Capt.), b Barnes	4	— c Gunn, b Barnes	0
W. W. Armstrong, c Smith, b Barnes	4	— b Foster	90
V. T. Trumper, b Foster	13	— b Barnes	2
V. S. Ransford, c Smith, b Hitch	43	— c Smith, b Foster	32
R. B. Minnett, c Hobbs, b Barnes	2	— b Foster	34
H. V. Hordern, not out	49	— c Mead, b Foster	31
A. Cotter, run out	14	— c Hobbs, b Foster	41
H. Carter, c Smith, b Douglas	29	— b Barnes	16
W. J. Whitty, b Woolley	14	— not out	0
Byes 5, l-b 4, n-b 1	10	Byes 14, l-b 7, n-b 2, w 1	24

Total 184

Total 299

Fall: 0, 5, 8, 11, 33, 38, 80, 97, 140, 184

Fall: 28, 34, 34, 38, 136, 168, 232, 235, 298, 299

	O.	M.	R.	W.	O.	M.	R.	W.
Barnes	23	9	44	5	32·1	7	96	3
Foster	15	2	52	1	38	9	91	6
Hitch	7	0	37	1	5	0	21	0
Douglas	15	4	33	1	10	0	38	0
Hearne	6	0	8	0	1	0	5	0
Woolley	·1	0	0	1	3	0	21	0
Rhodes	—	—	—	—	2	1	3	0

Hitch, 1 n-b.

Foster, 1 w.
Barnes, 1 n-b.
Hitch, 1 n-b.

England—

J. B. Hobbs, c Carter, b Cotter	6	— not out	126
W. Rhodes, c Trumper, b Cotter	61	— c Carter, b Cotter	28
J. W. Hearne, c Carter, b Cotter	114	— not out	12
G. Gunn, lbw, b Armstrong	10	— c Carter, b Whitty	43
C. P. Mead, c Armstrong, by Whitty	11		
F. R. Foster, c Hill, b Cotter	9		
J. W. H. T. Douglas (Capt.), b Hordern	9		
F. E. Woolley, c Ransford, b Hordern	23		
E. J. Smith, b Hordern	5		
S. F. Barnes, lbw, b Hordern	1		
J. W. Hitch, not out	0		
Byes 2, l-b 10, n-b 4	16	— Byes 5, l-b 5	10

Total 265

Two wickets for 219

Fall: 10, 137, 174, 213, 224, 227, 258, 260, 262, 265

Fall: 57, 169

	O.	M.	R.	W.		O.	M.	R.	W.
Cotter	21	2	73	4	....	14	5	45	1
Whitty	19	2	47	1	....	18	3	37	1
Hordern	23·1	1	66	4	....	17	0	66	0
Kelleway.......	15	7	27	0	....	7	0	15	0
Armstrong	15	4	20	1	....	12	1	22	0
Minnett........	5	0	16	0	....	2	0	13	0
Ransford.......	—	—	—	—	....	1·1	0	11	0

Cotter, 3 n-b.
Minnett, 1 n-b.

Umpires: R. W. Crockett and D. Elder.

Five

CRICKET'S UNSINKABLE SHIP

When Warwick Windridge Armstrong first played Test cricket, in 1901, he looked like a young Australian gum-tree —tall, willowy, graceful. When he last played for Australia, in 1921, he looked like a big Moreton Bay fig-tree planted on the field—he was then 42 years old and weighed 22 stone. In the photograph of that 1921 team in England, Armstrong rather suggested the liner *Queen Mary* surrounded by tugs and it was understandable that he was called by his team 'The Big Ship.' In bulk, in performance, in domination of the general cricket scene, he was Australia's Dr. W. G. Grace.

In first-class cricket Armstrong was one of only three Australians who made over 10,000 runs and took over 500 wickets, George Giffen and M. A. Noble being the others. Armstrong's record was 16,164 runs at an average of 46; and 832 wickets at 19 each. In all Tests, he made 2,873 runs at 38 an innings and he took 85 wickets at 31 each. To complete the record, he never lost a toss as an Australian captain.

He died in 1947, aged 68, leaving an estate worth £90,000. The assembling of so many runs, wickets, bulk and money would have been a busy enough life for an outstanding man, but, in addition, Armstrong never shirked a difference of opinion with officialdom and he ran into plenty of disagreements on the field proper. Sometimes—as if he didn't have enough to occupy his time—it almost seemed that he went looking for trouble.

Armstrong was strong-willed and stubborn, but also a man of high principle. He gravitated naturally into the Big Six dispute of 1912 when, on the evidence, the Board of Control was at fault in not honouring its promise to the players that they could choose their manager for England. The players plumped for Laver; the Board wouldn't agree and so the Big Six—Trumper, Hill, Armstrong, Cotter, Carter and Ransford—refused to tour.

These were times of high tension. Public meetings of protest were held to support the players. What is more, Clem Hill, who had previously been chosen to lead the side in England, highlighted a meeting of the Australian selectors in Sydney (the Warner-Douglas M.C.C. side was in Australia at the time) by discolouring the eye of Peter McAlister in a very willing set-to. McAlister was known as a 'Board' man.

That period marked the passing of control of the game from players to officials (if you except Sir Donald Bradman, no player in recent years has had any official influence worth mentioning). It was easy to understand why the players stood loyally by Laver. Not only was he a man of breezy personality but he was also a player. In addition to managing the two preceding Australian tours of England, he had been the side's outstanding bowler in the Test series. This, of course, was a remarkable achievement, yet it carried no weight with the Board. The Board won this struggle (though the tour was a horrible fiasco) and ever since has sent its man as manager to England—none outside the Board have the presumption to nominate. Not since Laver, however, has an Australian manager bowled a ball in first-class cricket in England. This, calling to mind a few of the managers, can only be regarded as a distinct loss to the art of comic entertainment. Still, you can't have everything!

Trumper died, Cotter was killed at Gallipoli, and Hill and Ransford never again played Test cricket. Armstrong and Carter did—and Armstrong still had ahead of him his biggest rows with officialdom.

It was only natural that a man as hefty as Armstrong was in the early 1920s should have been slow in his movements. He was hit badly in a Shield game in Adelaide but went on to Sydney, through his native Melbourne, to play against New South Wales. There he dropped a brick on the morning of the game. He told his team his legs were so painful that he couldn't play. He was supported in this by Dr. Roy Park, a member of the Victorian side.

Armstrong still had enemies in Victoria from the rumpus of 1912 and they stormed against him. They saw their chance to sink the 'Big Ship' and they fired their torpedoes with gusto. They said he should have notified the association of his condition earlier. Without calling him before them, the Victorian selectors dropped him from the State side to play England. Here was a pretty how-d'ye-do—the Australian captain dropped from his State team!

The populace began to roar. Public meetings were held in parks and a fierce controversy—very much pro-Armstrong on the whole—began in the Press. The Victorian association held a meeting on the subject behind closed doors. It was, obviously, a stormy gathering but out of it came vindication of Armstrong.

So the 'Big Ship,' unscarred, sailed serenely again into home waters.

Armstrong resumed his captaincy of the Australian Eleven and led his team to a 5-0 record win over the M.C.C. team. He made three Test centuries with an average of 77 and received several thousand pounds from a public testimonial which was begun when the controversy was at its height.

Not even a bad attack of malaria (he had spent some time in New Guinea during the war) could put him aside. The 'shivers' came upon him just before he was going out to bat in a Test. He sent to the bar for two 'stiff' whiskies, drank them without water—ambled out and made a century!

More seaworthy than ever, Armstrong sailed on to England to weather a few more cyclones in 1921.

That was the year when Englishmen were called in large numbers to the Test cause. Some 29 played in the series, only Douglas and Woolley playing in all five Tests. Armstrong's captaincy job was made simple by the possession of McDonald and Gregory, probably as good a fast-bowling combination as any in the history of the game, and this at a time of decided slackness in English strength. This Australian side was distinctly talented. Some say it was the greatest ever but certainly it was an easy one to lead. If Gregory and McDonald didn't break through—and they usually did— there were Mailey, Armstrong and Macartney to give them a spell. The batting order placed itself; so did the men in the field. Without doubt, Carter and Oldfield were the two best wicket-keepers any country had sent away in the same touring team.

The 'Big Ship' moved placidly and remorselessly on, ramming without mercy anything in sight that looked like a cricket team.

He was flayed by the English Press for not making Kent follow-on after that county finished almost 500 behind on the first innings. Even his own team thought him over-bearing in this and demurred in the dressing-room; but he silenced them with an autocratic wave of the hand. 'Put 'em on and do as you're told,' he barked at his openers. 'There's a Test coming on and I'm not over-working my bowlers for anybody.'

There was nearly a team insurrection over that decision. His own side liked his decision to bat again as little as the Kent men.

At the end of the game, Lord Harris, president of the county club, said Kent would be 'very happy to see ten of the Australian team again.' Nobody needed two guesses as to the 'uninvited' one.

The upset over Kent was only a zephyr compared to the storms still to break at Old Trafford during the Fourth Test and at the Oval during the Fifth.

Lionel Tennyson had replaced Johnnie Douglas as England's leader for Manchester. The first day of play was washed out and the poet's descendant made a forlorn bid for victory by declaring at 5.40 p.m. on the second day when only four wickets had fallen. Tennyson, however, had overlooked the important point that after no play on the first day, this game was now a two-day one, with a consequential change in the closure rule.

Tennyson came on to the field, clapped, and motioned the Australians in. No sooner had he done so that Hanson Carter, the Australian wicket-keeper (who, as far as knowing the rules was concerned, was Australia's Frank Chester), called out to Armstrong in his perky, shrill voice, 'He's wrong, Warwick. This match is now a two-day one. He can't close after 4.50.'

'You sure, Sammy?' said Armstrong.

'Certain,' said Carter.

'Right—stay where you are,' Armstrong called to his team, and ambled off to the pavilion to find Tennyson.

'You can't close, Lionel,' said Armstrong.

'Be damned to that,' exploded his lordship, 'we have closed and that's all there is to it.'

'Get the rule book,' grunted the 'Big Ship.'

So they got the rule book and, sure enough, found that Carter was right.

Tennyson apologised and out went Armstrong to join his men again. 'Thanks, Sammy,' he said to Carter; and then he called for the ball.

But the crowd wasn't happy about the delay. They believed that Armstrong was throwing his weight about, as usual, and they began to hoot the Australians vigorously.

With that, Armstrong went to earth to wait for the hulla-baloo to subside. It didn't, of course. It grew worse. (It also grew worse at Nottingham in 1938 when, after receiving orders from Bradman in the pavilion that I was not to shape up to bat if the crowd continued its slow hand-clap as the bowler was running up, I, too, did a 'sit-me down'.)

Tennyson came on to the field and, with an umpire, walked around the ground explaining in places to the crowd that he had made an error, that Armstrong was right.

The crowd simmered down. Armstrong rose from the turf, bowled, and the game went on. In the general upset he, alone, knew that he had bowled the over before Tennyson made the premature closure. So Armstrong became the first man in history to bowl two successive overs in a Test innings.

Then came the Oval and the final Test. The game finished with England 8-403 (declared) and 2-244 against Australia's 389. It was apparent long before the game finished that it would end in a draw and after tea on the final day Armstrong summoned four non-bowling members of his team—Pellew, Taylor, Andrews and Collins—and told them to split the bowling between themselves for the rest of the match. Then he himself lumbered off to—of all places—the boundary!

The Kennington crowd didn't like a Test being treated like that. They yelled and booed at Armstrong's bulky back; but he stood as bleak and as impervious as an iceberg. A blowing newspaper came towards him. He trapped it with a foot, picked it up and casually glanced at it.

So he fiddled away the last minutes of a Test career extending over 20 years. It was typical of Armstrong. He just didn't care a hoot what the other fellow thought.

He crossed swords in that same year with Lord Harris, the autocrat of English cricket. They were sitting at the Imperial Conference and the subject of betting on cricket matches was mentioned. Lord Harris pooh-poohed the idea that anything of the kind occurred.

'Are you sure, Lord Harris?' asked Armstrong.

'Certainly,' replied his lordship with some heat, 'people just don't bet on cricket. Silly rot to say they do.'

Armstrong took the subject up next day when conference re-assembled. 'If you would like a couple of hundred on our next Test,' he said to Lord Harris, 'I can arrange it for you.'

Lord Harris didn't speak to Armstrong for the rest of the conference.

In his later days, in a Shield game in Melbourne, Armstrong was fielding in the slips when a ball was snicked to the fine-leg boundary. The big fellow ambled out after it, recovered the ball, and was raising his arm to return the ball when a spectator at his back shouted, 'Come on, Armstrong. Throw it in.' Armstrong at once dropped his arm, walked slowly back to his position in the slips and then softly lobbed the ball back to the bowler. He was not a man to take dictation from anybody.

Armstrong came to cricket in the Golden Age of the game, when the Australian side included Trumper, Hill, Darling,

Trumble, Noble, S. E. Gregory, Duff, Kelly, Howell and Jones. The English team included MacLaren, Hayward, Tyldesley, Quaife, Jessop, Gunn, Lilley, Jones, Braund, Blythe, Ranjitsinhji, Fry and Jackson.

Armstrong thus made his bow in a period of great talent. He could not hope for a high batting position in that team and in his first Test, on the home ground at Melbourne, he batted number nine. He was twice not out with four and 45. At the end of the series, however, he had established himself by topping the averages with 53, although his slow leg-breaks failed to take a wicket.

He was, in the main, a front-of-the-wicket batsman, using his reach and weight to drive powerfully; he was also a superb square-cutter. His bowling was genial and deceitful. He twisted his wrist for leg-spin, but the angle of wrist at the moment of delivery gave the ball top rather than side spin. He got many wickets by sheer bluff—pretending to bowl leg-spin when letting loose a top-spinner.

His length was never loose. Major Philip Trevor, a noted English critic of the period, once wrote, 'Armstrong's accuracy of length is extraordinary. If I were choosing a side for which Armstrong was available, and found myself a little weak in batting, I should be inclined to exclude one of my bowlers, and to include a good batsman instead, for Armstrong is worth two ordinary bowlers. He at one and the same time stops the batsman from scoring and taxes his defence. And he does more than that. He rests his comrades, both fieldsmen and bowlers.'

His first Test wicket was a good one—Ranjitsinhji clean bowled at Birmingham in 1902 for 13. This was the Indian Prince's worst season ever, with only 15 runs in four innings. He never again played against Australia but his wicket was the only one Armstrong got in the series.

Like many an overseas cricketer on his first tour there, Armstrong found the English turf difficult to cope with. He averaged only 13 for seven Test innings. He had to play 30 Test innings before he scored his first century but possibly the innings that gave him most joy was his 90 at Melbourne, in 1911, against the superb attack of Barnes and Foster.

There was a glimpse of things to come when Darling gave Armstrong, at Nottingham in 1905, the task of bowling for a draw. Armstrong put all his men on the leg-side and at slow and slow-medium, pumped the ball down on an immaculate length just wide of the leg-stump. That went on for hour after hour, his figures at the end reading 52 overs, 24 maidens, 67 runs, 1 wicket.

It was interesting that this should have been at Nottingham, the home of Harold Larwood who was to bowl even more 'interesting' leg-theory in the years ahead. Johnny Tyldesley, back in 1905, was the only one to circumvent Armstrong's tactics. This he did by drawing away, wide of the leg-stump, and hitting Armstrong to the deserted off-side—a method that Australians of a later day could have attempted against Larwood had he been slow to slow-medium!

Like Bradman and Jardine, Armstrong had the 'killer' spirit well developed as a captain. He didn't believe in gestures to the 'enemy' and it was fair enough that his long run of successes should have been broken in 1921 when Archie MacLaren, who maintained that the Australians were not invincible, came out of retirement to justify his claim. It was at Eastbourne, after the Tests, and the game took a quick dip against MacLaren when his side was bundled out for 43—Armstrong taking 5-15. Australia made 174; Mac-Laren's side replied with 326 and for the first time the Australians realised that their unbeaten record stood in danger. They failed by 28 runs; and, accordingly, English cricket rejoiced.

Armstrong was not as apt a campaigner as Bradman. Caesar-like, Bradman stipulated how many Test men should be played against him in the Scarborough Festival of 1948—and then promptly played his own full Test team! It was in 1948 that Bradman became the first Australian captain to lead an unbeaten team in England, a feat narrowly missed by Armstrong.

In all ways, then, Armstrong was one of the big men of cricket; but he was a gruff and domineering man. I met him once on a Sydney racecourse in the 1930s and found him full of contentious stuff. He didn't think much of Bradman—many bowlers in his team would have clipped his wings. No, he didn't agree that Tate and O'Reilly were in world class as bowlers.

This, of course, was arrant nonsense—but I sensed that the 'Big Ship' hadn't been picking the winners and was feeling somewhat out of sorts.

The Australian Prime Minister, Mr. Menzies, told me of the occasion when I collected a 'pair' against England at Adelaide. Concerned at my fate, Mr. Menzies turned back to Warwick, who was puffing his belly-bowl pipe like a destroyer getting up steam for sea. 'That's a terrible thing to happen to a young cricketer, Warwick,' said Mr. Menzies, 'how can you account for it?'

Warwick never wasted words. He took the 'funnel' from his mouth and uttered through the side of his mouth, 'Can't bat.'

I used to meet him again just before he died, when our paths were along Darling Point Road in Sydney. Sometimes another international in Hunter Hendry, who played under Armstrong, would join us. Armstrong was inseparable from a huge, crooked-stemmed pipe and he was the soul of affability. I tried to draw him in conversation of cricketers and his times but he preferred to talk of other things.

'Many people in cricket hated me,' he once said, 'and I guess—I certainly hope—many people liked me. But what does it all matter now! It's all over and forgotten.'

Armstrong will never be forgotten. The opinions of those who play under a skipper count more than those who are on the outside looking in and Armstrong's men, of varying generations, all plumped solidly for him though one or two thought him no great tactician. He was hard, but fair, and always spoke his mind. You knew where you stood with him, and he stood nonsense from nobody—which suggests what a pity it was that a decade or so stood between him and Jardine! Slow in movement, big in target, Armstrong would have been beaten black and blue by bodyline but he would have retaliated on the field very promptly and his attitude would have been so full of thunder that bodyline would have died in one Test.

Which, as I see it now, would have been a very, very good thing.

Six

A VERY REMARKABLE TEST MATCH

You would have to search the records a long time to find a more memorable Test match than the one England and Australia played at Sydney from December 11 to December 17, 1903. From the cricket viewpoint it had everything—collapse, recovery, superlative batting, high-class bowling, brilliant fielding, and—for those who find interest in crowd behaviour—the most remarkable outburst of barracking known to the game up to that period in Australia.

P. F. Warner led the visiting side and it is especially interesting to note that at the height of the barracking hullabaloo, when Clem Hill was given run out by Umpire Crockett, the English captain wanted to lead his team from the field, though he was persuaded against such action by the Australian captain, M. A. Noble. I say this is especially interesting because P. F. Warner was one of the co-managers of the English side in 1932-33 when the tactics of the English captain of the time, D. R. Jardine, caused crowd reaction just as bitter as, and certainly more prolonged than, that on the afternoon of Tuesday, December 15, 1903. In the 1932-33 series of incidents, moreover, the M.C.C. offered to withdraw its team from Australia—an offer not accepted by the Australian Board of Control, the main reason being one of finance.

That team of 1903 was the first one sent out by the M.C.C. The two countries had met four times in the preceding six years and Australia had triumphed on all four occasions. It was a pity Warner did not have with him leading amateur batsmen in MacLaren (who at the time was feuding with the M.C.C.), Ranjitsinhji, Fry and Jackson; but his side was rich in bowling and all-round talent. Warner, moreover, was to prove a shrewd and successful captain, taking the Ashes home by three wins to two.

Cricket at that period had not been made water-tight (or should one say water-logged?) by those men who enjoy making rules. This was to come later though, to be sure, it was odd that no prior arrangement had been made about the closure or the follow-on. In the preceding interstate games, at Melbourne and Adelaide, the two captains agreed that the batting side could declare its innings closed any time after lunch on the second day. Australian interstate cricket had a curious rule that a side in a minority of 200 runs *had* to follow-on; in matches against the Englishmen, the rule was that a side having the advantage of 200 runs should have the option of making the opposing side follow-on.

M. A. Noble, who was to become the Australian captain (this appointment was made only on the morning of the Test), believed that the follow-on rule should not apply to any match being played out, as these Tests were.

Warner cabled to England for instructions and was authorised to waive the rule applying to the closure. Thus, neither side in this series had the power to declare its innings closed, which was remarkable as the timing of a closure is one of the game's greatest attractions.

Some modern teams, seemingly, do not regard as important results in county or interstate games prior to the Tests. Warner was not of this opinion. Time beat him against

South Australia, but his side romped home by an innings against Victoria and by an innings against New South Wales. This latter win gave the tourists great heart as New South Wales had seven of the men who were to play in the First Test.

Incidentally, there was then a cycling track encircling the Sydney ground and the tourists had found that in the strong sunlight it produced a pronounced glare. The officials gave it two coats of pale green paint to soften that effect. The track was pulled up in 1920, being considered at last too dangerous for cricketers.

Noble won the toss and batted on a true, fast and brown pitch on a dull, close morning. I have said that Warner's men, because of their previous feats, went into this game with confidence. Well, within 10 minutes this feeling had zoomed to a zenith, for Australia had lost Trumper, Duff and Hill—considered, by Australians at least, as the three most classical batsmen of the day—for 12 runs.

Duff and Trumper got singles for back-cuts in the first over of the day off Hirst, medium-fast left-hand. Then came Arnold, medium-fast right-hand, upon which Trumper shaped again for his favourite back-cut. The ball, however, came up sharply and, instead of getting it with the stomach of his bat, Victor got it on the shoulder and it flew into slips to Foster, who dived and grabbed a brilliant catch in his left hand, ricking his side as he fell. That was an auspicious start for what was to be a memorable game for Foster.

Hill began with a quick single and Duff got another. Hill clipped Arnold to leg for four. Hirst bowled a fairly tight over and then Duff faced Arnold. Like Trumper, Duff tried to back-cut the first ball but didn't gauge its pace correctly and was caught behind by Lilley. Two for nine—and all because of the back-cut!

The critics sharpened their pencils. Here was a limitless Test with two Australians trying the most chancy of all strokes in the first few minutes of the game, and that without first gauging the pitch or the bowler!

Out strode the Australian captain, M. A. Noble. He got a fast-run two from the first ball and then watched, very despondently, Hill flick and fall to Hirst at the other end. Another attempted back-cut! Three down for 12.

Thoughts of some onlookers went back to 1894 when, on the same ground in the First Test of a series, Tom Richardson had Lyons, Trott and Joe Darling back for 21. Australia then recovered to make the record Test total of 586 (Syd Gregory 201, George Giffen 161), though England won by 10 runs.

Arnold and Hirst were making the new ball swing in the air and fly off a fast pitch. The English fieldsmen were admirable—fast and safe. Noble and Armstrong concentrated upon defence, and, so relieved were the spectators after the early tinkerings, they applauded every time a batsman allowed a ball to go by outside the off stump. They had seen more than enough of the stylish back-cut.

Hirst bowled unchanged for 80 minutes, yielding only eight runs. Arnold, too, gave nothing away, and it wasn't until Warner brought on Braund and Bosanquet, with spin, that the score began to move. At lunch it was 59.

After lunch Armstrong brilliantly square-drove Hirst for two fours in one over. Warner put Relf on the boundary at point. Noble (who, a few weeks earlier, had made 230 against South Australia at Sydney) was very safe, and the score passed 100.

At 118, Bosanquet sent up a perfect 'wrong-un' which Armstrong failed to identify. This delivery, an off-break bowled with a leg-break action, was then quite new to the game. It was the 'mystery ball' of cricket. Armstrong was completely befuddled, playing one way with the ball breaking the other. It came behind the big fellow's back and broke his wicket.

But bowlers of wrong-uns, down through the years, have mixed 'tripe' with triumph, and Bosanquet, the 'father' of the wrong-un, was no exception. Accordingly, Noble and Hopkins helped themselves happily off full tosses and long hops. Now Rhodes came on with his left-handed spinners, but the batsmen scored 50 in 40 minutes. Noble was 80 at tea.

Later the Australian skipper was in a grand cutting mood. As one critic wrote: 'he "legged" Relf and, assisted by items, got to 95.' Helping himself to more 'items' he got to 100 in 205 minutes, and up came the 200.

Hopkins hit eight fours in a breezy 39 before Hirst broke through. There were clouds in the sky now and Howell, the Penrith bee-farmer, came to the crease instead of Gregory in order to put some zest into the score. He hit a four and a single and was then caught on the edge of the track by Relf off Arnold. Gregory got a neat 23 before succumbing to Bosanquet's wrong-un, and at stumps Noble was not out 132. A true captain's innings.

Next day the Australian innings soon folded up—for 285. Arnold, Rhodes, Hirst and Bosanquet shared the wickets. Noble's innings, finished off by a brilliant catch by Foster at short-leg, was masterly in every way. He had certainly risen to his first responsibility as a Test captain.

England made a bad start. Warner snicked Laver to Kelly and the first wicket fell for no score. Tom Hayward made a stand with Johnny Tyldesley, but England's fourth wicket had fallen by 117. Foster was in at number five and he and Braund stuck together, though Foster never looked like lasting. He was always in trouble. Remarkably, Gregory dropped him at cover—a chance which the adept little cover-point would have taken five times out of six. At stumps on the second day Braund and Foster were still there—England 4-243. Foster had taken three hours to make 50.

On the following day Foster changed his tactics. He began then to unlock his shoulders and his feet, moving well down the pitch to Noble, Armstrong and Howell, and he drove with tremendous power. From looking like Scotton and Barlow, the old English stonewallers, he suddenly blossomed into brilliancy. He drove the powerful Australian spin attack completely off its length. Then he hooked it.

Foster saw Braund go for 102, a highly creditable innings; Hirst bowled by Howell for none; Bosanquet caught off Noble for two; and Lilley caught off Noble for four. Braund fell (the fifth wicket) at 309, and Lilley (the eighth wicket) at 332. The Australian bowling had fought back to make the honours almost even again. But now Foster danced down the pitch and demoralised the length of the spinners. He thrashed them with off, on, and straight drives, and while Relf made 31 he made almost 100. This ninth wicket put on 115.

Relf went and Rhodes came in No. 11. (Eight years later he was to come in with Hobbs as No. 1 and No. 2.) Rhodes showed faultless judgment while making 40. His defence was impregnable. While he was there the score leapt—and for the last wicket!—from 447 to 577. Noble held Foster at last, for 287, off Saunders.

Foster had given the Australian attack the most severe thrashing it had ever known. His 287 far surpassed W. L. Murdoch's 211 at Kennington Oval in 1884. He batted only seven and a quarter hours—from 50 on he averaged almost a run a minute—and he hit 37 fours. It was difficult for anybody to realise that Foster on Saturday and Foster on Monday was the same person, because his batting on Monday was freely acknowledged to be the most brilliant ever seen from an Englishman in Australia. It was a record score, made in his very first Test innings against Australia, and as Noble led his men off he lined them up and they clapped Foster heartily as he walked down the lane. The members joined in: they gave him three resounding cheers and clapped him from view. Foster had scored two more than the whole Australian total!

The Australians now were footsore and generally tired—and 292 runs behind. Noble sent in Gregory and wicket-keeper Kelly to see out the late afternoon, which they did, scoring 16.

On Tuesday morning Arnold bowled Kelly, whereupon Duff joined Gregory. There were no early back-cuts this time. The Australians were still 256 behind on the first innings and were very conscious of the fact that they had been flogged as no Australian attack had before been flogged, not even by Grace, Ranjitsinhji, Fry, Jackson or any other Englishman. It would be tough enough even to get back into the game, and so Gregory and Duff batted very cautiously. They didn't probe for runs; they took them when they offered.

Rhodes, bowling with admirable flight, spin and length had Gregory caught behind with the score 108, and every-body noted what a master Lilley was at holding the chances. Hill came next and began brightly. The score passed 150 and edged towards 200. Meanwhile Rhodes, very keen on his first tour of Australia, was bowling leg-breaks to Duff on the off-stump with a tight off-side field. He barely bowled a loose ball. At 84, with the total 191, he tempted Duff into a mis-hit and Relf took the catch on the off. Duff had been very safe, and had also batted in his usual stylish fashion.

Now came the lithe Trumper, walking up the little ramp, emerging through the white gate to the cycling track and, while fiddling with his cap, passing on to the grass. The Hill rose to him. Harry Altham has written the 1902 season in England: 'On every sort of wicket, against every type of bowling, Trumper entranced the eye, inspired his side, demoralised his enemies and made run-getting appear the easiest thing in the world. To try to reduce to words the art of this consummate batsman is almost an impertinence. He had ease, balance and perfect naturalness that made him perhaps the most fascinating batsman to watch in the history of the game.'

C. B. Fry had said: 'He had no style, and yet he was all style. He had no fixed canonical method of play, he defied all orthodox rules, yet every stroke he played satisfied the ultimate criterion of style—the minimum of effort, the maximum of effect.'

And P. F. Warner had written of Trumper, after that tour of 1902: 'No one ever played so naturally. Batting seemed just part of himself, and he was as modest as he was magnificent.'

Now was to come an innings to be ranked even higher than any that Trumper had played during the preceding year in England. To begin with, he was very careful, looking at all the wares and taking 30 minutes to get nine.

The two leading batsmen of the day, Trumper and Hill, were now together and the fight, slow to be joined, slowly grew hot. The bowlers never let up, nor did the fieldsmen. But gradually, at first by defensive play and then by sound and beautiful batsmanship, the two Australians got on top. The running between wickets was superb and the crowd roared with glee as 250 came up. This was Australian cricket —indeed, the game of cricket—at its best.

But nobody was prepared for the dramatic crash just ahead.

Braund came on to bowl from the Randwick end. Trumper late cut his first ball to the fence for four. It was a stroke of sheer elegance and the crowd roared appreciation. The next ball was also cut to the fence, finer, but again for four. The crowd roared louder. This was the superb touch, the highly skilled placement, the whippy wrist work of the master. Braund tried to trick Trumper by a fast ball, but it was wide and went through for four byes. Then the whole Hill and the Members' Stand rose and cheered as Trumper, with perfect timing, scorched the grass wide of cover for yet another four. A stroke, that, to live in memory. And now from the crowd came gales of laughter at an anti-climax, for Trumper played the next ball quietly back along the pitch.

'You've got him tied down, Braund,' called a wag from the Hill.

The last ball of the over Trumper drove wide of mid-off. It went off towards the grandstand with Hirst in pursuit. The batsmen ran one; they ran two—the crowd yelling as if it were a game of football—they ran three; and they turned for four as Hirst threw. It would be a close thing and both Hill and Trumper sprinted. The crowd was roaring continuously.

But the throw slipped out of Hirst's hand and veered off towards the sight-board. Hill had clapped on such speed that he overran his end by about 10 yards and had a long way to go when Trumper called him for the overthrow, the fifth run.

The four runs had made the crowd delirious. The overthrow, as an overthrow always will, brought yells of 'Go again' and 'There's more in it.' The excitement bubbled, with the crowd urging Hill on and on. Relf had the ball now and returned well towards the Pavilion end, towards which Hill was running.

The ball passed behind Hill, and Lilley, taking it, whipped

the bails off. Hill had run some 15 yards past the wicket and on returning he was told that he had been given out.

Hill stood in amazement. Apparently he couldn't conceive that he was out, as the ball had passed behind him. Nor could the crowd at right angles to the wicket believe that Hill had not beaten the ball home.

A crowd in ecstacy now turned into one in an ugly mood. Hill's reception of the decision spurred them on, and from the Outer—and also from the Members' Stand—came bursts of booing. Crockett was the umpire who had given Hill out and the crowd now began to croak, 'Crock-Crock-Crock-Crock.' The noise went on undiminished for minutes from all the ground and when Noble came to bat he found that Warner was very agitated. The English captain had walked towards the Members' Stand to ask for silence, but to no avail. The ground re-echoed to 'Crock-Crock-Crock-Crock.' It was like a marsh full of bull frogs on a rainy night in spring.

Warner wanted to take his men from the field, but Noble persuaded him to continue play.

Warner said later: 'I was fielding at deep mid-on to Braund and thus wasn't in a position to see whether Hill was out or not, but Foster, who was standing at short-leg, and Hayward, at deep point, said they thought Hill was out by at least a foot.'

What has to be appreciated, of course, is the disappointment and reaction of both Hill and the crowd to sudden tragedy in a moment of elation and enjoyment. Trumper and Hill were piling on the runs. In this over had come 4, 4, 4 (byes), 4, nil, and a 4 seemingly turned into a 5 but suddenly turned back into the loss of Hill's wicket.

In after years Hill admitted that 'possibly' he was out. All the evidence would seem to suggest that he *was* out.

Anyway, the crowd croaked for the rest of that tumultuous

day. The coolest man of all was Trumper. In Braund's next over he hit him for four successive fours and then a two—38 off two overs. Trumper wiped off the deficit and at one stage scored 60 in 40 minutes. He was sheer perfection. He bounced Rhodes on to the track and he hit Relf, off successive balls, for two fours and a two to bring up his century. From 90 to 100 in three balls!

Bosanquet tricked Noble by flight (Lilley stumping him) and Armstrong was very uncomfortable against Bosanquet, A memorable day ended with Trumper 119 not out and the total 5-367. Rhodes, unerring in length, was England's best bowler.

Crockett, the umpire, booed off the field at the end of play, left for home by a back gate.

Trumper had given the English attack its first trouncing of the tour. A little rain that night bound the pitch for the next day. Armstrong made 27 and Hopkins 20, but the tail was feeble. Trumper continued as before and at the end was 185 not out in a total of 577. This total left England 193 to win in the last innings.

Lilley, the English wicket-keeper, was greatly impressed by Trumper's innings. 'I consider this one,' he said, 'not merely his own masterpiece but the finest I have ever seen played from my position behind the stumps. Our English bowlers were all in splendid form and the fielding was brilliant, but even against such a fine bowling combination as Hirst, Rhodes, Bosanquet, Braund and Arnold, he never gave the slightest chance. From the first ball to the close he played with perfect confidence and ease and never gave the slightest suggestion that he would get out.'

'His footwork,' Lilley went on, 'was perfection. It enabled him to make his shots to the off with delightful ease. He hit the ball with such perfect timing and so hard that our fieldsmen just had no chance of cutting off his strokes. He played every stroke in the game.'

Lilley added that during his long service behind the stumps he had enjoyed many opportunities of studying good and perfect batting by Englishmen and Australians, but in his opinion they had all been eclipsed by this innings by Trumper. And, to round off the tribute, the English wicket-keeper said: 'If Trumper had remained to double his score—which he might well have done had he not run out of partners— I should never have tired of watching him.'

That, surely, is one of the most graceful tributes known to the game.

Wilfred Rhodes was one bowler not subdued by Trumper. There had been speculation in England as to how he would fare on this tour. Some critics believed he would be unable to overcome the perfection of Australian pitches, yet Rhodes, in the second innings of his very first Test in Australia, bowled 40·2 overs (10 maidens) and took 5-94. These are remarkable figures when it is borne in mind that Trumper was in full flow. Rhodes's figures in the first innings were 17·2, 3, 41, 2, so that he shared with Foster a remarkable first Test in Australia.

One other interesting point: Trumper, Duff and Hill, who made only 12 between them in the first innings, made 322 in the second knock and Trumper was left not out. Yes, cricket certainly is a game of ups and downs!

So to the last innings. Warner and Hayward opened again but not with good fortune. Howell uprooted Warner's stumps for eight, with the total at 21, and there was jubilation among spectators as Noble brilliantly snapped up Johnny Tyldesley for nine, with the total 39. Foster came in to a tremendous reception and joined Hayward, of Surrey, in a dogged stand.

At this stage the cricket was as tense as it had been at any earlier period. The Australians were fighting hard—the fielding was brilliant yet safe, and the bowling full of attack and guile. On the other hand, the Englishmen were giving nothing away. They met determination and fight with determination and fight.

Up past 40, 50, 60 and 70 crawled the score, but at 81 Armstrong induced Foster to play forward and miss. In missing, Foster momentarily raised his back foot, upon which Kelly flashed the bails off. With one more run scored, Braund was out for none—caught Noble, bowled Howell. Now the game had taken a violent turn towards Australia.

In came Hirst. He took guard, looked around the field, settled down—and should have been out the very first ball. Laver, usually the safest of fieldsmen, dropped him at mid-on. Had that catch been taken, three English wickets would have fallen for two runs.

No more wickets fell that night, England finishing the day with 4-122. Hayward and Hirst fought on next day, and Hayward, after a grand innings that deserved a century, finished nine runs short and was out just before the game was won. Hirst remained 60 not out.

Had that catch been taken off Hirst's first ball the match could well have gone the other way. However, victory or defeat, after the first flush has worn off, means little in such a game. England won by five wickets and deserved to win.

It could be said, finally, that very few other games had contributed such outstanding individual efforts. Foster, Trumper, Noble, Duff, Rhodes, Armstrong, Hill, Hayward, Hirst, Tyldesley and Arnold—they all shone at different times, but right through the game ran cricket's noble story of reverses, recoveries, changing fortunes, challenge and counter-challenge, and throughout everything rich artistry with bat and ball.

The 'incident' was most unfortunate. Hill's reception of the decision undoubtedly encouraged and sustained an outburst which left a blot on the sporting name of Sydney, and on the Members' Stand in particular, which, as Warner pointed out, was not in a good position to assess the decision. And, of course, a Members' Stand should always behave with discretion and taste because a ground's standing is assessed by its members' behaviour.

'It seems to me,' said Warner in a gathering after the game, 'that the first rule of cricket is to obey the umpire implicitly, and especially an umpire of the ability and integrity of Crockett, who is considered to be not only one of the best in Australia but in the world. And when he was "booed" like that it was an insult to him and the game of cricket. Whether the batsman was out or not doesn't affect the question; but members in the pavilion who took part in the demonstration were not in a good position to say. But, regarding the whole incident, we are only too glad to tear the page out of the book and forget it for ever.'

'The umpiring,' said Noble, 'has given full satisfaction.'

'I am quite sure,' the Australian captain added, 'that if Mr. Crockett gave Hill out, then Hill *was* out. An injustice has been done Mr. Crockett. I say that officially.'

The Premier of New South Wales, G. H. (later Sir) George Reid, spoke for the community generally when he expressed deep regret that the 'unpleasantness' had taken place.

At this day, over half a century later, it does no harm to look back on that 'page torn from the book.' For certainly the outburst of the crowd—the 'Crock-Crock-Crock-Crock' that floated over the Sydney Ground on the afternoon of December 15, 1903, was a remarkable feature of a very remarkable game of Test cricket.

A VERY REMARKABLE TEST MATCH

AUSTRALIA *v.* ENGLAND

At Sydney, December 11, 12, 14, 15, 16 and 17, 1903
England won by 5 wickets

Australia—

R. A. Duff, c Lilley, b Arnold	3	— c Relf, b Rhodes	84
V. T. Trumper, c Foster, b Arnold	1	— not out	185
C. Hill, c Lilley, b Hirst	5	— run out	51
M. A. Noble (Capt.), c Foster, b Arnold	133	— st Lilley, b Bosanquet	22
W. W. Armstrong, b Bosanquet	48	— c Bosanquet, b Rhodes	27
A. J. Hopkins, b Hirst	39	— c Arnold, b Rhodes	20
W. P. Howell, c Relf, b Arnold	5	— c Lilley, b Arnold	4
S. E. Gregory, b Bosanquet	23	— c Lilley, b Rhodes	43
F. Laver, lbw, b Rhodes	4	— c Relf, b Rhodes	6
J. J. Kelly, c Braund, b Rhodes	10	— b Arnold	13
J. V. Saunders, not out	11	— run out	2
No-balls	3	Leg-byes 15, b 10, n-b 1, w 2	28
Total	**285**	**Total**	**485**

Fall: 2, 9, 12, 118, 200, 207, 259, 263, 266, 285

Fall: 36, 108, 191, 254, 334, 393, 441, 468, 473, 485

	O.	M.	R.	W.		O.	M.	R.	W.
Hirst	24	8	47	2		29	1	79	0
Arnold	32	7	76	4		28	3	93	2
Rhodes	17·2	3	41	2		40·2	10	94	5
Braund	26	9	39	0		12	2	56	0
Bosanquet	13	0	52	2		24	1	100	1
Relf	6	1	27	0		13	5	35	0

Hirst, 2 n-b.
Relf, 1 n-b.

Arnold, 1 n-b.
Bosanquet, 1 w.
Hirst, 1 w.

England—

P. F. Warner (Capt.), c Kelly, b Laver	0	— b Howell	8
T. Hayward, b Howell	15	— st Kelly, b Saunders	91
J. T. Tyldesley, b Noble	53	— c Noble, b Saunders	9
E. G. Arnold, c Laver, b Armstrong	27		
R. E. Foster, c Noble, b Saunders	287	— st Kelly, b Armstrong	19
L. C. Braund, b Howell	102	— c Noble, b Howell	0
G. H. Hirst, b Howell	0	— not out	60
B. J. T. Bosanquet, c Howell, b Noble	2	— not out	1
A. A. Lilley, c Hill, b Noble	4		
A. E. Relf, c Armstrong, b Saunders	31		
W. Rhodes, not out	40		
Byes 6, l-b 7, n-b 2, w 1	16	Byes 4, w 2	6
Total	**577**	**Five wickets for**	**194**

Fall: 0, 49, 73, 117, 309, 311, 318, 332, 447, 577

Fall: 21, 39, 81, 82, 181

	O.	M.	R.	W.		O.	M.	R.	W.
Saunders	36·2	8	126	2	....	18·5	3	51	2
Laver..........	37	27	116	1	....	16	4	37	0
Howell	31	7	113	3	....	31	18	35	2
Noble	34	8	99	3	....	12	2	37	0
Armstrong	23	3	47	1	....	18	6	28	1
Hopkins	11	1	40	0	....	—	—	—	—
Trumper	7	1	12	0	....	—	—	—	—
Gregory	2	0	8	0	....	—	—	—	—

Noble, 2 n-b, 1 w.   Saunders, 2 w.

Umpires: R. W. Crockett and A. C. Jones.

Seven

THE RICH MEMORIES OF
H. L. COLLINS

Herbert Leslie Collins, captain of the renowned Australian Imperial Forces team after World War I, captain of New South Wales from 1920 to 1926 and captain of Australia in the 1924-25 and 1926 series against England, never sought any honours on the cricket field. They simply came to him. Yet, after his retirement, nobody in officialdom sought any counsel from Collins. He became—and still is—one of cricket's more-or-less forgotten men in Australia.

They gave Collins many nicknames. A popular one was 'Poker Face,' and it was a good one, too, because his face was inscrutable. They called him 'Lucky' Collins and 'Horse-shoe' Collins when he was winning toss after toss against Arthur Gilligan in Australia in 1924-25. (In mock rage, Gilligan picked up Collins's lucky half-sovereign after losing a toss in Adelaide and jocularly threw it away, and it was never found again—at least not by Collins!)

Collins played big cricket before World War I, including some against the great Syd Barnes—'he hid his hand before he delivered and you never knew what was coming along.' He was in the dressing-room at Sydney Cricket Ground, playing his first Sheffield Shield game for New South Wales against Victoria, when Victor Trumper, losing the toss on a wet pitch, came in and said, 'What about it, "Mauly"?' (another nickname—no doubt because Collins bowled with his left arm). 'Do you feel like opening with me?'

Collins did open and saw Trumper, on a horrible pitch, beaten thoroughly by the first ball of the match from Jack Saunders. (I write of this happening in the chapter on Trumper and tell of Trumper's remark up the pitch to Saunders, 'It's you or me for it, Jack.')

'I'll never forget that innings,' Collins recalled. 'It was the greatest innings I ever saw on a bad pitch. The first ball beat Vic completely, but the second ball Vic bounced on the Hill of the Cricket Ground and over into the Agricultural Ground next door. What an exhibition for a young cricketer to watch from the other end!—not that I, or anybody else, stayed long with Vic in that innings.'

Collins, after the war, was quickly called in for the A.I.F. side. Australian army headquarters were in Horseferry Road and, with shipping woefully depleted by the war, thousands of Diggers were left in camp in England on a long, long wait before beginning the voyage home. Instructions were given that the troops were to be 'fed' on sport to while away the waiting hours. Cricket was a first choice and an itinerary of matches was arranged against county and private English teams.

There were some well-known cricketers among the Australian troops—Kelleway, Macartney, Collins, Pellew, Winning, Ted Long, Cyril Docker and others. Macartney, of course, would have been a very strong link but he was anxious to get home to Australia and went on an early ship.

From all over England came Australian troops for a trial one day at Kennington Oval. Collins recalls that there were about 20 nets in action and the scene looked like Moore Park,

Sydney, on a Saturday afternoon, when junior matches are in full swing.

Collins was one of the selectors and the team was to include 14 players. They had agreed upon 13 and were stuck for the last man. Then somebody pointed out a gangling youth who was heaving arms and legs in all directions as he bowled. The selectors called him up. Had he played cricket in Australia? Yes, he had, a little—with the North Sydney third-grade and Veterans' teams.

'Well,' said Collins, 'we have to get somebody to fill the last place so it might as well be him.'

Nobody had thought to ask the Cornstalk his name, so they sent for him again. His name was Gregory. That was a good start, anyway, the selectors told themselves. It didn't occur to them that he might have been one of THE Gregory family, the most famous cricket family in history; nor, of course, did they foresee that they had in their grasp one of the greatest all-rounders the game of cricket was to know— J. M. (Jack) Gregory. He got the final place in the team simply because he was unusual in appearance and the selectors had to fill in with somebody. 'Give the job to the long bloke,' they said.

Gregory played in the first match of the tour, against Lionel Robinson's Eleven at Old Buckenham, in Norfolk. Robinson was an Australian who made a lot of money out of gold in South Africa. 'He won the Melbourne Cup with Victory and the Caulfield Cup with Lempiere,' said Collins, breaking off in his story of Gregory to touch upon his own other keen interest, the turf.

Gregory was fielded on the boundary and he came in at the end of an over wringing his right hand—he had trodden on it in the field! The old-stagers grinned. This chap was pretty clumsy. What about going into the slips? they asked him. Yes, the tall fellow said, he would like that. So he went into the slips—and remained there in later matches to become the most sensational slip-catcher cricket has seen. Other players may have taken as many catches but none had the reach, nor the uncanny anticipation, that enabled Gregory to snap up the ball in almost miraculous fashion.

In quick time the English crowds, starved by the war of years of good cricket, were flocking to see the sensational Gregory in action. Collins considers that in that year (1919) Gregory bowled the fastest and the best of his whole career.

It was during the third game of the tour, against Surrey at Kennington Oval, that Field-Marshal Birdwood, G.O.C. Australian troops, sent for Collins.

'Collins,' said Birdwood, 'I want you to take over the captaincy of this side from Captain Kelleway.'

Collins was staggered.

'Captain Kelleway is a good cricketer,' said Birdwood, 'but unfortunately he quarrels. I understand that he has already had three arguments—including one with the caretaker here before the game began. I'm sending him back on the next ship.'

But Kelleway didn't agree with the Field-Marshal. He refused to be 'sacked' and went to Brighton for the next match of the tour. Collins approached him as he began to unpack his bag.

'Charlie,' he said, 'this puts me in a pretty awkward position. Won't you think it over?'

'I'm playing,' said the dogged Kelleway.

But the other members of the A.I.F. team, after going into consultation, told Kelleway that they wouldn't take the field if he did. So Kelleway gave up—and went back to Australia on the next ship. He bore Collins no ill-feeling. He played under the latter's captaincy in both New South Wales and

Australian teams and (according to Collins) never gave him a moment's worry or trouble.

Gregory, though an immediate success, proved an embarrassment when he got a fast one through the gloves of wicket-keeper Ted Long and gashed his face. The A.I.F. team didn't have another 'keeper. The search for one was conducted through various units, and at headquarters in Horseferry Road somebody told the questing and worried Collins that in the neighbourhood was a young chap who had done a bit of wicket-keeping somewhere. The informant didn't know his name but offered to take Collins to where his man lived.

Very soon, then, Collins was led to a dingy apartment near Horseferry Road, beneath street-level, and there he found a smallish, quietly-spoken chap, in khaki, writing letters home.

'I believe you keep wickets?' said Collins.

'Well, yes, I have a little, back in Australia.'

'How would you like to keep wickets for the A.I.F. team?' asked Collins.

'Oh, no,' said the other, 'I'm not in that class.'

'Well,' said Collins, 'we have to go to Oxford tonight on the 9.30 train. Be at Paddington at nine. Got any flannels?'

'Not even a shirt.'

Then began a feverish hunt for some cricket togs. Collins remembers that the new chap sat in a corner of the railway compartment, a few cricketing odds and ends tied in a bundle, and scarcely uttered a word during the whole of the run to Oxford.

In the first over of the match, the new wicket-keeper caused whistles of excitement among his team-fellows. What is more, by the end of the morning's play, a new star had come into the cricket firmament. He was W. A. Oldfield, and he was the best wicket-keeper Collins ever saw.

When the players trooped in for lunch, a disconsolate Ted Long mooched into the dressing-room. 'Well, Herbie,' he said, 'you won't be wanting me any more, now? I guess I can catch the next ship home.'

However, Long stayed on, as second wicket-keeper.

At this time, Pellew and Johnnie Taylor were establishing themselves as remarkable fieldsmen, both being fast, sure catchers of the ball, and superb throwers. The whole team, in fact, captured popular imagination in England. It gave delight wherever it played, and it gave, too, many personalities to the game.

Collins, for his part, returned to Australia to lead a New South Wales team that was good enough for a Test match. Subsequently (1921) he returned to England under Armstrong's captaincy, and was delighted to be in a team that included Ted McDonald and Jack Gregory.

'I recall,' says Collins, 'walking off the field at the end of England's first innings in a Test, when they had been shot out for just over a hundred. One of our young chaps said to me, "That was a pretty disgraceful batting effort, wasn't it?" I replied, "Thank your stars that you are with, and not against, McDonald and Gregory. If our side batted against them, we mightn't get even the century, as England did." '

We were in a club in Sydney, having dinner, when I was speaking with Collins on days and players of the past. He fell silent for a moment and then asked, 'Did you ever see Ted McDonald bowl?' No, I hadn't; he was before my time. 'Pity,' said Collins. 'He was one of the true "greats" of the game. He used to glide to the wicket like a snake.'

'Prime Minister Menzies,' I said, 'once told me that his action suggested silk running off a spool.'

'That's a better description than mine,' said Collins. He went on to pay high tribute to both McDonald and Gregory;

as good an opening pair, he said, as any opening batsmen would wish—or not wish—to meet.

I couldn't persuade Collins to talk of himself. He made a Test century in his first Test against England, but when I asked him about that, and about other episodes in his own career, he merely shrugged and went on to speak of others.

The last thing you could say of Collins would be to describe him as a 'gusher.' He speaks with cool deliberation and a fitting appreciation of values and opinions, as befits an Australian Eleven captain of his time and deeds. He won his captaincy by sheer qualification on the field; certainly not through the politics of the game. He was shrewd and knowledgeable, a real student of cricket.

I tried to persuade him to tell me of plans he had set. He would relate only one instance.

The Old Firm of Hobbs and Sutcliffe were giving the Australians the usual amount of trouble in Melbourne during a Test match. Just before the home team came on to the field again, after lunch, Collins spoke to Ponsford, who fielded at deep fine-leg to Jack Gregory's bowling.

'Jack will open the bowling,' said Collins to Ponsford. 'Now, just before he bowls the fourth ball of the over I want you to leave fine-leg and walk some 40 yards squarer and come in about 15 yards. That is, of course, if Herby Sutcliffe has the strike. I don't want to be waving my hands. It's up to you. If you move, without me coming into it, Jack will bowl a short ball and, I think, Sutcliffe will play the hook. You might get a catch.'

No operation could have been better conceived or carried out—up to a point. As Gregory walked back to bowl the fourth ball, Ponsford—with Sutcliffe unaware of what was happening behind him—'went walkabout' and got into position. Gregory bowled short, Sutcliffe hooked, and the catch carried straight into Ponsford's hand. But—he dropped it!

Poor Ponsford! Usually a very sure fieldsman, he spent the rest of the day apologising to Collins and Gregory. Sutcliffe went on to make 176. Also, he scored a century in the second innings.

One other example of shrewd captaincy came up in general conversation. The batsman need not be named but he stood with a two-eyed stance, this leading to a disposition to force the ball to the on-side. Collins played *three* mid-ons to this chap and completely frustrated him.

Further to the matter of field placing, Collins remarked that he could never understand why captains in Australia, when up against Wally Hammond, failed to station a man on the boundary at cover. 'That,' said Collins, 'is the first position in which I'd place a man against Wally—he was such a perfect cover-driver.'

While paying tribute to Sutcliffe's temperament, Collins suggests that he owed many of his successes to Hobbs, who frequently kept him out of trouble in both Australia and England. Nevertheless, he doesn't imply that Sutcliffe was not a remarkable cricketer in his own right.

A noteworthy episode recalled by Collins occurred when Hobbs opened against Australia for Surrey at the Oval. Naturally, on his home ground, against the Australians, and before his favourite crowd, Hobbs was eager to do well. Gregory bowled two balls to him and the third got past the bat and just gave the bails the merest flick. They fell gently in the slip-stream. So faint was the flick that the ball wasn't deflected at all as it carried through to Oldfield.

Having failed to hear any hit of the ball against the bails, Hobbs stood his ground. Collins, standing at short-leg, looked back to the umpire and appealed. The umpire gave Hobbs not out.

'What happened, Bert?' asked Hobbs of the Australian.

'The ball just touched your bails, Jack,' replied Collins.

'Oh, well,' said Hobbs, 'if I was bowled I think I had better go'—and he turned about and walked to the pavilion.

A great test of character, that, to accept a 'blob' in front of his own crowd and against the Australians, particularly when the umpire had given him 'not out.' And Hobbs, of course, was the Oval's idol.

No cricketer stands higher with Collins, in the matter of sportsmanship, than Jack Hobbs. Also, the Australian regards Hobbs as the best judge of a run he has seen and the best cover-point as well. He was still taking short runs with consummate ease at 50 years of age.

'The man who took a risk with Hobbs at cover was completely ignorant,' says Collins. 'He played with a batsman like a cat with a mouse, luring him on. He had a deadly short-arm throw and five times out of six could knock the stumps over from cover. As a batsman, he was one of the best that cricket has known, particularly on wet wickets. His century against us at the Oval in 1926, when England regained the Ashes, was a gem—it was made on a very difficult pitch, and, as usual, it included shielding of Sutcliffe. I said to Jack when he topped the century, "You have never played better than this." Hobbs thought for a moment and then nodded. "Yes," he said mildly, "I think I have played pretty well." '

Collins didn't like the 'feeling' that crept into cricket in the time of Jardine and Bradman. His own men, he admitted, played the game pretty hard, but there was always good feeling with the opposition. He thought little of Bradman's captaincy after the war and was sure he needled the Englishmen unnecessarily. He saw Bradman behind the Pavilion at

Adelaide after that poor Test match of the 1946-47 series when the Australians so obviously played for a draw.

'I have written an article for my Sydney newspaper about you,' Collins said.

Bradman nodded.

'In case they don't print it in full,' said Collins, 'I'll tell you the theme of it. I've suggested that cricket would be a better game now if you got out of it.'

From one Australian captain to another, that was stringent criticism.

Bradman passed on.

Like many others, Collins cannot understand how Bradman so dominates the game and the Board of Control in Australia—on the Board one minute, off it the next, selecting teams for the West Indies and England and then criticising them in the Press.

When Collins went to England, as captain, in 1926, an approach was made to him by a Beaverbrook representative to write a series of articles on his cricket experiences. Sensationalism had not then entered cricket journalism and Collins was required to write only straight, sober stuff. The fee was £1,000—big money in those days. Accordingly, Collins worked with a newspaperman on the ship travelling to England. But, nearing the end of the voyage, the manager of the Australian team, Sid Smith, questioned Collins regarding his constant association with the newspaperman.

'I'm writing a series of articles for publication in England,' said Collins.

'But your contract says you can't,' said Smith.

Collins had been under the impression that the contract referred to the cricket in England only; but he deferred to Smith and told the newspaperman that the deal was off.

'What I should have done, of course,' says Collins, 'was

to allow the articles to be printed and then be fined the nominal sum of £50 after the tour. That, I recall, is what happened to Bradman, Miller and Lindwall.'

I met Collins during the trial match of 1956 at the Sydney Cricket Ground. I have always felt close to him since the days, in the middle 1920s, when he dropped out of our Waverley side for one game and I—at the age of 16—was included in his stead. But, whereas Collins opened, I was sent in No. 11. I got a few not out and, as we had to follow-on, was asked whether I would care to keep the pads on. I did 'care,' and, having made a score, stayed in that position thereafter.

In that Sydney trial game, we watched together some aspirants for the English tour, and Collins, unhesitatingly, named several who would be complete failures if they were sent to England. He was absolutely right. He looked at their footwork, disregarded the trueness of a beautiful Sydney pitch, and evaluated their prospects on turning pitches.

Later, he questioned me on how they had set about playing Laker. Did they make a concerted attempt to hit him off his length? Was it a sensible attempt or did they just blaze at him? I told him that Laker bowled well on helpful pitches and that the Australians, on their part, showed lack of intelligence and craftsmanship. 'That's what it looked like from 12,000 miles away,' said Collins.

It was on the Old Trafford pitch, where the Australians on two successive visits to England (under Hassett and Johnson) panicked in time of stress, that Collins himself played an unforgettable innings of just on five hours for 40 runs to save a Test for Australia. He was a superb fighter; he was also one who often bluffed, as befits a good poker player.

I relished the story he told me of the First Test in Sydney in the series of 1924-25. It had been fine for a week before the match and Collins didn't bother to look at the pitch before tossing. He won, and batted. As he took guard and marked his spot he noticed that a little moisture came up with his sprig-mark. There would be early life in the pitch!

'I'll never forget that period before lunch,' said Collins. 'The first ball from Tate whipped off the pitch and hit Strudwick, the wicket-keeper, in the neck. Strudwick stood back, the only time he ever did so to Tate. Ponsford came in and was morally bowled three times in his first over from Tate. I walked down the pitch and said, "Don't be afraid of Tate. He can't bowl." It seemed a stupid thing to say, in the circumstances, but I wanted to boost Ponsford's morale. The truth was that I, too, was being turned inside-out by Tate; so I thought I would try a little psychology on him. I said to him, "It's no good bowling me that in-swinger, Maurice; I can pick it from a mile away." Tate looked at me and grinned. "Well, Bert," he said, "you know more about it than I do. I never know whether I am going to bowl a ruddy in-swinger or a ruddy out-swinger." '

Collins remembers Clem Hill visiting the dressing-room at lunch-time and saying, 'Well, that's the toughest bowling I have ever seen. If Tate had had any luck, your whole team could have been out twice before lunch.'

Collins had a high regard for M. A. Noble, who was worth his place in an Australian Eleven on any one of three counts—captaincy, batting or bowling. Noble was the best captain Collins knew. He didn't think much of the leadership of a few other captains I mentioned.

George Gunn, of Nottinghamshire and England, fascinated Collins at the wickets. He used to stroll out to Jack Gregory before the ball was bowled, whistling a tune the while, and pick and flick the ball at will. On one occasion Gunn hit Arthur Mailey over mid-on to a deserted place in the outfield. Collins, fielding at silly-point, heard the batsman call down to his partner, 'Two—maybe three.' But Johnnie Taylor took off from deep mid-off, ran some 40 yards in even time—as Taylor could—dived, and took an unforgettable catch. 'Well,' exclaimed the staggered Gunn, 'I'll be well and truly ——!'

Collins gave me some choice stories about Macartney, which I relate in another place. Then I asked him to nominate the four greatest batsmen he had known. He did not hesitate. 'Trumper, on his own,' he said; 'then Bradman, Hobbs, and —now prepare yourself for a shock—George Headley of the West Indies. I never saw a batsman whose footwork excelled Headley's.'

Blackenburg, a holy terror on the mat, spinning a fast wrong-un with his fingers, was the best bowler Collins knew in South Africa. He smiled when he thought of South Africa.

'We got there once,' he recalled, 'with almost every bowler injured or sick. I told Arthur Mailey he could expect to do more than a fair share of bowling. I put him on once at noon, when the game began, and he bowled until six o'clock. I, myself, bowled from noon until three.'

Collins greatly admired Dave Nourse and Taylor. He puts them definitely among the 'greats.' I remarked that, with me, Dudley Nourse was there, too; but Collins said that good judges in the Union didn't rate Dudley as high as his father, Dave. I made an allowance, here, for the pull in varying generations.

Collins greatly admired England's Len Hutton—another of the all-time 'greats.' He was less certain about putting Compton on that pinnacle.

'Had you seen Compton's 184 and 145 not out against the Australians in England in 1948, you would have no hesitation in putting him very high indeed.' I told Collins.

He agreed that an innings seen, and analysed, could be the only criterion. That, he said, was why he had been so impressed by Headley. Headley, he told me, had another warm admirer in the old English captain Archie MacLaren, who regarded the West Indian as one of the best batsmen he had ever seen.

Another opinion by MacLaren (as quoted by Collins) was that J. T. Tyldesley ranked as one of the greatest batsmen ever on all types of wickets—and certainly England's greatest on wet wickets. Various Englishmen who saw a famous match on a sticky pitch at Melbourne, in 1904, were inclined to put Tyldesley's 62 (out of the side's 103) on the same high level as Trumper's 74 (out of 122).

*   *   *   *

Collins and I rose from our table at last—we were the first to sit down and by far the last to get up. This tour through years of cricket and among famous players had exhilarated me, but as I said good night to my companion I felt completely despondent.

Here, I thought, when Australian cricket is in the doldrums, is H. L. Collins, captain of the A.I.F. team, captain of New South Wales, captain of Australia, a most likeable, most courteous man, a firm favourite in England on three trips, a man of discernment, knowledge, and clear judgment —here is this shrewd and intelligent fellow on the sidelines and nobody in the cricketing world of Australia seems to think of asking him, and men of his ilk, to come back to the game as administrators and instructors in order to give it new life!

Australian cricket, I reflected, has fallen into the hands of mediocrities—is, indeed, hampered by the limited outlook of little men.

Eight

YOU NEVER KNOW IN CRICKET

Early in 1926, Alan Kippax, brilliant Sydney batsman, was the centre of warm controversy. The Australian selectors closed their eyes to the centuries he was making almost weekly in Sheffield Shield games; and, moreover, closed their ears to the public clamour for his inclusion in the team to tour England.

Kippax found no place in the dozen players chosen at Christmas-time for England, and towards the end of our summer he was battling with other men—such as Woodfull, Victor Richardson, Punch, Love, Kelleway and Hornibrook —for one of the last places in the side. Under such circumstances, many players cannot do themselves justice. So keen are they to do well that they unconsciously tighten their muscles and it is not only in golf that taut limbs rule out freedom of stroke-play.

But Kippax rose above the mental hazards and on the very eve of selection he made a brilliant 271 not out against Victoria in Sydney. In view of what he had done before, this should certainly have gained him his place but, alas, the selectors, so far as Kippax was concerned, had hearts of stone. Woodfull, Ellis and Everett got the final places.

The wheel turned full circle in eight months. The Australians, with Wilfred Rhodes rolling back the years at Kennington Oval in the Fifth Test, were beaten in England—and there are never bouquets and champagne to welcome home a defeated team to Australia. Australian dissatisfaction with the original choice welled over with defeat and, accordingly, several members of that team of 1926 were marked for 'execution' as they lolled in their deck-chairs on the homeward voyage.

The first head to fall belonged to Syd Smith, the manager, who had also managed the 1921 team to England. He came from Gordon in Sydney and members of that club were just as incensed at the non-selection of Charlie Kelleway as the members of the Waverley club were over the snubbing of Kippax.

All high official positions in Australian cricket stem from the clubs. The clubs elect two delegates to State associations; this body, in turn, elects its members to the Board of Control and the Board distributes its plums—to Board members. High office is thus built on the lowly sands of club representation and these sands, as Smith found, are sometimes quick to shift. While in England, Smith lost the confidence of his club—and with it high office.

H. L. Collins, a selector of the touring team and its captain, played for the same club as Kippax; but Collins (together with other members of his touring side) found himself unwanted on his return and Kippax, the outcast, suddenly became the favourite. He was elevated to State captain. Alan's day had indeed dawned, and it was to last for eight influential years. Many another Australian had missed—or was to miss—a well-earned tour of England, but in Kippax's case the rank-and-file did everything possible by way of recompense.

At the time of which I write—late 1926—he was bringing his young team to Melbourne after a creditable win by four wickets over South Australia. Only two experienced cricketers, Tommy Andrews and Arthur Mailey, were with him and he thus had the burden, potentially crippling for any young captain to carry in first-class cricket, of having seven men new to top cricket. They were: Steele, Campbell (a young slow bowler whom Hammond was to 'kill' a few years later), Jackson (then only 17), McNamee, Phillips, McGuirk and Hogg.

A captain on such a tour, with so many new men, needs the qualities of a mothercraft nurse. He has to guide, humour, teach, inspire and understand all the varied personalities of his new men, many of them away from home for the first time. In Adelaide, for instance, Kippax had to impress upon one of his young bowlers that it wasn't the thing to put his cap on the ground to mark where his run began, nor was it necessary to call 'play' before each ball was bowled. Kippax, as you will perceive, had his teething troubles.

However, the win in Adelaide bucked his side up and the players had plenty of smiles for the photographer when they left the train at Melbourne. The caption over the photograph, when it appeared that afternoon, was 'Ready for the Fray.' In the same edition, a Victorian critic wrote that many runs should come from Ponsford, Woodfull, Hendry and Ryder, since all of them were in good form. Prophetic words!

So the day of the game came and Kippax won the toss. A good start, and he had no hesitation in batting. The hesitation was to come later—in the batting. After five hours of streaky endeavour, the New South Wales side was out for a rather colourless 221.

The next day (Saturday) was Christmas Day so that the game was put aside for two days. It began again at 11·30 on a bright Monday morning.

As usual, the two Bills, Woodfull and Ponsford, opened

for Victoria. A wicket should have fallen early. When Woodfull was seven, Ponsford mistimed a savage hit at a no-ball from McNamee, and the ball flew high to Kippax at mid-on. Woodfull, evidently, had not recovered fully from his Christmas dinner; anyway, his reflexes were muddled and he began charging towards Ponsford's end. As all schoolboys know, nothing is to be gained by running for a stroke off a no-ball unless the stroke is to the deep and there is more than a single in it—and, as all schoolboys further know, the only way in which a wicket can be lost off a no-ball (excluding the theoretical ways of interference, assault and so forth) is from a run-out. It follows that Woodfull—who, perhaps, was committing the only known indiscretion of his life—was badly at fault in going for the run. Moreover, it was Ponsford's call and he stood his ground, yelling at Woodfull, 'No, no: go back!'

Woodfull stopped and was stranded, halfway down the pitch, as Kippax caught the ball and sized up the situation. As so often happens on such occasions, time to think can lead to trouble. Quick, impulsive action is often best, ruling out errors of judgment.

McNamee crouched over his stumps, waiting for the return. Now, that same McNamee was a priceless wit but a hopeless fieldsman, one who was apt to grab at the ball. Bearing that fielding weakness in mind, and knowing there was plenty of time, Kippax sent in a perfect slow lob. It was destined to land plumb in McNamee's hands.

Alas, though, McNamee couldn't suffer the agony of waiting. The ball seemed to mesmerise him and it drew him forward. He grabbed at it—and at the same time—fell over the stumps, fumbled the ball, and then dropped it! In the midst of this horrible muddle, Woodfull raced safely back to his crease.

I have drawn the circumstances of this incident in some detail because, though the first wicket should have fallen for 17, it didn't fall until 375!

Woodfull made no other error until he snicked a catch to Ratcliffe off Andrews when 133. That was bad enough for New South Wales but at stumps the position was worse with Ponsford 334 not out: Hendry 86 not out. The one wicket had fallen for 573.

Mailey had bowled 28 overs that day, at a cost of 148. Only four maiden overs were bowled all day and Ponsford, who rarely scored behind the wicket, got many runs from a short-arm jab, a stroke he had learned at baseball, which carried the ball over mid-on's head. His on-side play was faultless, his feet getting his body into quick and perfect position. During the whole day he never gave anything that resembled a chance.

The spectators trooped to the ground next day in great numbers, wondering whether Ponsford would break Clem Hill's Sheffield Shield record of 365 not out, made for South Australia against New South Wales in season 1900-01.

But Ponsford didn't break the record. This, next day, was how a Melbourne newspaper described what happened:

'The almost ecclesiastical calm of the Melbourne Cricket Ground yesterday in those tense moments before Ponsford's wicket fell was an indication of the tremendous interest Australians have in the breaking of records.

As cricket, it was slow, but none would have had it otherwise. The dropping of those single runs into the slot of time, gradually lengthening into the tens that crept up on the record for Shield matches, held by Clem Hill for over a quarter of a century, was sufficient excitement. Impudent play would have been resented. Only a cricket d'Artagnan would have taken artistic liberties in such a duel.

When the fatal ball broke the wicket, it broke the crowd's Sabbatical quiet. Thenceforward exhortations and witticisms, impossible before, were the portion of the players. The crowd could no longer help their hero.'

Ponsford was out at 352. He snicked a ball on to his foot and it rebounded to the stumps. He turned, surveyed the fallen bail, and said with great feeling, 'By cripes, *I am* unlucky!' That remark staggered the New South Welshmen almost as much as did the score.

So, to the disappointment of the crowd and the relief of his opposition—who had come to perceive the genus of amaranth in his bat and his bulk—Bill Ponsford trudged reluctantly to the pavilion, not to sip nectar and tender thanksgiving to the gods but to meditate darkly on how Fate had cruelly crossed him at 352, only 14 short of the record he had set his heart on. Naughty Fate!

'The champion,' wrote one critic, 'began quietly, too quietly, as he afterwards admitted. He added only 18 in 41 minutes to his over-night score but, for all this, he almost beat the clock with his 352 in 363 minutes, with 36 fours.'

Hendry, a New South Wales player of other years, sacrificed his wicket at 100; Love, another former New South Wales player, was out for six; King went for seven; but then came Jack Ryder, and he committed, first, assault and mild battery on the groggy attack and, finally, sheer murder.

Ryder made 295—the first 100 in 115 minutes; the second in 74; his final 95 in 56 minutes.

His score in the book read thus: 1 1 1 1 1 1 1 1 4 4 1 1 1 4 1 2 1 4 1 1 2 1 1 1 1 1 1 1 1 4 2 1 4 1 4 2 2 1 1 1 4 1

4 4 4 1 1 2 1 1 1 2 1 2 4 4 1 3 1 1 1 1 4 1 6 1 1 4 4 2 4 4 4 1
1 2 6 2 1 2 2 4 2 2 4 2 1 1 4 4 2 1 1 1 6 1 1 3 1 4 1 2 1 1 1 2
4 2 1 1 1 2 1 2 2 1 4 4 2 4 4 4 2 1 4 1 1 6 1 1 2 4 6 4 *

Six times—a record for such games—Ryder hit the ball out of the ground. One hit, off a full-toss from Mailey, struck the verandah of the Smokers' Stand; another went into the reserve and narrowly missed smashing the clock. This caused a heartfelt sigh in the dressing-room, for the story was that six cases of champagne would be presented to any batsman smashing the clock on the Melbourne Cricket Ground—though a subsidiary item was that nobody, least of all Ryder, knew who had promised the champagne.

'Hard luck, Arthur,' somebody sympathised with Mailey in the dressing-room during an adjournment as the slow bowler was taking a much-needed rest.

'Well, you can't get wickets if the catches are not taken,' replied the whimsical Mailey.

'Catches?' asked the outsider, puzzled, 'I didn't see any catches.'

'There's a chap in the Outer dropped Ryder twice already off me,' said Mailey.

The crowd roared like football barrackers as Ryder was hitting his sixes. Apart from the two mentioned above, the other four were hit against the breeze, down into the Outer.

Off five overs from Mailey, Ryder hit 62. He was 275 when he faced up to Andrews, who also bowled slows. Ryder hit the first ball for four; the next for six; the next for four; the next for six, and, trying to reach his 300 in the grand manner, mis-hit the fifth and was caught by Kippax.

There is no more enthusiastic sporting crowd in the world

* If you are academic enough to try and catch me out by adding up this glut of runs, I hope you go as cross-eyed over it as I did. Moreover, I intentionally left out Ryder's final scoring stroke, which was a six!

than the Melbourne one when it is whipped up, and Ryder certainly did some whipping that day.

The carnage didn't finish with Ryder. Hartkopf, Liddicut and Ellis continued to push the New South Wales attack around and it fell to Ellis to hit the stroke that brought the 1,000 up. Jack Ellis was—he still is—a vital, cheerful fellow and as he made the eventful stroke to the outfield he whooped, 'Come on, there's three in it. Three in it and the thousand up! Long live Victoria!'

Fortunately for New South Wales, Ellis and Morton ran themselves out, but before the innings finished Victoria had tallied 1,107—beating the 1,059 Victoria had made against Tasmania, which had been the world's record score in a first-class match. Kippax led from the field a footsore, humiliated team, their 'eagerness for the fray' (as the newspaper caption had it on their arrival) now considerably subdued.

Naturally, the Melbourne newspapers 'went to town' over the remarkable score. R. W. E. Wilmot (father of Chester Wilmot, author of *The Struggle for Europe*) wrote in the *Age*:

'It takes a special type of brain to be a record-breaker in anything, and Ponsford seems possessed of one which believes that records exist to be broken and he is the one to do it. His batting was that of a master. When he hit, he hit hard and that for more than five hours. It was only towards the end of the day that he showed fatigue. The crowd of 22,348 saw wonderful batting, and, though revelling in seeing all those records broken which New South Wales had so sedulously established against Victoria, they could not help sympathising with and admiring the courageous fight put up by the visitors. One remarkable feature of the play was that the crowd—and a crowd can quite often be cruel—cheered the batsmen, the bowlers and the fieldsmen. There was an entire absence of jeering.'

This was kindly comment: it differed from that which advised the visitors to bring a comptometer operator, and not a scorer, next time they came to Melbourne.
This is what the *Argus* had to say:

'It will be the talk of the cricket world for a long time to come. There has been no other achievement like it in first-class cricket. Enthusiasts, taken completely by surprise, are discussing the likely causes of this startling revelation of the acme of batsmanship. Was it that Woodfull, Ryder, Ponsford and Hendry reached their zenith on the one occasion, or was it that the New South Wales team was of inferior quality? Our opponents were without some of their best players, but who would say that against the same side the same set of Victorian batsmen would again compile more than 1,100 runs? They might not even be equal to 500. Psychology is the safest refuge for all but the quidnuncs. It was Ponsford's hour and the glamour of the deeds he performed inspired his teammates. New South Wales may be the next to find the hour and the man.'

Wise words. A country lad, named Don Bradman, had just been invited to Sydney for a trial. He was to put even Ponsford into the shade—and just around the corner, also, was the return game between New South Wales and Victoria in Sydney.
Although the Victorian newspapers ran to great praise of the event, the Sydney *Daily Telegraph* took rather a crusty view of it. An editorial ran:

'In the heyday of Spofforth and Turner, Trott and Giffen, to mention only a few of the great Australian bowlers of a bygone generation, the batsmen were considered lucky if they got into double figures; today they are considered unlucky if they don't get a hundred. After all, you can do only a certain amount of things with a cricket ball. You may bowl fast, medium or slow. You may give the ball certain spin. You may send down a googly. There is a scientific way of meeting every ball and science cannot go wrong on a billiard-table wicket. How easy it is may be gathered from the huge score just completed by Ponsford, who doesn't bother at all about the science of the game but just uses his quick eye and quick foot and punishes everything that comes along.'

A pretty hard (and ignorant!) critic, this fellow, but having suggested a smaller ball, a narrower bat and a fourth stump, the Great Oracle of the newspaper office called it an editorial day and, no doubt, pushed off to his club to have a few reminiscent snifters.

The New South Wales players were leg-weary when they batted on the fourth day. They were all out for 230 and Victoria won by an innings and 656. Kippax was learning captaincy the hard way but he was a light-hearted chap who always saw the humour in things. One other point must be stressed. Despite the murderous onslaught, Kippax always had his bowlers aim at the stumps. There was no wide leg or off-theory and this, undoubtedly, contributed greatly to the fact that Victoria's 1,107 was made in the incredible time of 574 minutes.

This was the Victorian score-card:

```
Woodfull c Ratcliffe, b Andrews  . . . . . . . . . . . . . 133
Ponsford, b Morgan . . . . . . . . . . . . . . . . . . . . . . . . 352
Hendry, c Morgan b Mailey  . . . . . . . . . . . . . . . . 100
Ryder, c Kippax b Andrews  . . . . . . . . . . . . . . . . 295
```

Love, st Ratcliffe b Mailey 6
King, st Ratcliffe b Mailey 7
Hartkopf, c McGuirk b Mailey 61
Liddicut, b McGuirk 36
Ellis, run out 63
Morton, run out 0
Blackie, not out 27
    Sundries 27
                                    ————

Total 1,107
Fall of wickets: 1-375; 2-594; 3-614; 4-631; 5-657;
      6-834; 7-915; 8-1,043; 9-1,046; 10-1,107.

BOWLING

	O.	M.	R.	W.
McNamee	24	2	124	0
McGuirk	26	1	130	1
Mailey	64	0	362	4
Campbell	11	0	89	0
Phillips	11·7	0	64	0
Morgan	26	0	137	1
Andrews	21	2	148	2
Kippax.......................	7	0	26	0

McNamee and Mailey each bowled a no-ball.

*   *   *   *

Just two weeks later, in Sydney, New South Wales made 469 in the return game against Victoria—and then toppled the champions out for 35! McNamee, who took 0-124 in Melbourne, this time took 7-21!

Apparently, the leader writer of the *Daily Telegraph* was not at his desk that week. There was no illuminating article on cricket. Perhaps he had a mild attack of gout, which was a pity, because it would have been interesting to know whether he would have advocated a bigger ball, a smaller stump— or whether he just thought that McNamee had produced a performance of which Spofiorth, Turner, Trott of Giffen might have been proud.

As to the game itself—as somebody once said, you never know what's around the corner in cricket.

Nine

THE CHAMPION WHO WAS COLOUR-BLIND

Many cricketers have had their names blazoned on posters *after* the event, but William Harold Ponsford, of Victoria, is probably the only one in history to have his name on posters *before* the event. It happened to him in Sydney early in January 1928, following the most remarkable month ever experienced by a cricketer in Australia. Nothing like it has happened since.

Although I'm not specially keen on statistics, it seems desirable here to cite a few figures. I think Ponsford's 1,146 runs in December 1927, made in five innings at an average of 229·20, represent the outstanding batting performance (in one month) of all time. His innings were 133, 437 (breaking his own world record of 429), 202, 38 and 316. These scores were the end of a string of 11 centuries in 11 consecutive matches in Australia. The others were 102 in 1925-26; 214 and 54, 151, 352, 108 and 84, 12 and 110 in 1926-27; and 131 and 7 before the flood of runs surged in full force in that December of 1927.

It was all this that led to Ponsford being 'postered.' With a rare touch of business acumen, the New South Wales Cricket Association did something hitherto unknown to the game— it had big posters printed and tied to telegraph-posts in the

The grace and power of Victor Trumper's drive caught by the informed
camera of G. W. Beldam.

Jack Hobbs jumps out to drive—compare with the frontispiece portrait of Trumper. The great players of their day did not hesitate to leave their ground to punish slow bowling.

Warren Bardsley in the nets, where he perfected his patient craft.

S. F. Barnes—Warwickshire, Lancashire, Staffordshire, and England:
he mastered great batsmen on batsmen's wickets.

Warwick Armstrong—'The Big Ship.' The biggest man in Australian
cricket of his time.

Paul Estripeaut, the French cricketer (after a surf at Bondi).

Picnic lunch at Lord's. *Foreground—left to right:* Bill O'Reilly, Ian Peebles, the author, and Lord Birkett.

C. G. Macartney. A late-flowering genius of Australian batsmanship.

Alan Kippax. The stylist, once eclipsed, but eventually recognised in his own State.

Bill Ponsford, the solid, commanding, but over-sensitive record-breaker.

Work begins on the Melbourne cricket ground for the 1956 Olympics.

The task completed. The world's greatest cricket stadium. Will a cricket match ever fill it?

The 'Governor-General'; Macartney in imperious batting mood.

Dudley Nourse batting in the First Test against the M.C.C. in December 1938.

The skill and power of Norman O'Neill. Beautifully balanced, O'Neill hits one to the boundary in a Sydney grade game.

The catch of a lifetime. Norman O'Neill brilliantly catches Sam Loxton off his own bowling at Melbourne Cricket Ground.

Peter May, England's captain. A text-book model for the drive.

Ian Craig bends the knee to Surrey's spin attack at The Oval.

The catch of the Sydney season. Philpott, of New South Wales, flies through the air with the greatest of ease to catch a West Australian batsman in a Sheffield Shield match.

city and suburbs. They hit Sydney in the eye. 'PONSFORD,' they ran, 'COME TO THE CRICKET GROUND AND SEE THE WORLD'S GREATEST BATSMAN.'

The invitation was cordially accepted, the attendance being 67,614 over the days of play and the gate-takings £4,606. Both were records for a Shield game in Sydney. But there the records ended. Ponsford certainly didn't contribute any. In fact, he made only six runs in the first innings and two in the second! As was sometimes his habit against fast bowlers, he shuffled across to the off against Jack Gregory, leaving his leg-stump open to be hit; and in the second innings Gregory again figured in his dismissal, taking a typically sensational catch in the slips.

Still, it wasn't often that Ponsford failed and this was one of the two worst first-class games he knew in Australia. He had jumped into the headlines in the 1922-23 Australian season when he made 429 against Tasmania—not a Sheffield Shield state but enjoying the status of first-class games—and that tally eclipsed A. C. MacLaren's 424, which had stood since 1895 as the world's record first-class score.

Five years later, again on his home ground of Melbourne, Ponsford improved on his own record by making 437, this time against Queensland and in a Sheffield Shield match. However, Bradman was now on the horizon and Ponsford's record endured for only two years when Bradman toppled it (also against Queensland) with 452 not out in Sydney.

That score of 452 not out remains the world's record. But not even Bradman equalled Ponsford's feat of making two first-class scores of over 400. Aptly, in a sense, Ponsford retired from cricket after the 1934 tour of England, during which he teamed with Bradman to put on 451 in the Oval Test (Ponsford 266, Bradman 244) and 388 at Leeds (Ponsford 181, Bradman 304). These partnerships, in order, were for the second and fourth wickets and are record ones in the Australia-England series. They were the only occasions on which Australia's great record-breakers got together in a Test as a 'firm,' although this was something that had been eagerly awaited since Bradman shot into the records' list in the late 1920s.

As was to be the case with Bradman later, Ponsford had his wings clipped by Larwood. The speedy Englishman scattered his stumps for two in the first innings of the First Test at Brisbane in 1928 and had him caught behind the wicket for six in the second innings. In the first innings of the next Test, in Sydney, he had made only five when a ball from Larwood fractured a bone in his hand. Ponsford played no more in that Test series. He was left to lament some 'famous last words' that appeared under his name at the beginning of that season in a Melbourne newspaper. 'Larwood,' he had said, 'is not really a fast bowler!'

Ponsford came back to make his favourite Test score of 110 at the Oval in 1930; but Larwood loomed up again in the next series in Australia—the bodyline period. Larwood clean-bowled him for 32 in the First Test at Sydney; Voce clean-bowled him for two in the second. As a remarkable fact, Ponsford was dropped for the next Test, appearing on the field in the incongruous role of a drink-waiter. But he played a very plucky innings of 85 in the following Test at Adelaide—that match of extreme bitterness—and then was shot out for three, by Larwood, in the second innings. Larwood bowled him for 19 at Brisbane and caught him for nil off Allen in the second innings.

That was the end of Ponsford's Test career in Australia— the selectors clean-bowled him before the final Test began.

Obviously, Larwood gave Ponsford much anxiety, and there was certainly substance in the claim that fast bowlers—

the best of them, that is—sometimes found a chink in his armour, or, to be more precise, caused a flutter in his temperament and a stutter in his footwork. That was something no slow bowler ever did.

Indeed, it can fairly be said that from the 1920s onward cricket knew no greater batsman than Ponsford against slow bowling. O'Reilly once told me he would sooner bowl against Bradman than against Ponsford. He gave himself some chance of breaking through Bradman's defence—sound as it undoubtedly was—but the job against Ponsford always struck him as being virtually hopeless.

Like most famous Australian players, Bill Ponsford came into cricket at an early age. He was a few days short of 16 when he played his first game, for St. Kilda, in Melbourne pennant cricket. He quickly made an impression with sound defence, an equable temperament, and a marked keenness for the game. Yet, strangely in the case of one who was to make mammoth scores, the century eluded him time and again in the pennant games.

He was a good scorer, ranging from the 60s on to (once) a tally of 99; but he still had not made a pennant century when he was chosen, at the age of 20, to play against Johnnie Douglas's M.C.C. team of 1920-21. He wasn't a success. He made only six and 19, and, as the cricket selectors of Victoria have usually been conservative—those in New South Wales have often been just the opposite—he was relegated to pennant cricket again.

In the season of 1921-22 he gave the Tasmanians a slight taste of what was ahead, making 162, and in the next season came that record 429 against them. Ponsford's name immediately became news. He moved up into the Victorian Shield team again, this time to stay until he himself cried 'Enough' in 1934. He played his first Shield game against

South Australia and made 108 and 17. He played his first Test against England in the next season, and, as in the Shield game, began with a century. He says to this day it was the hardest-earned century of his career.

'I was 24, and a very nervous young man,' says Ponsford of this match. 'I can never seem to remember with any accuracy much about cricket dates and statistics, but that day on the Sydney Cricket Ground, December 19, 1924, although nearly 33 years behind me, is as fresh as today and much more memorable.

'Maurice Tate was a big-shouldered, 15-stone giant, with a deceptively short run. He came in flat-footed and swung his arm over. He was no express and I thought I saw the ball well. I went to make my stroke. The ball swung a little, hit the pitch, and fizzed through like a flat pebble off a mill-pond. It beat me, beat the wicket and beat the 'keeper, Bert Strudwick. It went for four byes.

'The next ball, I swore, would not do the same humiliating thing. It did—although this time Strudwick took it. The third ball I watched as if it were a bomb. But again it swung at the last moment, came off the pitch like a Larwood bouncer, went through me and wicket-keeper as well, and shot to the fence for four more byes. Little "Tich" Freeman was bowling leg-breaks at the other end. I got a four off him, and was so relieved at missing a "blob" that my confidence, so shattered by Tate, returned. I made a century, which I think was chanceless, and we won the match, on the seventh day, by 195 runs.'

Thus Ponsford told his story many years afterwards. But he omitted some important details. At the other end was Herbie Collins, the Australian Eleven skipper. Those who saw Ponsford make his shaky start against Tate (the sheen had gone from the ball, Ponsford coming first wicket down with the score at 46), will never forget how Collins strolled up to him at the end of the over, had a talk, and then kept Tate's bowling exclusively to himself until the younger man had recovered his poise.

This, so they say, was a classical example of how one man can make a century for another if he has the ability, the intelligence to work the strike, and the team-spirit to protect somebody in trouble

Maurice Tate, that day, almost shed tears of frustration because Collins wouldn't let him 'get at' Ponsford. Ponsford made 110 in his first Test innings against England; Collins made 114.

The former Australian Eleven skipper (one of the most modest of men) prefers that I should not record the details of the conversation he had with Ponsford at the end of that 'nightmare' over, but he emphasised that he will always remember Ponsford's gesture when he returned to the dressing-room after making his century. The team, naturally, made much fuss over Ponsford, but he postponed most of the slaps on the back and the handshakes and went across to Collins to take his hand. 'This chap,' said Ponsford, 'deserves most of the credit.'

(Writing of Larwood recalls my own first Test innings against England, also in Sydney. I should have got off my 'blob' first ball through placing a single from Larwood, but when half-way up the pitch I saw my partner at the other end with his hand up, countermanding my call. I turned, scrambled, and finally dived, narrowly escaping being run out. One or two of our men, in that series, were not at all eager to get down to Larwood's business end!)

Ponsford made another century in his first Test series of 1924-25—128 in the Second Test at Melbourne—and he finished the five games with the splendid figures of 468 runs at 46·80. Nevertheless, he never again scored a Test century in Australia against England. Like many others, he was eclipsed by Bradman's tall scoring in the Tests in England in 1930—Ponsford made 330 Test runs at 55 an innings and Bradman 974 at 139.

On figures, however, Ponsford finished his career in England in a blaze of glory. Whereas on his first trip, in 1926, he made only 37 runs in three Test innings, on his final tour he made 569 runs at an average of 94·83; and in so doing he shaded even Bradman, whose figures were 758 at 94·75. But—and this is an important point in relation to both Ponsford and Bradman—there was no Larwood and no Voce in 1934. Both were stood down by Marylebone in the aftermath to bodyline.

Whichever way you look at the Ponsford record—at his figures or when he was in the midst of a big score—he was a truly great player. He crouched a little at the crease, the peak of his cap pulled characteristically towards his left ear; he tapped the ground impatiently with his bat while awaiting the ball, and his feet were so eager to be on the move that they began an impulsive move forward just before the ball was bowled. This was the shuffle that sometimes took him across the pitch against a fast bowler; but, that aside, his footwork was perfection. I never saw a better forcer of the ball to the on-side, and for this stroke his body moved beautifully into position.

He used an extremely heavy bat—'Big Bertha,' he called it —and an umpire with an inquisitive mind was delighted when, before play in Sydney one morning, he put a width gauge on 'Bertha' and found it to be too wide. All that this proved—and even though Ponsford had to lay aside a favourite bat—was that the constant meeting of the ball with the middle of the bat had flattened and squashed the willow.

Those watching the Victorian at practise the night before had noted that not a single ball passed him in 15 minutes!

Ponsford could play every orthodox stroke in the game, and he added a few unorthodox ones of his own. Those who watched him over the years detected a change in his shoulders later in his career—he turned his right more to the bowler —and, whereas he was a strong cutter of the ball in his early days, towards the end he showed a partiality for the on-side. The theorists might ponder upon this.

Against the modern trend of leg-side bowling, with many an off-break bowler delivering from around the stumps, I think a batsman makes himself more comfortable and better able to play on-side strokes if he adopts, for the occasion, a slightly two-eyed stance. Not, mark you, that Ponsford ever stood two-eyed, as Kelleway and Ryder did.

On returning from the 1934 tour of England—and after making 266 in his last Test—Ponsford put his bat aside when it was still full of runs. His retirement shocked Australia. He was then only 34 years of age. Possibly the retirement of Woodfull (as well as other factors) influenced him. The pair were given a testimonial in Melbourne in 1934 and it was known that Woodfull intended this to be his last first-class match. Play was in progress when Ponsford announced that he, too, intended to retire.

Practically throughout their careers, the two Bills had been batting partners for Victoria and Australia, and they were close friends off the field. Their records are strikingly similar: Ponsford 13,819 runs, Woodfull 13,392, each at an average of 65. Woodfull made 49 centuries and Ponsford 47. Their Test records are also similar—Ponsford 2,122 runs at 48, Woodfull 2,300 at 46. Each hit seven Test centuries.

Strangely, on the part of one so gifted, Ponsford allowed himself to get very worried by cricket. He worried particularly if rain threatened during a match, though he was more proficient than most leading Australians on rain-affected pitches. He worried, too, whether he would be chosen in teams or for tours. Larwood worried him; Bradman too, I think, worried him, because he came so soon after all those Ponsford records—records which took so much out of Ponsford. Moreover, I fancy he did not relish the prospect of playing under Bradman's captaincy.

Accordingly, those closest to Ponsford were not really surprised when he packed away his cricket gear and took out his fishing rod. He was always a keen fisherman; indeed, during one Test he could not field because his feet had become sunburnt when he fished on the Sunday. In the post-war period he agreed to play in a certain match with former internationals, but when the day came he wasn't there—he had gone fishing. Curiously, he soon lost his devotion to cricket. Chasing records, no doubt, took too much out of him.

Ponsford had a strong sense of humour. He was full of satirical fun in the dressing-room, and he made a typical remark in the war period when he was being examined for service and was found to be, of all things, colour-blind—a fact which he had never known. He could not distinguish red from green and the puzzled doctor asked him how he had known when the new ball had lost its red sheen in cricket.

'Well,' said Ponsford, 'I suppose I always knew that a ball was red at the start of an innings. When it became worn I never worried about what colour it was—only how big it looked to me.'

By the same token, many bowlers will tell you that Bill Ponsford invariably batted as if the ball were as big as a football. He was, I think, the best all-round batsman Victoria has ever produced.

Ten

THE BEST TEST I HAVE KNOWN

Well, now, that covers a lot of ground, a lot of time and a lot of Test matches. I've seen some very exciting Test matches and I've seen some pretty dull ones (especially during the past few years when captains have been parsimonious in their outlook on the game), but as Tests 'viewed' cannot possibly compete with Tests 'played,' from the viewpoint of personal interest, I'm going to plump very solidly for a Test in which I played. That Test produced two of the greatest innings of this century and other critics, with no personal part in the game, might also consider this particular Test the best they ever witnessed. Even though it finished in a draw!

The time was late December 1935. Victor Richardson's team of Australians had won the First Test against South Africa in Durban, and, although the Springboks a few months earlier had taken the series from England in England, they were deep in the depths of despondency as the Second Test came due at the Wanderers' Ground, Johannesburg.

It had been a sad home-coming for them. Jock Cameron, a champion wicket-keeper, one of the hardest and most scientific hitters known to modern cricket, and a prince of good fellows, was stricken with enteric fever on the voyage from England and had died. This cast an immediate blight over the tour and, in addition, Grimmett and O'Reilly, possibly the best spin-bowling combination known to Test cricket, had driven a feeling of inferiority into the Springbok ranks. Tremendous bowlers, these two, completely unlike in their tactics. You could bat for two hours against the two masters and not get a loose ball. Often, as I crouched at short leg with Vic Richardson, driving home still further the threat of O'Reilly in particular, I felt pity for the Springboks as I saw their creased looks of intense concentration and worry.

Fleetwood-Smith was the third of the spinning trio. He, being a left-handed googly bowler, was entirely different from the others, but every batsman had moments of anticipation against him. He was likely to bowl the best batsman in the world head, neck and heels (as he did Hammond once on a true pitch in Adelaide in 1937), and yet every now and then you would get a loose ball from 'Chuck.'

Our batsmen were in fine shape, we had Oldfield behind the stilts, and our fielding was said to be up to our highest standards. This, I suppose, was because we had more than a fair sprinkling of young chaps and because, too, we would regularly spend some two hours at fielding when net practice was over. We had the zest of young fellows who knew that to get the best out of a game you must put all you have into it. We loved the exhilaration of living and being on a cricket tour. And we were happily led by a chivalrous warrior, Vic Richardson.

Well, then, to Johannesburg on this late December morning of 1935. Though we had been walking over the provincial sides, the South African enthusiasts were sure there was something better around the corner. Many families from Durban, Cape Town and the outlying veldts breakfasted outside the Wanderers' Ground that day, waiting for the gates to open.

Herby Wade won the toss, gave a happy signal to his

dressing-room, and a hearty cheer ran around the ground. First blood to South Africa.

Elation, however, soon turned to dejection. Ernie McCormick (one of the richest wits in the game and the most delightful of team-mates) was in his best fast-bowling form that morning. He did not share the feeling of those athletes who are distressed by the high altitude of Johannesburg, 5,700 feet above sea level. The ball behaves differently compared with sea-level grounds, and many a fieldsman, shaping for a catch in the out-field, will find the ball carrying farther in the rarefied air, only to finish over the fence.

McCormick, this day, was as fast as any bowler I have known. He had two other similar spells—one at Brisbane and one at Lord's, both later—and he revelled in the conditions of this fast pitch. At lunch, South Africa were 6-78, their backs and hearts broken. McCormick, at one stage, had these figures: 9-4-26-3. And then came Grimmett to rub it in, as usual.

I can well recall the anguished 'Oh!' that circled the ground when McCormick sent spinning the leg stump of Dudley Nourse, certainly South Africa's greatest batsman of modern times. Nourse was then in his middle twenties, of average height, splendidly built, and the son of Dave, who, himself, had hit his Test centuries for the Union and was to make a half-century against us in Cape Town towards the end of the tour.

'Dudley will get us out of this mess,' the crowd had hopefully murmured as he swung through the gate, a picture of fitness and confidence. But Nourse could not put his bat on McCormick, who, apart from his great burst of speed, was swinging the ball late from the leg. So to lunch, with the locals in a state of dejection—but we enjoyed ours!

The Springboks doubled their score after lunch but were

all out for 157. O'Reilly had thundered into the breach and, bowling his leg-breaks and bosies to an impeccable length from his height of six feet three inches, he tied the batsmen into many an awkward knot.

We came to bat just after tea and by stumps that night were ahead with seven wickets in hand. Brown and I were having a happy tour and put on a century opening partnership at better than a run a minute. McCabe was forcing it home in his own brilliant manner when he was dismissed right on time.

The South African newspapers, I remember, told a doleful tale next day. It was in this innings that I remarked to Richardson, who had taken my customary New South Wales position of silly short-leg to O'Reilly, that I would like more fielding work to do. 'Come and join me,' said the bright Victor, and along I went to make a double leg-trap. The two of us, up so close, had many a narrow escape from decapitation, but we pegged the batsmen down for O'Reilly. It was strange, therefore, knowing what risks we were taking, to read next morning that we 'were being unsporting in fielding so close to the batsman.' The batsman had the solving of that little problem all in his own hands!

It was a docile, glum crowd next morning—but not for long. Chud Langton, one of the best medium bowlers I have known, soon got to work on a perfect pitch and under a cloudless sky. He knocked back Richardson's stumps; he baited Chipperfield in the fine-leg trap; and, with us having last use of a pitch not long laid, we began to have some apprehensive thoughts of what this bowler would do to us on a wearing pitch in the fourth innings.

Darling, a spectacular left-hander who never gave the grass much chance to grow under his feet or in the direction of his drives or pulls, was in great form. So, too, was Oldfield, as neat with the bat as the gloves. From 5-174 we shot up to 5-209. 'Getting out of the woods,' we told ourselves as we watched from the pavilion. But then came one of the most brilliant pieces of fielding I have ever seen. Oldfield hit a ball hard and wide of mid-off and called. Darling came on. Langton threw out his right hand at top speed, gathered the ball, wheeled, and threw the stumps over. Darling was out by a foot to as thrilling a piece of fielding as one could ever hope to see.

The crowd began to chortle again. In the next five minutes —through the medium of Bruce Mitchell—they went crazy with excitement and joy. Mitchell was a grand opening batsman and a very safe slip field, though in the Brisbane Test of 1931 he gave himself the most awesome nightmare for the future by dropping Bradman three times off Neville Quinn before he was 20—and the Don made 226! Mitchell was also a very fair bowler of leg-breaks, walking just two steps to the bowling line, and in one over on this hectic day he took three wickets for three runs. No wonder the spectators became almost hysterical with excitement.

The stands were crammed when play re-commenced after lunch. This Wanderers' Ground, since taken over for extension of the railway yards, was in the heart of the city and spectators flocked there during the lunch hour.

Mitchell's bowling again made us reflect. If he could turn like this on the second day, what could we expect on the last? No doubt the Springboks were thinking: 'If Bruce can turn like this, what will O'Reilly and Grimmett do?'

There must have been some feverish planning in the Springboks' dressing-room, and it was soon obvious what the policy would be. They had decided that this was their day. The portents were clear and they would continue to attack.

As a true captain should, Herby Wade came first to practise what he preached. No leader from behind was Wade.

Spurred on by his first-innings success, McCormick bowled again as fast as human could, but this time he lacked accuracy. Twice in his first over wide balls went for boundaries. There was a yell when, in the second over, point mis-fielded and Siedle went for a run. Wade shouted 'No,' Siedle jammed on his brakes, turned—and narrowly beat the throw home. Exciting stuff!

In his second over, Wade beautifully hooked McCormick twice for four. Then came another thrilling pull for four. Siedle also got two fours in the one over from O'Reilly, one a powerful pull, the other a scorching straight drive. Forty came up in 30 minutes. Richardson made quick bowling changes. It was tense, dramatic cricket. Grimmett came on. Wade thought there was turn where there wasn't, the ball came straight and fast with top-spin, and out he went, l.b.w. Grimmett, the fox of cricket, smiled broadly. He loved to see batsmen play where the ball wasn't.

Grimmett and Fleetwood-Smith bowled four successive maiden overs. And now a hush fell over the crowd, only the crack of bat against ball breaking the expectant silence.

Rowan had come to the crease. Siedle, remembering Wade, played for a straight one which broke—and 'tinkle, tinkle' went his bails. Grimmett, as he was wont to do, clasped his arms and smiled again—expansively. 'You old fox, Clarrie,' we said, as we thumped him on the back. His grin of delight, when such things happened, was one of the sights of the cricket field. He loved to diddle a batsman out.

Rowan, the 'Talkative' (so called because he kept up a running conversation with bowler, fieldsman and 'keeper all the time he batted) was kept defending as hard as he talked.

'Wasting your time there, Vic,' Rowan would say as he played a dead-bat to O'Reilly. 'I hope you see home again, Fingo,' he said to me as he crashed into a no-ball from O'Reilly and Richardson and I dropped to the ground as if in an air-raid.

Richardson had the decisive, if not the final, word. 'There's your passage ticket, Eric,' said Vic as Rowan feverishly played where the ball wasn't against Grimmett and up went the umpire's finger as Grimmett spun round, index finger aloft, and put the question.

'I'll get you next Test,' hissed the irrepressible Rowan as off he went.

So we had fought back again, thanks to Grimmett, whose figures at this stage read: 10-4-20-3. Wonderful bowling.

Mitchell came at No. 4 this time and Nourse No. 5. Nourse was not himself. Even so early in the tour we had considered that his weakness, if he had one, was against pacy bowling. Richardson must have thought hard as Nourse came to bat. McCormick should have come on immediately for Nourse, but Grimmett couldn't be taken off and Fleetwood-Smith was also on the spot. It was a difficult decision. Richardson went on with spin.

Nourse batted as if in a nightmare. He stabbed feverishly, his footwork indecisive. Mitchell thumped two fours off Fleetwood-Smith and another in the next over, but Nourse just couldn't get the ball away. He was, of course, facing a 'pair' and he had the large crowd as uncomfortable as himself —as one feels uncomfortable when watching somebody in distress.

Grimmett was teasing Nourse unmercifully, but eventually, after playing four maidens, Nourse got him past cover for four. He had been 25 minutes getting off his 'pair'; but now was to come one of the greatest innings in Test cricket, and perhaps the greatest ever played by a Springbok on his home soil.

Nourse found himself immediately. He stroked now with precision and confidence, and there was a great yell from the crowd when, at the end of Fleetwood-Smith's next over, Richardson tossed the ball to McCormick. This purgatory of spin bowling, said the crowd, was over at last. Thrilling and admirable as it was, it was too uncomfortable to watch. Here, now, was McCormick!

The crowd hadn't heard Richardson say, as he tossed the ball to McCormick, 'Grum, Drong.' A team on tour—a good team, that is—works like a machine and two contractions of nicknames were enough to suggest that there was no spell yet for Grimmett. McCormick, ever the wag, swung his bowling arm several times—and then threw the ball to Grimmett. Mitchell, who could hit when in the mood, tucked Clarrie away for three fours in that over. The crowd loved it.

So to tea, with South Africa 3-132—Mitchell 28, Nourse 14.

'Stoke yourself up, Drong,' said Richardson to McCormick at tea. 'You look like having a long lease of that top end.'

'And about time, too,' chipped in Grimmett, 'You ought to be ashamed of yourself, leaving all the hard work to young chaps like me!'

'Who said you were coming off, Grum?' said Richardson, bantering Grimmett, as he always did. 'You've just started to bowl. And no more experiments with Bruce Mitchell, either. Get stuck into him.'

McCormick paced out his long run after tea. In that very first over Nourse snicked one that flew high to the clutching hands of the jumping Chipperfield and Richardson in the slips. Luck was with the batsman, and the ball went through, untouched, to the fence. The crowd gasped in relief.

Then came a three and a two through the slips, upon which

Richardson gave McCormick more slips, until he had five in all. Nourse accepted the challenge and once, twice, thrice he cut McCormick through the massed slips to the fence. The crowd roared with glee and then shouted approbation in the next over as Nourse calmly ignored every ball from McCormick, all teasingly outside the off stump with the slipsmen crouched, their tense fingers expectant for the catch.

Nourse overtook Mitchell in the thirties, forced Grimmett superlatively off his toes for four, picked McCormick square for four, and then on-drove him for four. Fast, anticipatory fielding by Darling saved another four. Then came O'Reilly, to curb Nourse with four successive maidens. Nourse broke the sequence by drawing back to his stumps, standing tip-toe, and crashing O'Reilly with a short-arm back-swing between Richardson and myself. To the fence, again—and we withdrew a yard.

Up came Nourse's 50 in 90 minutes, with eight fours. Take out his abortive first 25 minutes and his 50 came in 65 minutes. Not even Cyril Walters had treated Grimmett and O'Reilly like this in the preceding year in England.

Nourse surged on, his feet twinkling, his bat scourging. Out and back, out and back, his body never still, never retaining its initial position of the stance. Mitchell, like the sensible man he was, withdrew into passive obscurity.

Nourse almost went at 65, Fleetwood-Smith getting one hand to a hefty pull off Grimmett. Next ball, Nourse savagely hooked Grimmett for four, where there was no fieldsman.

The new ball came at 210. McCormick had four slips but Nourse got him through immediately for four. Oldfield snapped Mitchell up off McCabe (134 minutes for 45) and Nourse had made 76 of the 129 partnership—a partnership which redeemed the reputation of South African cricket because it quelled, for the first time, the great Australian spin attack.

Still Nourse sailed on. Off four successive balls from Mc-Cormick, he took eleven with two successive fours out through the alert off-side field—drives in the classic manner, timed to perfection, the bat swinging against a stiff left leg and the ball sounding off the bat like a sweet chime.

Nourse stood at 98 as the last over came. 'Dudley, Dudley, Dudley!' chanted the wildly excited natives in their special stand on the far side of the ground. I went down near them, to field on the fence and there saw a mass of dark faces, with white teeth gleaming in anticipation of Nourse's hundred that night. On the opposite side of the ground, no noise came from the whites. They sat like monks in contemplation.

The garish day finished at last, with Nourse still 98 and still not out. The Springboks were 161 ahead—with six wickets in hand. We could, we told ourselves in the pavilion that night, lose this game. But what an innings from Nourse!

We were to find next day that the innings had barely begun. As Nourse came in with Dooley Briscoe, a sharp nor-westerly was stirring up dust, and O'Reilly and Grimmett inspected happily the now very worn patches at both ends. This was the first time this pitch had been used. It had stood up well to all the pounding feet but now it was breaking.

Nourse, immediately and majestically, moved to his century with a push for two off Grimmett. The crowd rose to him. O'Reilly was troubling him, the big fellow spinning and jumping the ball up smartly from the turf, but Nourse eventually got him square for four and then thumped him to the off for another four.

The sun was blazing and Nourse, too, warmed up, peppering our hands on the off-side. It was exhilarating to be in the middle of this and Billy Brown, Darling and I, on the off-side,

pitted our wits and our speed against Nourse, trying to an-
ticipate his shots, trying to manoeuvre him away from the
strike. We were earning our biltong!

Gradually Nourse became dominant. He hit Grimmett off
for Fleetwood-Smith; he took seven in successive balls
from O'Reilly; he drove Fleetwood-Smith straight for four;
he murderously pulled him. Then, in the 160s, he hopped into
Fleetwood-Smith, missed, was stranded, and Oldfield, for
once, didn't pick the turn of the ball. It was the left-hander's
bosie, deceiving batsman and 'keeper, and Nourse scrambled
back as Oldfield fumbled.

Nourse hooked O'Reilly for four and Nicholson hit him
high into the pavilion for six. At lunch the score was 5-370,
Nourse 179.

Dark clouds came up during lunch and the mineral-laden
sky looked ominous. The light was now bad and rain came.
For 15 minutes we were off while a swarm of natives covered
the pitch. Fleetwood-Smith took the ball and a handful of
sawdust. Three times, off successive balls, Nourse hit him
to the leg boundary. A single then, and Nourse was 200 in
276 minutes.

Now Nourse began to loft the ball. He hit Grimmett back
over his head while Nicholson went and Langton came.
Langton hit Fleetwood-Smith for six and Nourse now surged
boundaries in all directions until it became a flood. He swept
past all South African records, and, on this worn pitch against
some of the greatest spinners ever, he humbled us well and
truly.

Richardson tried to control the game, but it was no use.
'Got any ideas, Chuck, about Dudley?' he said once to Fleetwood-Smith.

'Yes,' said that bowler, 'Shoot him.'

We just had to wait until the end of Nourse came.

It came at last, McCormick brilliantly catching him at point. A. D. Nourse, c McCormick, b McCabe—231. This score should be entered in the cricket book of all time, in letters of gold.

Nourse hit 36 fours and batted for 298 minutes. As we were leaving the field for tea we lined up to meet General Smuts. 'I, too,' he said with sparkling eyes, 'have done some hectic chasing in my time!'

Bob Crisp (then a journalist, now a farmer in England) had a merry 35 and the innings finished for 491. It was the Australians, now, who were dragging the chain.

Vic Richardson was the best possible captain to play under. He never stood over his men, but jollied them along and gave them credit for knowing the game. No long string of tedious orders from Victor.

'Now then, you two,' he said as Brown and I padded up, 'work it out for yourselves in the middle. It's going to be tough. I'll leave it to you.'

We needed 399 to win on a fourth innings pitch, and at the rate of almost a run a minute. As we had managed only 250 in the first innings, 399 was something stiff.

'G'luck, Nugget,' I said to Brown as we walked towards the middle, with me to take strike.

'Same to you, my friend,' said Brown with a smile.

'One thing, Bill,' I said, 'is that "Buster" Nupen would have made our job much harder here.'

Bill Brown nodded in agreement. We had been regaled since our arrival with tales of how great a bowler Nupen *had been* on matting pitches. Now that turf had come to all South African Test pitches Nupen had been put aside—and that was a consoling thought as Brown and I went out to bat. The truth was that Nupen was a great spin bowler on *any* pitch!

You would never wish for a better opening partner than Bill Brown. He always came at your call, you could rely on his, and he never hogged the strike. His smile, however, was a little wry. We both had an idea it was going to be hard going.

It was not Bill's day. Nicholson soon snapped him up behind off Crisp. Then came Stan McCabe, with his quick walk, always anxious to start proceedings. Stan was a bad 'pavilion waiter.' He had much waiting to do with Ponsford and Bradman in England in 1934, as they piled up huge partnerships, and he was always pleased when his job commenced.

Nourse had been superlative in his final stages, but now McCabe began to play, from the very beginning, every bit as wonderfully as Nourse had done. He batted with effortless ease. He never lunged; he always stroked. He was built very much like Nourse—medium height, solid, square shoulders —and there was a definite similarity between their styles. McCabe had whippy, powerful wrists and he was a master of placement.

It was 4.20 o'clock on the last day but one, with Australia 1-17 and the light wretched, with dark black clouds looming for the certain storm, and the pitch thoroughly unreliable. But in 40 minutes McCabe never made a false step, stroke, or error of judgment. In 40 minutes he made 51—40 of them from boundaries.

I left it all to McCabe. At 4.55 the light was shocking. It was a ticklish position for us. We still had a long way to go and we knew that we had a very long tail. Stan was vice-captain and we had a mid-wicket conference.

'I can hardly see the ball,' said Stan.

I smiled. 'No foolin'?' I said.

'Well, you mightn't think so,' said McCabe, in his modest,

shy manner, 'but I've got my work cut out to see it. We have all day tomorrow. This is a good start. I think we had better give the light a go.'

'Umpire,' I called, 'how is the light?'

We got the appeal immediately and left the field 1-85, of which McCabe was 59.

'Well done,' said Richardson, as we got in, 'you did the right thing. I didn't want to lose another wicket tonight.'

This last day should have been a battle all the way against the clock as well, yet inside an hour, on a turning, dusty pitch that was a bowler's dream, McCabe tore the Springbok attack to tatters. Sometimes the ball would rear and turn amazingly, but McCabe was either right out or right back, and every time he played a stroke he seemed to find a gap in the field. My orders were to hold tight and leave it to McCabe.

Our 100 came up in 85 minutes, with boundaries coming from McCabe at an almost incredible rate. He ran to his own 100 in 90 minutes. An appeal was made for a slip catch, but the umpire was with McCabe.

With the total 194, Mitchell spun one off the dust round my legs and just flicked the leg bail. I had made 40 in a hard struggle to keep out shooters and big and sudden breaks— which made McCabe's innings at the other end seem like a crazy dream to me. He had made 148 of our partnership of 177.

The Springbok attack was well tamed, but not beaten. McCabe's wicket was the one they wanted. If they could get him, they reasoned, the other Australians should be easy.

Darling came to give McCabe support, and to see the 200 go up in 166 minutes. McCabe ran to 150 in 145 minutes and at lunch he was 159. He had made his century before lunch, joining Trumper, Macartney and Bradman in achieving this feat.

At lunch we were 2-217. The clock, too, was beaten. But,

though we now looked certain to win, we knew that this match could well be over in an hour.

The light, after lunch, was as murky as a tunnel. In the distance, vivid flashes of lightning lit the sky, and now the prospect was certain rain.

A new ball was due and McCabe and Darling had to fight hard. McCabe got a high one luckily through slips and then, in quick succession both he and Darling were dropped in the slips.

McCabe brought up the 250 in 199 minutes, but Darling, who had commenced delightfully, was now hard put to it to sight the ball. Thunder was crackling and erupting and the forked lightning was almost frightening to behold. McCabe snicked one again into the slips and Robertson, diving, failed to hold it.

Then came an historic appeal. Herby Wade, from the field, appealed against the light! The umpires agreed, the players came off, the rain tumbled down, and in 15 minutes the pitch was under water. We Australians were only 125 off victory, with three hours left for play.

So ended what I still think was the greatest Test I have known. It had every ingredient of exciting, fighting Test cricket, with the fortunes changing almost hourly. The bowling, the fielding, the tactics were always interesting, and in Nourse's 231 and McCabe's 189 not out (he hit 29 fours) it gave cricket two of its greatest innings ever.

Said Wade at the finish: 'It has been a wonderful game of ups and downs, both sides being on top at different periods. The Australians were definitely on top when bad light and rain brought the close. The game was played in the best spirit. These Australians are a splendid lot of cricketers. I want to congratulate McCabe on his classical innings and Grimmett on his great bowling.'

Said Richardson: 'Unfortunately, a very fine finish was nipped in the bud by bad light and rain. The South Africans fought back splendidly in their second innings and set us an almost herculean task to collect 399 runs on a dusty, wearing pitch; but it is a pity that, despite McCabe's individual record Test score and a very fine knock by Fingleton, which set us well on the road to accomplishing that task, finality was not reached.'

In retrospect, I think it best that the game ended as it did. Both sides deserved to win: neither side merited defeat.

SOUTH AFRICA *v.* AUSTRALIA

Match drawn

South Africa—

	1st		2nd	
B. Mitchell, c Oldfield, b McCormick ..	8	— c Oldfield, b McCabe ...	45
I. J. Siedle, c Chipperfield, b McCormick	22	— b Grimmett	34
E. A. Rowan, lbw, b Grimmett........	38	— lbw, b Grimmett	13
A. D. Nourse, b McCormick	0	— c McCormick, b McCabe	231
J. Briscoe, b O'Reilly	15	— b McCormick	16
H. F. Wade, b O'Reilly	0	— lbw, b Grimmett	30
A. B. Langton, c Fingleton, b O'Reilly .	7	— b McCormick	16
A. Nicholson, st Oldfield, b Grimmett..	27	— lbw, b Fleetwood-Smith	29
J. R. Crisp, b Grimmett	8	— b O'Reilly	35
J. B. Robertson, b O'Reilly	17	— b McCormick	3
G. Bock, not out	9	— not out	2
Leg-byes	6	Byes 13, l-b 19, n-b 5..	37

Total 157		Total 491	

Fall: 11, 46, 50, 68, 70, 78, 112, 126, 139, 157

Fall: 50, 89, 90, 219, 291, 397, 440, 454, 466, 491

	O.	M.	R.	W.		O.	M.	R.	W.
McCormick	16	5	36	3	....	26	3	129	3
McCabe........	6	2	11	0	....	9	1	30	2
O'Reilly	20·2	9	54	4	....	35·3	15	91	1
Fleetwood-Smith	6	2	21	0	....	21	5	93	1
Grimmett	15	5	29	3	....	58	28	111	3

McCormick, 4 n-b.
O'Reilly, 1 n-b.

Australia—

J. H. Fingleton, c and b Langton	62 —	b Mitchell............. 40
W. A. Brown, c Crisp, b Robertson ...	51 —	c Nicholson, b Crisp.... 6
S. J. McCabe, c Robertson, b Langton..	34 —	not out 189
L. S. Darling, run out...............	42 —	not out 37
V. Y. Richardson, b Langton	2	
A. G. Chipperfield, C Rowan, b Langton	0	
W. A. Oldfield, c Briscoe, b Mitchell ...	40	
C. V. Grimmett, b Mitchell	7	
W. J. O'Reilly, b Mitchell	0	
E. L. McCormick, b Mitchell	4	
L. O'B. Fleetwood-Smith,. not out.....	5	
Sundries	3	Sundries 2

Total 250   Two wickets for 274

Fall: 105, 127, 168, 170, 174, 209, 241,   Fall: 17, 194
241, 242, 250

	O.	M.	R.	W.		O.	M.	R.	W.
Crisp	15	1	49	0	....	17	3	62	1
Langton	32	6	85	4	....	22	6	54	0
Mitchell	7·3	0	26	4	....	15	1	73	1
Bock	14	2	49	0	....	9	0	42	0
Robertson......	13	0	38	1	....	13	3	41	0

Eleven

'EVIL SPIRITS' AND 'BUMPERS'

Twenty years separated the two West Indian teams that visited Australia, but in skill, temperament and outlook on the game the two were as close as today and tomorrow.

When the luck of the game ran their way, they sparkled like champions. They were then brimful of the confidence that enables cricketers to attempt the things that make them great. But when the fight was from the rear the West Indians, or at least some of them, wilted perceptibly and let matters drift. The men from the isles of spice and sun became depressed much too easily.

G. C. Grant brought the team of 1930-31 to Australia; John Goddard brought the one of 1951-52. Grant's side had the greater opportunities because his tour was well arranged, with the customary games against the States before the Test series began. Thus, Grant's men were able to accustom themselves to Australian conditions, grounds and players. But the later visit of Goddard's team, brought about by the spectacular successes of the West Indians in England, was arranged at the last minute and the visitors were into the thick of a Test series soon after they landed. Had this not happened—had they been able to experience Australian conditions in earlier games against the States—they would have been a tougher Test proposition. However, the fact appears to be that the West Indians usually labour under an inferiority complex against the Australians.

The islanders' troubles, it would seem, extend into super-stition. After the side had lost the first two Tests against Australia, and also matches against New South Wales, South Australia and Western Australia, one of Goddard's greatest difficulties was to persuade some of his men that the team was not dogged by evil spirits. He got them out of the trough to win the Third Test (in Adelaide) by six wickets, but then, at a vital stage of the Fourth Test (in Melbourne) down went some of the bundles again and Australia gained a sensational victory by one wicket. The visitors, clearly enough, did not possess the capacity to 'sew up' a Test when they had it, so to speak, in their laps.

Grant's side included two magnificent cricketers in George Headley and Learie Constantine. Weekes, Worrell and Wal-cott had many meritorious innings in England before coming to Australia but, as seen in Australia, none of them measured up to Headley as a Test batsman. Weekes was a glorious stroke-maker, a hitter of the ball. Worrell stroked with classical artistry. Walcott, big and powerful, hit with tremendous force, but in six Test innings could manage only 87 runs, averaging 14·50. He seemed often to be off-balance and distinctly open to an early yorker.

So far did the three W's fall short of their English per-formances that it was Gerry Gomez, the all-rounder, who finished first in Test averages in Australia. He averaged 36. Worrell was next with 337 runs at 33·70. Weekes was only seventh on the Test list, with 245 runs at 24·50.

After the disappointing loss in Melbourne, Gerry Gomez, using a made-to-order breeze for in-swingers at Sydney, took 7-55 and the Australians were bundled out for only 116 in the last Test. Here was the chance for the West Indies to show, finally, that there was little between the teams. Alas, though, the evil spirits returned—in the persons of Miller, Lindwall and Johnston—and the West Indians were spirited out for a woeful 78. The Australians made 377 in the second innings and the West Indians were beaten by 202 runs. Stollmeyer, a good fighter, made 104. The next highest score was that of Rae, 25.

Thus the tour finished on a dismal note and John Goddard, the victim of a 'palace movement' that deposed him from the captaincy for the final Test, spoke bitter words after the match. Some cricket writers were having dinner with West Indian pressmen that evening and chanced to meet John as he stood waiting, with Weekes and a few others, for a lift.

John addressed his remarks to Bill O'Reilly and myself. He complained that Australia's fast men had bowled a surfeit of bumpers throughout the tour. 'We didn't expect such an uncricketlike welcome,' he said.

I was to have a similar experience next summer after the South Africans had been humbled at Sydney, in the Third Test, by a pretty blistering bumper attack from Lindwall and Miller. The Springboks had taken the Second Test in Melbourne by 82 runs, and the Australians decided to 'turn on the heat' in the next Test in Sydney. They did so, winning by an innings and 38 runs.

The manager, Ken Viljoen, called me aside after the match. 'I thought,' he said, 'we had come to Australia under a gentlemen's agreement that there would be no bumpers.' The captain, Cheetham, was with Viljoen. I told him that the matter had nothing to do with me since I was not a cricket legislator. Also, I told him who I thought was responsible for perpetuating bumpers in Australian cricket and who he should approach in the matter.

Lindwall and Miller, strangely, got no more Springbok

wickets. Neither took a wicket on the passive Adelaide pitch in the Fourth Test (Miller bowled only three overs in the match) and both were stood down from the final Test at Melbourne. I don't suggest that they were suspended because of bumpers; the fact was that the selectors wished to try Archer and Noblett with a view to selection in the 1953 team to tour England. This was the Test the Springboks won to give them equal honours with Australia.

To return to the West Indians. Goddard was very wrathful about the dose of bumpers his side had been given. He had a doleful Weekes by his side as he recalled what that player had been through in the match—he lost his wicket once to a bumper when he submerged like a submarine but left his bat aloft like a periscope so that the ball hit the bat and shot straight into the air.

O'Reilly and I could tell Goddard only what I, later, was to tell Viljoen and Cheetham. Like a certain notability of old, we washed our hands of the matter. Anyway, what a country sows in sport, as in other things, so does it reap. In loss of standing in the game, in decrease of the game's popularity here, Australia has suffered retribution for relying so much upon the intimidation of bumpers to win Tests in post-war years.

Whereas we should have enjoyed a rich spectacle of batting by those gifted warriors from the West Indies we saw, instead, much fevered ducking to earth as if a flock of doodle-bombs was whistling overhead. Spectators soon tired of the weaving and ducking. They wanted to see cricket, not the antics of the boxing stadium.

With such circumstances in mind it is well not to be dogmatic about the ability of Worrell, Weekes and Walcott. Certainly, however, one could not place any of them on the same Test pedestal as George Headley, that batsman who came 20 years previously with Grant's team, and who played a memorable century-innings against a strong Australian spin attack in Melbourne. Elsewhere in this book I write of how highly H. L. Collins rated Headley; and another who speaks in the warmest terms of him is C. V. Grimmett, who is not given to idle compliments where batsmen are concerned.

Learie Constantine was another West Indian of pronounced potentiality. On his day, he was in the very top bracket of fast bowlers—in the class of Larwood, Lindwall and Miller. He was the finest fieldsman to his own bowling that modern and near-modern cricket knew; and, in addition, he was about the cleanest big-hitter of modern times. Constantine didn't merely slog, he was a scientific hitter. Those who saw him in action will not soon forget his three prodigious sixes at Sydney in 1931 against New South Wales—he put one ball half-way up the Hill, another on the roof of the Paddington stand and the third high on the roof of the Sheridan stand. If you know the Sydney ground you will realise that these were remarkable hits. Moreover, on that day Constantine hit with full-blooded force along the ground.

Yet that was one of only a few good innings he played in Australia. He had then just completed an engagement in the Lancashire League, and he seemed to be a trifle jaded before the Australian tour was half-way through.

So much for Constantine and Headley. I don't think the later West Indian side (1951-52) possessed two cricketers as good as that pair although, overall, Goddard's side had much the greater potential through possessing, in addition to the three W's, Ramadhin and Valentine.

There were times when, as Valentine bowled, I thought I was watching the best left-handed bowler I have ever seen.

One of his characteristics was to rub his left hand on the ground to get grit for purchase. He did this before the start of every over, and he did it while awaiting the return of the ball after being hit to the boundary. He spun the ball much more in Australia than, for instance, England's Verity or Australia's Bill Johnston. He had an even sharper spin than Ramadhin, and he gave the Australians more trouble in the first innings of the First Test in Brisbane than did his fellow bowler. He took there 5-99, his victims being Morris, Miller, Harvey and Hole—an imposing bag. Ramadhin took 1-75, and in the second innings his figures were 5-90.

Valentine took 24 wickets in the series, splendid bowling for a left-handed spinner on covered Australian pitches. He was a cheerful soul who played in spectacles. Alec Bedser told me once that he watched Valentine field at The Oval, Surrey, and noticed that, when fielding, he often went in an opposite direction to the ball. Alec suggested that Alf should make some inquiry about Britain's free optical services, which he did, and ever afterwards he played in glasses.

I saw Valentine once on an Adelaide beach, when the West Indians had a day off and most of them were in the water. I asked Alf wasn't he interested. 'No, sur, Jack,' he said, 'if dem sharks have an appointment with Alf Valentine dey'll have to come right on up to de hotel shower to see him. Yes, sur.'

Len Hutton, a grand teller of a tale, had spread some fearsome stories in Australia during the previous year concerning the 'black magic' of Sonny Ramadhin. He declared that a dark ball came out of a dark hand, often against a dark background of crowd, devoid of a sight-board, and he defied any batsman, at first meeting, to tell which way the ball was spinning, from off or leg.

'Never met the like of him before,' said Len, who was not

one to underestimate the difficulties of a batsman. In fact, the further he got across Australia the more gloomy was the picture of Ramadhin that he painted for the interest of Australian batsmen.

To a group of players in Melbourne, on one occasion, Hutton was demonstrating how Ramadhin held and delivered the ball. Presently he turned to 'Big Jake' Iverson (whose unorthodox grip had made him a much discussed bowler) and said, 'By the way, Jake, how do you hold the ball?'

'I guess,' replied "Wrong Grip Jake," 'that you'll see soon enough for yourself—in the field.'

The 'black magic' tales that preceded Ramadhin to Australia induced Morris and Miller to go to Newcastle, New South Wales, where the West Indians were to play their first game. Their special idea was to sit behind the little West Indian and try to fathom his break. He bowled both off- and leg-breaks, but not with wrist twist. He spun by flicking his fingers down either side of the ball, and with a quick action he was, as Hutton declared, very hard to pick.

The Australians, at the beginning, made heavy weather against Ramadhin. Three times in successive innings he took Hassett's wicket. Once, as he was leaving Hassett in Melbourne, Ramadhin said to the Australian captain, 'So long, Rabbit, I'll have the hutch open again for you in Sydney!' Hassett's reply was typical: 'I'll have you flat to the boards, screaming for mercy, before I'm finished with you!'

Now the Australians began to indulge in bluff against Ramadhin. As Miller came in to bat he made a point of walking towards the little bowler and saying as he twirled his bat vigorously, 'I'll give you some stick today, Sonny.' And, in fact, it wasn't very long before the Australians had fathomed Ramadhin and were indeed giving him 'stick.'

He took six wickets in the First Test at Brisbane, but in the second one at Sydney his figures were 0-143 and 1-53. He took 14 Test wickets at an average of 50, and only 22 wickets on tour at an average of 42. It was a poor return after all the tales of 'black magic' we had heard of him.

Twelve

WHEN BLUFF BEAT THE
WEST INDIANS

The last day of the Fourth Test against Goddard's West
Indians, played in Melbourne in January, 1952, was one of
brilliant sunshine, but the pitch—with its grass dying after
years of use and the soil obviously sour—was suspect.
Apart from the wear of years, the ground had suffered because American troops took it over during the war and they,
knowing nothing about cricket, had no reverence for the
strip in the middle.

Hassett (23 over-night) resumed batting with Harvey (21),
and the pair poked the pitch like doctors pressing a suspect
stomach. The Australians were 1-68 and needed a further 192
to win. So far it had been a low-scoring game, the West
Indians making 272 (Worrell 108—Miller 5-60) and the
Australians replying with 216 (Harvey 83, Miller 47—Trim
5-34). The West Indians had the chance to forge far ahead
in their second innings but Johnston, Miller and Lindwall
dismissed them for 203 (Stollmeyer 54, Gomez 52).

With the cracks widening in the pitch as the game went on
it was apparent that runs would be even harder to get on this
final day. Moreover, in Valentine and Ramadhin the West
Indians had the spinners to make the most of the pitch. The
visitors were favoured to win and, having won the preceding

Test in Adelaide, they had the rosy prospect of carrying the series to the final game in Sydney.

In his first over Ramadhin made a ball keep so low as to cause Harvey to wince. Trim, fast-medium, came on at the other end and the scoring was slow. The batsmen were so intent on defence, waiting for the ball to do the unexpected, that they were rarely in position for an attacking stroke. In 20 minutes only six runs were added. Ramadhin's tactics were obvious—every ball was in line with the stumps. As usual, he never seemed to angle for catches.

Harvey at last pierced the field with a superb on-drive off Ramadhin. Then came Valentine. Bowling round the stumps, he presented Hassett with a full-toss on the leg-side which was deftly tucked away for four but, in the same over, the bowler drew Harvey forward as if by magnetism. Harvey's feet, usually so definite when they moved forward, were now hesitant, as if they didn't approve of the order from above, wherefore the ball spun sharply past his groping bat and rapped the middle stump.

This was the perfect ball—and Harvey's wicket was the one the West Indians wanted most. More than Hassett, he had the capacity to cut loose and put on quick runs. The Australians now were 166 behind, with eight wickets to fall.

Jack Moroney, whose Test chances in Australia had been strangely limited when set against the favours accorded certain other players, had not faced Ramadhin before the first innings. In that innings he had shown a cordial desire to keep away from the little spinner and thus he came, at this stage, with no great show of confidence.

Valentine appealed loudly for l.b.w. against Moroney off the first ball, and in the same over he dropped him—dropped a caught-and-bowled chance that was really a 'sitter.'

The Australians were now struggling. Ramadhin had

bowled seven overs for seven runs. Some of us onlookers, therefore, began thinking that Miller, instead of Moroney, would have been a wise recasting of the batting order. Two defensive batsmen together give an attack a chance in such circumstances to get on top. Anyway, Ramadhin soon had Moroney l.b.w. again, and when the following batsman, Miller, had scored only two he clipped his bails off against Valentine. Just 12 months before, in Adelaide's Test, Miller had chopped his bails off against Douglas Wright—and that when his tally was 99!

The Australians were now 4-109. The six men left to Hassett had contributed 23 in the first innings and here, now, the pitch was taking much more spin and the West Indians were dominant and aggressive.

Hassett himself should have been out immediately after lunch, but Guillen missed a stumping chance on the leg-side off Ramadhin.

Ramadhin and Valentine changed ends at this stage. Why they did so wasn't apparent since both had bowled well at their chosen ends before lunch. However, runs came slowly, very slowly, and at 144 Goddard took the new ball. We wondered whether Ramadhin would rub it immediately in the dust, as he had done at Brisbane in the First Test, but this time Goddard spelled his spinners.

Worrell and Gomez now bowled wide leg-theory to both batsmen causing me to wonder why the West Indians had bothered to change the ball at all. Graham Hole was swinging furiously at the leg-theory and missing completely until he suddenly connected with a ball from Worrell. The ball went off at high speed and from Gerry Gomez, close in at leg-slip, came a whoop like that of an Indian—Red variety. The whoop circled the ground as Gomez tossed up the ball. He had taken the catch of his career.

Hole had been batting 54 minutes for his 13. The score was now 5-147 and Australia needed 113 to win. The odds were heavily in favour of the West Indians.

When Lindwall came in Goddard took off Gomez (four overs for one run) and called back Ramadhin. Lindwall hit him immediately to leg for two and then got a four and then two more fours to leg. He scored 14 in the over. It was a worrying over for Goddard. He cast anxious eyes towards the pavilion to see if Trim would appear. The fast-medium West Indian had bowled splendidly in the first innings for 5-34 but, for some reason or other, he didn't return after lunch.

Goddard, no doubt, would have liked to recall Valentine but he evidently remembered that Lindwall had thrashed him in the first innings of the First Test at Brisbane when he top-scored with 61, and he didn't like to run the risk again at this stage. Moreover, as shown against Ramadhin, Lindwall was obviously eager to 'kill.'

Worrell now bowled an outrageous 'shooter' to Lindwall. The ball never left the turf but, luckily for the batsman, it was pitched wide of the stumps. Again Goddard looked towards the pavilion. Where was Trim? Why didn't he come?

Ramadhin bowled a maiden over to Hassett. In the next over, however, Lindwall slammed the spinner for three and then gloriously square-cut him for four. In this period Lindwall scored 29 to Hassett's eight. Then, to the obvious relief of the West Indians, Lindwall mis-timed a square-cut off Ramadhin and was caught behind—a dangerous nuisance was out of the way.

Now, with 68 needed, the shrewd Hassett decided to adopt the role of hitter. He swung Valentine to leg for four and then beautifully square-cut him for another four. In fact, whereas he had occupied 70 minutes going from 71 to 80, he rattled through the eighties in a matter of seconds. His

defence all day on a pitch helpful to spinners had been immaculate and now, with little support remaining, he had
decided to make an offensive thrust for victory.

Ramadhin bowled a maiden over to Ian Johnson and in
the last over before tea Hassett swung Valentine fine again.
Weekes, half-way to the fence at fine-leg, leaped feet into the
air but the ball sailed over his fingers. Hassett was 95 at tea;
Australia 6-204. When the players emerged again, Trim was
still absent. Hassett again swept Valentine fine for four and
went to his century in 303 minutes. It was one of his best
innings, full of courage and responsibility. Then, at the other
end, Ramadhin had Johnson caught behind.

Ring, as was his habit, came bustling out, but this time
looking at the board and doing a quick sum. Australia still
needed 42 but now, Valentine, bowling round the stumps,
had Hassett l.b.w. for 102.

Langley was the next man in. He sneaked a quick single to
avoid his 'pair'—and then was l.b.w. to Valentine. Australia
9-222. The last wicket needed 38.

The match seemed as good as won for the West Indians.
The result of the series would hinge, then, on the meeting at
Sydney.

Bill Johnston, as amiable a fellow as ever pulled on a pad,
emerged in his usual cheery manner while the crowd of
30,000 or so chirruped in anticipation. Bill's angular batting,
with his feet moving back and his bat moving forward,
was always good for a wholesome laugh. But it wasn't good
enough to endure this crisis. Anyway, that was what the
crowd thought. That was also the idea of the local con-
stabulary for Johnston had gone only a few yards through
the gate when a dozen men in blue solemnly moved out after
him to encircle the ground and prevent spectators from
visiting the pitch at the end of the match.

Ramadhin and Valentine were in conference as Johnston approached the wicket. So were Goddard and Stollmeyer. They set the field together, carefully and precisely. Ring paced about, obviously ill at ease.

Johnston prodded his bat both backwards and forwards and, to the amusement of the crowd, missed the ball. From the depths of the grandstand rose a cry 'Come on the Tigers! The Tigers can do it!' But, in fact, no onlooker really believed that the two 'Tigers' (both Ring and Johnston came from Melbourne's Richmond club, known as the 'Tigers') could pull the match off. What the batsmen thought on the point was known only to themselves.

As Ramadhin bowled to Ring the West Indians surged in and out like surf on a beach. This, it seemed, was one possible Test victory against Australia which they had no intention of throwing away.

Ring sneaked a single and at the end of the over all the players, including the batsmen, went into groups of conferences. Goddard and Stollmeyer again meticulously arranged the field and for several balls Ring poked a very uncertain bat at Valentine. Obviously this hefty batsman needed one good boundary, right from the centre of the bat, to bring him confidence. At this stage he seemed to be paralysed by the occasion. Then came a streaky, lucky three for a snick. Johnston stole a cheeky single. Following that, just the right type of ball came from Valentine and Ring gave it all he had. It was a clean hit and the ball flew high to the deserted outfield for four. This was just what Ring needed. He now had assurance. He waited again for the right ball and swung. This time he played the golfer's hook and the ball sailed away over long-on for yet another four. The crowd roared with delight as Ring and Johnston sneaked a single off the last ball. The over had yielded 13 runs.

Another West Indian conference occurred before Rama-dhin bowled the next over. They realised that every well-pitched ball would get the 'treatment' from Ring. He swung furiously, and connected, against Ramadhin, but this time Atkinson made a brilliant one-handed save and a possible four was limited to two. Australia—20 runs to go!

Goddard directed Atkinson to go further out, but no sooner had the captain turned his back to marshal his forces elsewhere than Ramadhin brought Atkinson in. What should a fieldsman do in such circumstances? Clearly, he should ignore the bowler. In this case the very next ball from Ramadhin was hit over Atkinson's head to the spot Goddard had placed him!

Again, now, there was an animated conference as Goddard placed his field afresh. Signs of panic were evident.

A well-run two followed, after which Ramadhin almost bowled Ring. As Johnston grinned Ring paced round and round the stumps like an expectant father outside a maternity ward. Ramadhin came up to bowl, dropped the ball, and had to start again. His delivery was the last ball of the over. Ring tapped it and ran. Johnston, with long legs, arms and bat flaying the air, was off too, and Weekes dashed in from cover for the run-out. Alas, though, the fieldsman fumbled and the batsmen got home. Only 13 runs to go now, and the crowd was roaring like the surf crashing on Bondi cliffs in a southerly buster.

Worrell now bowled. Ring and Johnston stole another single. Johnston crouched low over his bat, tapped one and galloped off. Stollmeyer raced in, picked up smartly and threw the stumps over, but again the batsman was safe. Stollmeyer careered off after the ball but the momentum of Ring and Johnston had taken them both well past the stumps.

Why, one wondered, did the West Indians allow the

Australians to get away with this tip-and-run stuff? They should obviously have had a man up close on either side of the pitch to stop it. But once again Ring tapped, Johnston surged, the West Indians converged, the ladies squealed and the Outer roared—and again the batsmen scampered to safety.

Now only 10 runs were needed. When the deficit was further reduced by another quick single Ramadhin held the game up through leaving the field. It was said later that he, like Trim, was suffering from leg-strain, but I knew many a Test bowler who would have stayed on to the end, even if he had to call for crutches. However, Valentine—honest, plugging, smiling Alf Valentine—was still fighting on, rubbing his hands in the dirt and spinning the skin off his fingers.

Johnston tapped a ball six yards down the pitch and off went the Australians again. Their policy, in the belief that the West Indians were thoroughly flustered, was to run for everything. Ring, when running, got a flying start, but Johnston was still well out of his crease as Valentine, following through, fielded the ball. The bowler wheeled—and held the ball. Behind the stumps stretched the boundary, with nobody backing up, and Valentine wouldn't risk over-throws.

Guillen, the wicket-keeper, emitted a lusty appeal as Ring played and missed. But Guillen was alone in his appeal and the Outer roared ridicule at him. From a square-cut by Ring they ran three (Christiani making a bad return), and now they had only five runs to go with two balls left in Valentine's over.

Johnston collapsed on the next ball, smothering it, amid loud laughter from the crowd. Next ball he square-cut like a champion and they ran three. But Johnston, in his anxiety, ran one short and so Australia still needed three.

Worrell bowled to Johnston a shooter that never left the

ground and brought up a spurt of dust. But it was wide of the stumps and Johnston, after fanning himself in relief and smiling broadly, settled down again and got a single to fine-leg. Now only two were needed.

Worrell walked back slowly, very slowly, and tried hard to find a shooting-patch on the stumps. Ring pushed him past mid-off for a single—to make the scores equal. Now honours of the series were with Australia. Worrell ran up, Johnston prodded, the ball trickled to fine-leg and the batsmen ran one. The match was over!

Late that evening Bill Johnston's throaty laugh was still echoing in the dressing-room. 'Actually,' said Bill (with tongue in cheek) 'the issue was never in doubt! I had with me my favourite bat. Not a mark on it. And Doug Ring and I understand each other. I was only sorry we weren't chasing another 50! I was just settling down to the job. But can anybody tell me why that pack of policemen followed me on to the field?'

Plenty could, but the real story of that late afternoon, from 5 p.m., when Johnston and the police walked out, to 5.35 p.m., when Johnston hit the winning run, was a story of colossal bluff that paid off. The two Australians decided that Ring would chance his eye, his arm and his luck, and the two of them would run for everything. It was this tip-and-run strategy that demoralised the West Indians and snatched victory from them.

I have seen no more blatant bluffing on a cricket field. To watch it in operation, and to mark its effects, was to realise why it is that West Indian cricketers on Australian fields have yet to do full justice to their ability.

Thirteen

ON THE STRAIN OF CRICKET TRAVEL

'Travel crowds a Test tour in Australia and imposes
a tremendous strain upon the players.' So said
M.C.C. captain F. R. Brown at the end of the 1950-
51 tour of Australia, in which all travelling was by
air.*

It was January 13, 1885. Arthur Shrewsbury's team of
Englishmen had just finished a match against a batch of
22 at Candelo, on the far south coast of New South Wales.
The next game, also against a team of 22, was against the
Shoalhaven district at Nowra.

A crow would have made quick work of the distance
between Candelo and Nowra, but on such a day it would have
been difficult to get the crow to try. The sky was black and
intensely moody; the wind was on the make; and the band
of Englishmen looked apprehensively at the little steamer of
500 tons as they gathered on the wharf at Tathra. Bags of
potatoes and numbers of squealing pigs were being hustled
aboard.

No road over the mountains connected Candelo and
Nowra. A long sea trip of 200 miles to Sydney in the slow

* Brown's team grew to 19 when Tattersall and Statham were flown out
from England. With such numbers, Brown and the leading professionals took
it in turns to have a week's rest. Brown went to a sheep station. Hutton sailed
leisurely from Sydney to Adelaide between the Third and Fourth Tests.

little vessel lay ahead of the Englishmen; and the irony of the business was that they would have to cover more than half that distance again as they came south by train and coach back to Nowra. They had one hope—a tentative arrangement had been made that, if conditions were suitable, a Government tug would put to sea off the mouth of the Shoalhaven River, tranship the cricketers, and bring them in to Nowra. But the weather made that arrangement seem very unlikely.

The captain of the little coastal tub met the cricketers as they came aboard, putting their cricket bags under a big spread of tarpaulin.

'Sorry to give you such a nasty day, Mr. Shrewsbury,' said the captain. 'I'm afraid, too, it will get worse. I don't think we will be seeing that tug.'

The weather did get worse. Land was soon lost to view in the low clouds and pelting rain. The winds lashed into stinging spray the tops of large Pacific rollers. Terrified, the pigs in their pens squealed louder and louder.

The English cricketers huddled like a group of bedraggled fowls under what cover the bridge could give. All were violently sea-sick. Lunch-time came and went with nobody venturing below to the pokey little dining-room. In fact, the odours from there made them the more wretched.

About mid-afternoon a sailor approached Shrewsbury.

'Message from the cap'n, sir,' he said. 'We are about off the Shoalhaven now but the skipper doesn't think the tug will come out.'

Shrewsbury grunted. He didn't care much what happened. Long ago he had cursed the little steamer, the tug, the Shoalhaven, and the very cricket tour of Australia. Also the squealing, squawking pigs. He wished, with all his heart, that he had left Australian tours to the one he had made five years earlier. On this January day there would be a big, roaring fire in the Trent Bridge Inn and he could have been standing there, pewter pot of ale in hand, yarning with his fellows of the Nottinghamshire eleven.

There remained eight hours more of this bouncing, jolting voyage to Sydney. It was almost dark now, but the passengers could see the rollers coming and could brace themselves against their charge. It would be worse in the dark, pitching and plunging; but even this could be preferable to changing at sea into the tug and then bouncing shorewards.

Shrewsbury had neither the heart nor stomach for anything more. He grimaced when he thought of his stomach. It had let him down long ago. In its place was a ball of pain. He wasn't exactly scared—just sick, sick of everything.

Five minutes later the same sailor came to him.

'The skipper would like to know, sir,' he said, 'if you could come up on the bridge and see him?'

Shrewsbury nodded. Holding tight to stanchions and rails, he timed his wobbly feet to the pitch of the vessel and scrambled up slippery steps to the bridge.

The engines had been cut down. Straining eyes on the bridge were sweeping the sea for a sight of the tug. There was now little daylight left.

'I'm afraid I will have to take you on to Sydney, Mr. Shrewsbury,' said the captain. 'I don't think the tug has come out. And I don't blame 'em, do you?'

Shrewsbury agreed. But just then came a shout, 'Tug on the starboard bow, sir.'

They looked and there, dimly, was the tug, a minute affair, riding high one moment and out of sight in the trough the next. Shrewsbury was sure he had seen bigger pleasure craft on the Trent.

The steamer changed course and lurched towards the tug but, obviously, it wouldn't be possible to get close.

Shaw, the English manager, was now on the bridge. He and Shrewsbury looked at each other, doubt and apprehension in their eyes.

'What about it, gentlemen?' asked the sea-captain.

'What do you think?' asked Shaw.

'It will be a difficult job getting you across,' said the skipper, 'but the tug has come out—and it will save you many more hours of this. I'll give it a go, if you will.'

England's cricket fields seemed to belong to another world as Shaw and Shrewsbury talked matters over. 'I think we should try it, Alfred,' said Shrewsbury, and added with a wry grin, 'if we go down, we take the honours of the rubber with us.'. (They had already won Tests at Adelaide and Melbourne.)

Shaw turned to the captain. 'Very well,' he said, 'we are willing to try it.'

They slipped and stumbled back to their fellows beneath the bridge. 'We are going to the tug,' said Shaw. 'Each man will take his cricket bag and be responsible for it. And— England expects that every man in the next half-hour or so will do his duty.'

Shaw counted out six men to do the first trip—himself, Read, Bates, Flowers, Briggs and Ulyett. They formed a line across the deck and handed six bags into the lifeboat, swaying on its davits.

'Just a minute, Johnny,' called Shrewsbury to Briggs. It had suddenly crossed Shrewsbury's mind that Briggs had hit 121 in the First Test. No need to throw discretion to the winds and the sea altogether. It would be policy to divide his stars. He pulled Briggs back and pushed the stonewaller Scotton to the deck-rail.

The davits were now letting the lifeboat down. Deftly, with their oars, the crew kept it from smashing against the side of the parent vessel; and then, again, when it hit the water.

Two by two, the cricketers stood on the rail, reached for the davits, and then went smartly, hand under hand and legs entwined around the ropes, to the craft below.

Smartly, ever so smartly, the davits were cast off, and away went the lifeboat from the lee of the steamer. The remaining cricketers could barely watch as the cockle-shell ran up and down and, sometimes, out of view. They feared for their fellows; they feared, even more, for their own turn, soon to come.

A Yorkshireman, Joe Hunter, was the only one who didn't cheer when, finally, the six cricketers were seen on the deck of the tug and the lifeboat appeared again from the other side of the tug. Joe had lost his voice completely!

Back came the lifeboat and huddled in the lee of the steamer. Oars were out again to hold it from smashing on the side. This time the cricket bags were slung overboard and the remaining six cricketers prepared to slide down the ropes. Joe Hunter, with Shrewsbury, stood near the rail, ready to go over.

'Are you all safe down there?' Joe called to the lifeboat.

'Yes.'

'Well,' said Joe, 'you stay where you are and I'm going to stay where I am.' He meant every word. He spoke from the bottom of his heart.

W. Barnes was another who declined to move at the last moment.

Off went the cockle-shell, back it safely came and was hauled aboard. The steamer tooted, the tug tooted, and each went its way, soon lost to the view of the other.

In less than an hour, the 10 Englishmen had landed at Nowra.

Hunter and Barnes continued their nightmare journey to Sydney, 90 miles away. Next day, still sore and ill from the voyage, they caught a train to go some 90 miles to Moss Vale. There they entered a coach to ride 50 miles over a bumping, winding track down the mountains. 'Keep an eye out,' the coachman told Hunter, as he shut the door on him. 'There may be bushrangers about.'

Twenty-one hours after they had left their comrades, Barnes and Hunter saw them again in Nowra. When Bobby Peel saw them he squealed like a pig, climbed to the cross-bars of a lamp-post and, assuming a voice stricken with terror, called out to Hunter, 'You stay where you are; I'm going to stay where I am.'

*　　　*　　　*　　　*

The weary tourists walked slowly up the steps of the landing-stage to their aircraft at Sydney. It had been a hard night. Following the day's cricket had been the social festivities. It would be a good idea, one or two thought, if they shut Sydney's night-clubs a little earlier. 'Oh, no,' they yawned—and there was another game to start in Melbourne in two days' time. Someone cracked the old jest, 'This would be a good tour if there were no cricket.'

They trickled to their numbered seats, buckled their safety-belts for take-off, and rang the bell for the hostess. Cushions? At least they could snooze the two and a half hours to Melbourne. The hostess brought them sweets so that their ears wouldn't block in ascent.

The mechanic below gave the thumb-up sign to the pilots. The flaps were wiggled in testing. Slowly, lazily, the four props began to turn and then to whistle and scream. Over the inter-com came the release from the control-tower. The big plane turned and ambled down to the beginning of the long runway.

Twenty minutes later it had turned over Botany Bay and was far down the indented coast of New South Wales, one of the prettiest pictures in all air travel. But the tourists were too tired to notice. They mostly slept.

Over Nowra, a gentle shudder shook the plane as it turned sou-sou-west and found a small pocket of disturbance from the hotter air over land.

The tremor, faint as it was, caused Eldred to wake.

'Tea and scones, sir?' asked the pretty hostess.

'No, thanks,' said Eldred.

'Perhaps a beer, whisky or cigarettes?' she asked.

'No,' said Eldred and turned out-board the better to slumber.

He looked through the window and blinked hard. Riding, ever so perkily on the wing-tip, was a gremlin. There was no doubt about that. He knew a gremlin when he saw one. You often saw them aloft—especially after New Year's Eve parties—but this was a most unusual one. It was dressed in cream flannels and a near-M.C.C. cravat. It wore, too, an old-fashioned cricket cap and the face sprouted a bushy moustache and side-levers.

For all the world, thought Eldred, like a photograph of old Shrewsbury. Odd, extremely odd, but perhaps the oddest thing of all was that the gremlin had its fingers to its nose.

'A rum show, what!' said Eldred—and dropped off again to sleep. He was so very, very tired.

Fourteen

CRICKET FAREWELLS*

Twiddling the peak of his cap, as is his wont, Len Hutton walked from the Sydney ground and into the pavilion depths just as the workman on the balcony above hauled down the M.C.C. flag for the last time.

Behind Hutton came Compton, surrounded, as he invariably was in Australia when play ended, by a doting band of the British merchant service who unfailingly convoyed him from the field and then, after depositing him at the dressing-room door, just as unfailingly convoyed themselves in the general surge to the members' bar. And behind Compton came Evans, his red-faced gloves tucked under his right arm and his left consolingly about a small boy who, like his ilk, thinks time and place of no autograph consequence.

In short time the pavilion had swallowed them all up and the sad thought grew that possibly no Australian ground will see again Hutton, Compton and Evans. In such a way did Grace, Trumper, Ranjitsinhji, the Gregorys and all the brilliant rest pass from cricketing sight. There is a moment in every cricketer's life when he's seen; another moment and he's no more, nor ever will be again.

Lord's could not comprehend in 1948 that it had seen Bradman for the last time. Thousands stood on the grass

* Published in London, *Sunday Times*, 1955.

174

in front of the pavilion and called for their hero. They found it hard to leave a sunlit scene where so often he had made the hours immortal; they found it harder to believe that he had gone from their sight for ever. So also with Hobbs in Australia in 1929. On his last day in Sydney he walked the full circuit of the ground with Noble while the crowd rose to him, singing 'Auld Lang Syne,' and the Hill presented him with a birthday fund.

Hutton and Compton for a surety won't be seen again in Australia. Evans might be, because 'keepers go till their knuckles grow callous, and Strudwick and Duckworth became as familiar on the ship's run to Australia as the Galle Face at Colombo.

Those who thrive on statistics will say that Hutton did this and that on our various grounds; that Compton once got two Test centuries in an Adelaide game, and that Evans knew peerless stumping days in addition to batting often with pronounced entertainment and success.

Others, however, will have richer memories.

Of Hutton here I will always recall the sheer brilliance of *the* perfect innings he played in Sydney nine years ago. It didn't pass 40 but it ran the gamut of the whole batting art. I see him again in his own elegant manner driving Lindwall straight and to the off; glancing—and he knew no peer in glancing—and forcing Miller, and all the time fiddling with his cap just before he settled down to the crease or cradling his bat as he ran. Those movements were part of Hutton. That classical innings gave me an imperishable memory.

Compton, like the majestic Hammond before him, has known some of his greatest and some of his poorest days in Australia. The latter are soon forgotten. Those who know genius will always carry the mental picture of Compton smacking the ball fine to leg as only Compton could; of the sheer beauty and thrill of his cover-drive and hook; of his impish run-out before the ball was bowled and, sometimes, his scamper back like a schoolboy caught helping himself to jam.

In Melbourne, once, when that weird bowler 'Wrong Grip' Iverson (who flicked off-breaks off his second finger with a leg-break action) was befuddling the Englishmen at their first meeting, Sheppard, who had been doing best of all, walked down the pitch and asked skipper Compton whether he (Sheppard) shouldn't change from defence to attack. 'Go on as you are, David,' said Compton, who had been in the most abject bother. 'Leave the antics to me.'

Evans, always tremendously vital, will live as the man who stood undaunted over the stumps to Bedser—as Strudwick did before him to Tate at his greatest.

Rich characters, all of them, fading from the scene, but their memories will remain. There is poignancy in thinking we will see them no more, poignancy and regret. When the last flag had long been furled I looked up from my Press work and saw in the gloaming a man in civilian clothes treading the pitch as if a pilgrim in Mecca. He walked, at last, towards the pavilion and then turned 'and took one long and lingering look, and took a last farewell' before he, too, went into the pavilion for the last time. It was Alec Bedser.

Fifteen

'HIS EXCELLENCY THE GOVERNOR-GENERAL'

I see him standing erect in the popping crease, his guard just taken, his strong jaw apparent, his alert brown eyes roving the field to pin-point the openings to be pierced, his bat aloft and twirling vigorously in his hands as if seeking a charge of electricity from the air—and, indeed, many a bowler and many a fieldsman did think it had been super-charged!

C. G. Macartney, the 'Governor-General' of Cricket!

I have asked many of Charlie Macartney's contemporaries why he was called the 'Governor-General,' but none has been able to tell me—at least, not precisely. Surely, though, the term arose from the manner in which he lorded the cricket field, entering it like one about to inspect the ranks, throwing challenges and exuding domination, dismissing bowlers from the crease as an official G.-G. would dismiss footmen from his presence when their duty was done.

It was a manner, apparently, which Macartney had about him from early in his cricketing career. He played his first series against England in Australia in 1907-08, but he was no great sensation then nor when he made his first tour of England in 1909. He was a member of the chorus, not a *prima donna*, once batting as low as No. 10. Nevertheless, everybody knew whom Victor Trumper meant when, on returning from that tour, he said, 'We are to lose the "Governor-General." He's going to New Zealand.'

Trumper didn't mean that he had had a hot tip from the Palace that the second Earl of Dudley was moving on. Not at all. He was breaking the news that C. G. Macartney intended to live, in future, in New Zealand.

Luckily for Australia (and I am inclined to think for cricket, too, because Macartney might not have developed in New Zealand), the little 'Governor-General' stayed in Australia, although 17 years more were to pass before he reached the zenith of his career. That occurred in England, in 1926, when he was 40 years of age.

Australia has had three great personal batting triumphs in England. They were achieved by Trumper (1902), Macartney (1926), and Bradman (1930); and an interesting point is that in their vintage years Trumper was 25 and Bradman 22. It is curious, therefore, that Macartney should have had his greatest year when he was 40, an age when a player is fast moving down the hill, if he has not, indeed, reached the bottom.

In Macartney's case, however, the apparent anomaly proved nothing other than what the cricket world missed from him because of the interruption to the game by World War I and the various illnesses and injuries that he sustained when the Englishmen were in Australia after that war. He played in only two Tests against J. W. H. T. Douglas's side in 1920-21—making a scintillating 170 at Sydney; he did not play in any at all four years later.

Macartney went to England with the unhappy Australian team of 1912—the side that toured without the Big Six, namely Trumper, Carter, Cotter, Armstrong, Ransford and Hill—but the edge was off that tour before it started. Macartney played the best innings of the series with 99 at

Lord's, and the manner of his dismissal typified the man and his outlook on cricket. Most batsmen of the period were wont to creep upon a century like a cat-burglar on his objective. Not so Macartney. He tried to hit F. R. Foster into St. John's Wood Road.

'I thought I could have hit it for six,' he declared later. 'Should have, too. Full toss. Made a mess of it!'

In his halcyon days, Macartney's stroking was pungent, crisp, deliberate. It was not always so. His cricket seems to have been in a continual state of evolution, for he was noted as a stone-waller when he first entered Sydney grade cricket. A critic of those days, Frank Iredale (who had Test experience behind him), wrote that Macartney had an ugly, defensive style. This statement strains imagination, but that it should have been written of him is proof that his game underwent remarkable changes.

At the beginning, he was a better left-hand bowler than a right-hand batsman. Whereas he averaged only 18 in the Tests in his first tour of England in 1909, he was second in the bowling with 16 wickets, averaging 16. At Leeds, where he was to win himself immortality 17 years later, he took 7-58 in the first innings and 4-27 in the second. Nor did he have any stipulated place in the batting order. He went up and down the list like a painter on a ladder. He was chosen against O. A. Jones's team in 1907-08 as an all-rounder and batted No. 7. About this time Duff was lost to Trumper as an opener —no doubt they were Australia's best opening pair of all time—and Macartney opened with Trumper in the next Test. He was moderately successful and again opened in the last Test; but in 1912 he found his position-by-right in the batting order and to the end of his cricketing days batted first-wicket-down for Australia.

I asked him once which batting position he liked best.

Back flashed the answer, 'Opening up. If you get on top of an attack early, you are on top for the rest of the innings. And if the first ball of a Test asks to be hit for six, why, you just hit it for six.'

That was his philosophy, expounded at the end of his career. It's not a philosophy one would recommend to a young batsman beginning his Test experience as an opening batsman, for I know what selectors would do if a wicket fell off the first ball of a Test through the batsman trying to hit a six! Macartney, however, held that every ball had 'a look on its face' as it came up the pitch towards him.

'It was labelled,' he said, 'either 1, 2, 3, 4 or 6. I leave out the 5. Too far to run.'

He left out too, you will notice, the defensive stroke for none. That didn't come into his consideration. He held that every ball was punishable.

In the late 1920s and early 1930s New South Wales had a delightful cricket coach named Jimmy Searle, whose every joint on his hands was knotted and gnarled through wicket-keeping breaks. Jimmy used to conduct mid-week games on Cricket Ground No. 2, when his 'Colts' would play Junior association teams. Many a first-class player came up through those games, and they were all the more enjoyable in that Macartney, Kelleway, Oldfield and other retired or active Test stars would often play with the 'Colts.' I opened once with Macartney, and as we walked out he said, 'Keep your eyes open for the first ball, son. I'll take strike.'

I thought he meant that there would be a quick, stolen single and I was doubly anxious to respond to the Great Man's call. But the first ball came hurtling back like a meteorite and was crashing against the fence while the umpire, the bowler and I were still prone to the grass as if in an air-raid. I picked myself up and met Charlie in the middle.

'It's always a good idea,' he confided, 'to aim the first ball right at the bowler's head. They don't like it. It rattles them. Then you can do as you like!'

It was the same man who rattled Macaulay—and England —at Leeds in 1926.

Unknown to Englishmen, the Australians that year held a high opinion of G. G. Macaulay, the Yorkshire spinner and seamer. He didn't play for the county against the visitors (playing instead in a Test Trial), and the Australians were apprehensive about him when he was chosen for the Third Test at Leeds, on one of his own Yorkshire grounds.

It was not often that the pugnacious Macartney feared a bowler. But he did Macaulay. 'This chap,' he said on the eve of the Test, 'could go through us. There's no better bowler in England. I want permission to "murder" him immediately.'

Collins, the captain, was ill and Bardsley was to take over the leadership for this match.

'You don't often talk like that, Charlie,' said Bardsley.

'No, but I know just what Macaulay can do to us if we don't nobble him first.'

So Bardsley agreed that Macartney could do as he wished with Macaulay.

It is well to know this background because it gave rise to one of the most brilliant innings in the history of cricket.

There were storms during the night and the groundsman switched to a new pitch next day because the original one had been flooded through the covers. The Australians, all of them, gathered in an anxious band around the pitch while the Englishmen were having great trouble in choosing their final team in the pavilion—and also, no doubt, discussing with Carr what he should do if he won the toss.

The three Australian selectors—Bardsley, Macartney and Ryder—locked themselves in a bath-room while they finalised their team. They, too, had to discuss what to do in the event of winning the toss. But, fortunately for them, Carr called correctly—and he put Australia in. That decision was to become one of the most discussed actions in Test history. Carr hasn't lived it down to this day. Even now, however, it might console him to know that Bardsley would have ordered the Englishmen to bat had *he* won the toss.

What did make Carr's decision slightly illogical was that, although he sent the Australians in, the left-hand bowler, Parker, had been dropped from the English side. Perhaps the Englishmen gambled on losing the toss!

The sun was out as the match began but it soon withdrew, a fact that didn't help Carr's intentions as he was hoping that sun on a wet pitch would cause it to 'bite.' It never did.

Bardsley was out off the first ball of the match—something that had happened only once previously, when (31 years earlier) Maclaren fell to Coningham in Melbourne. Sutcliffe caught Bardsley low at first slip off Tate.

In strode Macartney. He glided Tate's third ball through the slips for two, but then, off the fifth ball of the opening over, he snicked Tate to Carr, of all people, in the slips—and Carr dropped the catch. That was the most publicised missed catch in all history by the end of the day, because Australia, instead of being two down for two, didn't lose the next wicket until 235!

Poor Carr! Had he taken that chance Australia would have been on the run and, conceivably, might even have been out before lunch. So goes the game of cricket. I wonder if, even to this day, Carr does not have nightmares about both his missed catch and his decision to make Australia bat?

As everybody knows who has played the game, it is a simple matter to spill a catch, and more often than not it is the simple ones that go to ground. The best a fieldsman can do is practise, practise, practise, so that his fingers, loose and yielding, will time a ball and instinctively close on it. If his fingers are taut, stiff with anxiety and endeavour, out will pop the ball. Carr possibly tried too hard, or perhaps didn't quite sight the ball against the dark background of the crowd. At all events, the drop and Macartney's subsequent deeds made Carr the most criticised man in cricketing England.

Macaulay, playing his first Test for England, opened the bowling from the Pavilion end. His first delivery was a no-ball, which Woodfull hit for a single. Up came Macartney. He took guard, studied the field, twirled his bat, cocked his left foot at the bowler, as was his wont, and hit Macaulay for two to the off. The next ball he smashed almost for six, over mid-off. The 'murdering' of Macaulay had begun.

The whole Leeds crowd (which had uttered a painful 'Oh!' as Carr dropped Macartney) now began to exclaim 'Ah!' as Macartney unfolded his artistry. He smacked Macaulay for two more fours in his next over and in 40 minutes Australia had 50 on the board—40 of them to Macartney. In 79 minutes, up came the 100, Macartney's share being 83. In 103 minutes Macartney had scored 100, the first batsman since Trumper to hit a century before lunch. (Six years later Bradman was to hit, also at Leeds, a century before lunch, a century before afternoon tea, and yet another before stumps.)

At lunch Macartney was 112 and Woodfull 40. After lunch the 'Governor-General' went on and on, wielding his bat like a merciless flail. A close-set field that had encompassed him during the opening overs of the match, from Tate and Macaulay, had spread out, and it didn't close again for three hours. Macartney completely dominated the English bowlers, and none more so than Macaulay.

At 151, Macartney lifted Macaulay to Hendren and was out —after three hours' batting. The crowd rose and cheered him off. In the pavilion Archie Maclaren said, 'We have been looking at Victor Trumper all over again!'

That was the only wicket Macaulay took. He bowled 32 overs (8 maidens) at a cost of 123 runs. Macartney had deliberately set out to 'murder' him, and he so far succeeded that Macaulay was never again chosen to play for England against Australia—and that although he top-scored for England with 76 runs at No. 10, the sensational partnership of 106 for the ninth wicket with George Geary saving England from possible defeat.

So, too, in thinking of Carr's decision and Carr's dropped catch—no matter how sympathetic you may feel towards him—there is also the thought of what might have been Macaulay's career, in Test cricket against Australia, had Macartney, at Leeds in 1926, been dismissed for two runs instead of 151.

Sir Pelham Warner, whose experiences covered most of the greatest years in cricket, had this to say of the 'Governor-General's' innings:

'I say without hesitation that I have never seen a greater innings than that played by Macartney. Not even the immortal Trumper could have played more finely. And what higher praise could I give to any batsman, English or Australian?

'After his mistake, he made but one false stroke, a mistimed hit on the off-side just before he was out. He simply pulverised all the bowling with the exception of Tate's. Such stroke play I can never hope to see again. His timing of the ball was perfection itself, and every sort of stroke came in rapid succession.

'It mattered not what length the bowler bowled; runs simply flowed from his bat at an amazing speed. As quick on his feet as a Genee or a Pavlova, his steel-like wrists and powerful fore-arms reduced the bowling, always excepting that of Tate, to impotence. No Grace, no Ranjitsinhji, no Trumper, no Hobbs could have surpassed his cricket!'

That score of Macartney's was the middle of three Test centuries in succession. He charmed a Lord's crowd with 133 and he followed his Leeds achievement with 109 at Old Trafford. And in those three matches he also bowled 86 overs —not bad work for a man of 40!

Of his innings at Lord's, one well-known English commentator wrote:

'Everybody at Lord's was talking about Macartney's innings; it was so far above everything we had seen on the cricket field this season. How he makes his shots and where he gets the power from is a question everybody asks and nobody answers. He is gifted with a rare degree of limb-quickness and sight-keenness and is possessed of an immense belief in himself. His feet are those of a dancing master. His eye is like that of a hawk. His confidence is colossal. "Little Mac" has no respect for reputations or conventions. He doesn't wait to play himself in. He is not dependant upon the loose ball for runs. He thinks in fours.'

Leeds was for Macartney (as it was to be for Bradman) a happy scalping-ground. But his most remarkable innings of the 1921 tour, was the 345 he played against Nottinghamshire at Trent Bridge. He was missed in the slips at nine, and then stayed at the wicket until, four hours later, he was out for 345.

Seeking a comparison, we might say that had Macartney batted at the same rate as at Nottingham, and for as long as did Jackie McGlew the South African against the Australians at Durban in January 1958—572 minutes for 105—he would have rattled up something like 860. Colossal—impossible— but interesting!

Bert Collins said he saw Macartney play, in that Nottingham innings, an almost miraculous stroke. The ball was on its way from the bowler and Macartney had taken his bat back for a cover-drive. The ball, however, changed direction off the pitch, and Macartney, as quickly, changed direction in his down-swing. Where did he hit the ball? Clean out of the ground, into the street behind the pavilion, over long-off!

In that innings of less than four hours, Macartney hit four sixes and 47 fours. Australia made 675, and Notts, demoralised by a 'bat as crooked and as wicked as original sin,' could manage only 58 and 100—losing by an innings and 517 runs.

In 1926, at Old Trafford, Macartney played a dazzling innings for 160. It sent the spectators into rhapsodies. Many of the runs were made against the great Australian fast bowler Ted McDonald, who had an engagement with the county. Then, with the ball, Macartney had 27 overs (16 maidens), taking 4-15 in the first Lancashire innings, and in the second innings bowling 19 overs (12 maidens) and taking 1-19.

How good was Macartney as a bowler? In the opinion of one English critic, he was the best left-arm bowler Australia ever sent to England—but that view was expressed before the days of Bill Johnston, the three-in-one bowler: fast, medium and medium-slow spinners. Certainly, Macartney was a most polished bowler. He clean-bowled—clean-bowled, mark you—MacLaren (twice), Fry, Hobbs, Hirst, Warner, Rhodes and Chapman in Tests. What a haul!

Macartney had a graceful run to the line of about six or seven yards. With his powerful wrists he gave the ball terrific spin, and he had a compelling, curving flight with adroit change of pace. His best ball was one that came from the off with remarkable lift from the pitch. Watching him closely, I found that he invariably delivered this ball (he bowled around the stumps) from wide on the line. He cut his biggest finger across the seam with a quick flick, and this, with the angle of delivery, gave it an almost incredible whip and seeming break from the pitch.

Once, in a Sydney grade match, he clean-bowled Tommy Andrews with it, and Andrews, who had made two tours of England with Macartney, should certainly have known his wares.

'You won't get me again with that one, Charlie,' said Tommy before play began on the second day.

The 'Governor-General' grinned.

'Now, Tommy,' he called down the pitch when Andrews came to bat, 'you're sure you know it?'

'Yes,' said Andrews, 'I'm ready for you this time.'

'Right, off we go,' said Macartney—and in that very over he clean-bowled Andrews again!

Bert Oldfield told me that story. He kept wickets to Macartney in grade, Sheffield Shield and Test cricket, and rates him very highly as a left-hand bowler. What's more, you have to bear in mind that 'Little Mac' was a brilliant fieldsman, with sure hands and a quick flick of a throw.

In all Tests, Macartney made 2,132 runs at 41 an innings. In all first-class cricket he made 14,217 runs at 47 and took 366 wickets at 21. A remarkable feature of this record is that of his 48 first-class centuries not one was scored at Melbourne. Twenty were made in Sydney and one in Adelaide.

Charlie Macartney had no coaching when young. He watched the giants of his youth and then applied his own methods. In the summer he never varied his habit—not even when a Test cricketer—of arriving at Chatswood Oval (Sydney) at 6.40 each morning and leaving at 7.50, five days a week. A band of about 17 local players indulged in this practice, and Macartney found that the pace of a composition ball skimming off a dewy pitch was ideal for sharpening up his eyesight and his strokes. Moreover, nature had endowed him with the strongest possible pair of wrists. It was his wrists that allowed him to play so late—a short, sharp back-swing and then a convulsive whip at the ball that led you to believe you were watching magic.

Not only was Macartney the terror of cricketing bowlers. There was also apprehension on the Chatswood rink of a Saturday whenever he was playing on the local oval across the railway line from the bowling club. He never failed to lift a couple out of the ground—up and over the railway line and on to the bowling clubhouse roof or on to the rink itself.

Because of his audacity, because of his all-round compet-ence, the little 'Governor-General' will never be forgotten.

One of the most impressive of cricket photographs shows him striding down the steps of the Sydney Cricket Ground pavilion, the members all rising with applause and with rapt anticipation on their faces.*

Looking at this picture, you can hear in fancy the crowd on the Hill chanting 'Here comes the "Governor-General." ' And, without effort, you can guess that the 'Governor-General' is saying to himself: 'The first ball will have a look on its face as it comes along. It will be 1, 2, 3, 4 or 6. Some-how, I think it will be 4. Straight back past the bowler, eh?'

In the late 1940s, the compiler of an Australian *Who's Who* wrote to Macartney to seek his help. Macartney's answer was typical: 'I have no desire to appear in any publication of this kind, and I fail to see that any good purpose will be served by my name appearing. If you desire, of course, to publish my cricket history, well and good, but I would rather let it rest at that. I have gone over the particulars supplied on the

* Page 208, my *Cricket Crisis*.

attached, and they appear to be correct, but I have no record of figures, nor am I concerned with them. My only interest is in the manner in which runs are compiled and how wickets are taken, and in the good of the game.'

Those sentiments summed up the cricket story of C. G. Macartney.

Sixteen

MELBOURNE'S FACE-LIFT

The scene of more missed centuries and aching feet than any other in the world, the Melbourne Test ground was given a face-lift in 1955. Every pound of its 3,000 tons of black, unyielding Merri Creek soil was unceremoniously bull-dozed away so that the fall of seven feet eight inches in the ground could be corrected for the 1956 Olympic Games.

Fittingly, the C.O. of the bull-dozer knew nothing at all of cricket. While members of the committee steadied themselves, the driver of the bull-dozer lit a cigarette, put his machine into gear, slipped the clutch and, in five minutes, had taken an enormous scoop of revered turf that W. G., Hobbs, Ranjitsinhji, Trumper, Bradman, Hammond and countless others since 1877 had trod and patted into place.

Those who covered this ground in its entirety with Merri Creek soil have been solidly cursed down the years by batsmen, bowlers, fieldsmen and umpires as they tenderly rubbed their feet at the day's end. It had less give than a miser.

It was there that Larwood broke his boots, as well as the Australians, in 1932. By some odd quirk of fate they now hang on the bar-room wall of a Melbourne pub (the boots, not the Australians), a mute testimony of the day he turned the ground into turmoil as he came and went with successive boots. The surface of the ground had no yield at all. The soil was littered with sprigs that departed their soles.

This won't happen again. The new ground has Merri Creek soil only in the centre, for the pitches. The flanks are covered with red, pliant mountain soil, and a new, towering grandstand, its top flirting with the next life, has increased the ground's seating capacity to 120,000.

No other ground, not even Lord's, can quite compare with Melbourne in the stark intensity of its Test match atmosphere. It drilled into your very back as you walked out of the gate to take the first ball of a Test against England, and Australians who make a Test century there against England never forget the enveloping crash of thunder that greets the ultimate run. No crowd in the sporting world can make a noise like the Melbourne crowd. They showed that when the Australian girls were scooting home first in the 1956 Olympiad—and also when Kuts, the Russian, 'killed' the field in his immortal distance race.

No Test pitch knew such life in the opening hour of play. One always had to be ready for a good-length ball that made pace and lifted to the ribs. Possibly it was because of moisture still in the pitch from preparation—or, maybe, moisture from that subterranean stream that was discovered on Hutton's tour when, after the pitch had widened out into crumbling cracks on the Saturday's play (and after a blistering week-end, if you please), it miraculously came together again on Monday morning, almost as if it had been watered and rolled again. Some, including myself, thought it had. The Melbourne Cricket Club committee stiffly said it hadn't but, fortunately in a sense, the miracle favoured England.

Oddly, because of the early qualms it gave them, opening batsmen dominate the 52 Test centuries scored there by England and Australia—26 to each country.

Opening the innings there in 1877, in the first Test ever between England and Australia, Charlie Bannerman made 165 for Australia before a ball from Ulyett split his finger and Bannerman retired hurt. Five years later, Ulyett made the first century there for England.

Hobbs adored and adorned the ground, hitting five centuries for his country. Sutcliffe assumed his full majesty there, often allowing his lordship to spread from one day to the next. With Rhodes, Hobbs had an opening partnership of 323 in 1912. With Sutcliffe, he scored 283 in 1925; but the best partnership possibly seen on the ground was their 105 in 1929 on a vile 'sticky.' As I write elsewhere in this book, they fooled the Australians with tactics, and floored them by technique on a pitch infamous as the worst in the world after rain and under hot sun.

Bradman, by right, took five centuries there, but some great ones missed out badly—Trumper and Macartney for Australia; Hutton and Compton for England.

Which brings one to the longest list ever of missed centuries. They are Australia: Hill 99, Trott 95, Hassett 92, Tallon 92, Armstrong 90, Taylor 90. England: Tyldesley 97, Hendren 95, Ward 93, May 91. Both countries have known flocks of eighties.

Hill got additional pity because five years before he was out for 96 against England in Sydney. But, after this 99 in Melbourne, he made 98 and 97 in the very next Test in Adelaide. In 1912, in Adelaide again (his home city), Hill was out for 98 again, so that with his four centuries against England, a little more good fortune would have placed him in an unchallenged second position to Bradman with Test centuries.

One day, not far from the Melbourne ground, they picked Clem Hill up from the roadway after a tram accident. Unrecognised and dying, he was taken to hospital.

I have seen no better English innings on the famous ground than the 156 played by Reg Simpson with Brown's team of 1950-51. It was made in a total of 320 with Miller, Lindwall, Johnston and Iverson at their bowling best. The next time Simpson came to Australia he was rarely invited to play. His main mission seemed to be to find sunburn on the surfing sands, but this was not his fault.

Melbourne, as Old Trafford does in England, holds the record in Australia for the most exciting Test finish. This was in January, 1908, K. L. Hutchings (126), for England, being the only century-maker in a fairly high scoring game. England were seemingly well beaten at 8-209 but Barnes, Humphries and Fielder held on to raise the score to 9-282 for England to win by one wicket. It should have ended in a tie. Jerry Hazlitt, fielding up close, could have run up and knocked the wicket over when Barnes and Fielder dashed off for a very short run with the scores equal. Hazlitt should have tossed the ball gently to Carter, the wicket-keeper, but he let fly at the stumps with all his power—missed—and the ball went for four overthrows and England had won.

The longbeards in the pavilion still rate S. F. Barnes the greatest bowler Melbourne has seen. His five wickets for five runs in 1911 is immortal. So, too, is the first-ball dismissal of Bradman by Bowes in 1932. I was batting at the other end at the time and it is something I won't forget. How Bradman entered to the wild plaudits of the packed ground; how he was cheered all the way to the middle; how he went feet across the pitch to the first ball and hit it into his stumps behind his back. The silence, as Bradman walked away, was shattering.

Colin Cowdrey got the last century on the old soil, though May just failed in the next innings. The experts say the Melbourne pitch will be better than ever. Maybe. Ian Johnson is the new secretary of the ground and one of his first acts was to snare Sydney's most efficient wicket-maker, William Watt. Soon we will see Melbourne in its second phase of life but pitches don't immediately respond to face-lifts. Kennington has never been quite the same since one of Hitler's bombs lifted its upper crust in World War II.

Seventeen

MOSTLY ABOUT CRICKET WRITINGS

What's wrong with cricket?

That question has been the theme of critics since the game began. In these final chapters, attempting a quick cover of happenings in recent years, I shall not be able to resist the fashionable urge to declaim upon evils—perhaps real, perhaps imaginary—but my main premise can be stated immediately: nothing so much is wrong with cricket as with some who play it, officiate in it, tinker with it, or write about it. I myself, of course, am included in the last category, but rest on the excuse that writing has been my occupation for the last 30 years or so.

As I see the position, one of cricket's greatest difficulties is to contain the many who thrive upon it, either in a pecuniary or a publicity sense. And I don't mean the professionals who acknowledge themselves as such; these I have found in the main to be admirable, although the gains to be made have sometimes caused a few of them to become self-centred and assertive.

It is an odd thing—to me, at least—that a simple game of bat and ball should attract so many theorists, so many 'professors,' so many who will insist upon making the game more difficult and abstruse than need be. These, for the most part, are men who are forever wanting to tinker with the rules.

Such fellows should be made to do a 'Fuchs' with the penguins in Antarctica—although this might seem a little rough on harmless penguins who, very quickly, would be having their waddle analysed for the correct back-swing and follow-through.

I now run the risk of incurring caustic criticism from fellow-journalists who review books, but any close consideration of modern cricket must pay heed to the affinity between some players and some sections of the Press. It is the fixed practice of many cricket pressmen to write in the strain of 'I said to Bill Bloggs' and 'Bill Bloggs said to me.' The suggestion, of course, is that the writer is on the most matey terms with great men of the game—as well he might be. But close association with players can often be an embarrassment to a journalist, and also be a complete give-away.

The journalist who is 'fed' material can't always afford to be objective. For favours granted, he must often reciprocate with smooth comments about his source of information—every captaincy move must be right, every selection must be superb—or else his source will dry up. And, as in politics, if you analyse the drip of syrup you will trace the 'leak.'

Some captains in recent years have encouraged pressmen to call upon them in the dressing-room. This is fair enough if a doubtful happening stands in need of clarification, but it can be overdone, and I think it has been so overdone in recent years as to be a detriment to the game. The 'Let's-all-be-pals' attitude can lead to many excuses, to many condonations, to newspaper favouritism and protection. On the other hand, the writer who 'dares' to criticise big men in cricket is considered to be jealous, or maybe something of a crank.

I have noticed this affinity between some players and certain sections of the Press grow particularly in the post-war years. Individual players are considered to be the preserve of some newspapers long before they put aside the bat for the guided pen.

Then, on retirement, there comes an inevitable book of 'revelations' which, for newspaper serialisation, must necessarily be full of 'meat.' (The ghost-writer ensures that it is.) I am sure that many of these books of charges and counter-charges do the game harm, yet no one can fairly condemn cricketers for accepting the lure, particularly as the practice is common enough in other spheres, especially the military one. The diary, it would seem, is now an integral part of a Test cricketer's kit, and thus the modern dressing-room at a play-ing-ground cannot well be the comradely place it once was.

At the end of the 1956 tour of England, we held a journa-lists' dinner in London. The club comprised professional journalists who had written on a specified number of Test matches. We twitted one of our number who was said to have 'ghosted' a remarkable number of books for cricketers. He took it in good part and came back with the remark, 'Well, I must say my family live pretty well!'

That tour of 1956 had not finished when Keith Miller, who probably suffered from the many frustrations he had known in his cricket career, was letting off steam in a syndica-tion of his book in the Press. He lost a lot of popularity over that excursion: I think he indulged in rather too many 'inside' stories on people and certain happenings, although I could understand his outlook. In addition to previous snubs, he had little prospect of gaining, on his return to Australia, the 'bumper' type of benefit which both Bradman and Hassett enjoyed on retirement.

In the book under notice, Miller gave me credit for not writing a sensational story at the end of the 1953 Test series at Kennington Oval. He said I could have made a lot of money out of the story. No doubt. But I was being sufficiently rewarded for writing the type of material which my newspaper wanted, and I mention the incident now only to correct Keith (who was not present at the time) when he says that Hassett had asked me that day to leave the Australian dressing-room. If that were true, my decrying of the over-use of the journalistic path to the dressing-room would seem hypo-critical.

As Miller observed, Hassett and I were very friendly. The point is, however, that I have shunned dressing-rooms since I finished playing Test cricket. There have been only three exceptions.

Once was in Birmingham when Hassett sent a message across to the Press-box asking me to come to the room at the close of play. We had a delightful hour of reminiscences, over a few drinks, with two entertaining Englishmen, Tom Dollery and Eric Hollies.

Another occasion was when, at the end of the 1956 Test at Lord's, I went inside to ask the Prime Minister (Mr. Menzies) and the Australian captain (Ian Johnson) if they would come to be interviewed by me on B.B.C. television. They both did so.

When the Oval Test finished in 1953, with Australia losing the Ashes, I recalled from my own experience that a defeated team is not overloaded with friends. So, before settling down to the considerable job of reviewing the whole Test series, I thought I would pop up to the Australian room and offer a few words of commiseration. I had far too much work on hand to want to sit around and gossip.

When I went into the room with The Oval secretary, Brian Castor, I found Hassett giving an interview to two Australian journalists, who were covering newspapers rival to mine.

I said, 'If this is an interview, Lindsay, I had better be in it.'

Hassett's reply was, 'Pour yourself a drink and make your-self at home. I'll be with you soon.'

It was an awkward situation. 'No, thanks,' I said; 'if I can't be in on the interview, I'll push along.'

And I did.

Miller was therefore wrong in saying that Hassett asked me to leave the room, and, on that assumption, he suggests that I would have been justified in writing the story of 'happenings' much later in the day. Keith wrote the story which I didn't write, nor think of writing. It was a sensational item for newspapers which like their stories 'hot'—and I was the only journalist at The Oval when it happened.

Soon after the game had ended Castor took me out to have a look at the much-criticised pitch. On our way back we could see into the dressing-room, and it was apparent that some of the players, not all Australians, were 'letting their hair down' after all the worry and tenseness of the Test series. I grinned at the sight, having often been in a happy 'do' of the kind myself.

Some hours later, my work finished, I was having a drink and a chat with Castor and some members of the Surrey team, in his office, when a very harassed dressing-room attendant burst in and implored him to send for the police. There was a 'riot,' he said, in the Australian room upstairs. He gave details. Castor, not at all flurried, soon broke up the 'party.' Possibly he used my (journalistic) presence below to do so—but dog doesn't eat dog in the cricket world. Or he shouldn't.

For my own part, I mention the incident now—and pass by other 'highlights'—in order to make my position clear and to amend Keith Miller's impression.

Ray Lindwall also broke into print before that tour ended, probably as a newspaper counter to Miller. Both were fined by the Board of Control (as was Don Bradman in 1930) on returning to Australia. But it could well be argued that the manager of the side, W. J. Dowling, would have acted correctly had he sent both Miller and Lindwall home from Pakistan and not allowed them to play during the remainder of the tour. As Miller had very strongly criticised Ian Johnson in public, it must have been an acute embarrassment for the captain to have had his critic in the same dressing-room.

Australia's Board of Control has itself largely to blame for such happenings. Bradman knew he would be rewarded with a testimonial match in Melbourne at the end of his career; Hassett had a fair inkling he would, too. Miller and Lindwall, equally deserving such an honour, knew they wouldn't. They could see themselves departing the game with precious little of a tangible nature to remind them of their years of glory—and sacrifice.

It has to be recalled, too, that Sir Donald Bradman had been allowed to set some remarkable precedents so far as writing for the Press is concerned. He has *twice* been re-appointed to the Board after serving as a newspaper-correspondent on English tours. He wrote in England in 1956 on a team which he helped to select, and, indeed, he was the sternest critic of Ian Johnson's captaincy in The Oval Test. Clearly, Bradman should not have been permitted to serve two masters—I personally think he is a better writer than a selector—but possibly both Miller and Lindwall reasoned that what Bradman could do, with niceties of resignations and re-appointments, they might at least attempt.

The manager of that Australian team in England (W. J. Dowling), who is now chairman of the Board of Control, told me during the tour that he thought Australia would have to alter its laws to allow pressmen to hold official positions. He considered that Australia was turning its back on too much talent and knowledge. I agreed somewhat, thinking that possibly O'Reilly, Hassett and others might serve in some consultative capacity in the years ahead; but, seemingly, Bradman was the only one in mind—he is again a member of the Board and a selector.

Moreover, in an apparent attempt to be as accommodating as possible, the Board now has an odd rule to the effect that Australian selectors finish their job as soon as they choose a team. Thus, when the 1957-58 team in South Africa needed a replacement the job was done from South Africa, since the selection committee in Australia had been dissolved. Three selectors thousands of miles away, who knew nothing of current form in Australia, chose the replacement. Surely the three men who selected the original side should have done the job?

With his task of selection over, Sir Donald Bradman was free once again to tilt in the newspapers with anybody who criticised the Australian choice. Previously, he had clashed with those who thought more youth should have been taken to the West Indies and blooded for the 1956 tour of England; he clashed vehemently over the l.b.w. rule with Miller, and on this later occasion he fell into an argument with Frank Tyson, the English fast bowler, who claimed that beating South Africa was vastly different from beating England.

Few who know Australian cricket will dispute the belief that Bradman dominates the game in this country. Of all the international players who have appeared in Tests before and since the war, he alone holds any position of authority on the Board of Control. It will serve no purpose to name the other members of the Board, good and estimable citizens as they are, for they are unknown to cricket overseas, even though they choose Australia's skipper. (Also, by the way, they have the power to declare a player unfit to play for Australia for 'reasons other than cricket'; and they don't have to reveal the 'reasons.')

On such a Board, and particularly when it resolves into an interstate conference to decide the parish affairs of the game in Australia, Bradman has matters more or less his own way. I cannot imagine other members of the interstate conference arguing against him on matters such as changes of rules.

Surely it is not a good thing that any one man, however competent as a player, should have overriding powers in a national game. This would be open to criticism at any time, and especially is it a matter for question now, when tennis, golf, swimming and athletics have shot ahead of cricket in Australia.

In Adelaide not so long ago, one of a party of Asiatic journalists, meeting Sir Donald Bradman, asked him if he could account for the decline of cricket in Australia. The reply was curt: 'There is no decline.'

Bradman must be the only cricket follower in Australia who believes that. Indeed, the decline is most apparent of all in his own State of adoption, South Australia. Since Victor Richardson's days, South Australia has relied to a large extent upon talent imported from the other States. Curiously, since Bradman went to Adelaide, in 1934, South Australia has not produced a single outstanding batsman. Its best cricketer in years, Bruce Dooland, wasn't chosen in the Australian team for England in 1948, and, feeling as disconsolate as certain cricketers produced by New South Wales and Victoria, he moved on to professional cricket in England.

This table of South Australian effort in the Sheffield Shield competition of recent years doesn't read very well:

1949-50	..	..	.. Last
1950-51	..	..	.. Last
1951-52	..	..	.. Second last
1952-53	..	..	.. First*
1953-54	..	..	.. Second last
1954-55	..	..	.. Last
1955-56	..	..	.. Last
1956-57	..	..	.. Last
1957-58	..	..	.. Last

What a lamentable record this is for a State which once produced some of the greatest cricketers in the game— George Giffen, Clem Hill, Joe Darling, Ernie Jones, Victor and Arthur Richardson, and others. If then, why not now? The fact appears to be that South Australia began to topple when, reaping as much from Test-match profits as did New South Wales and Victoria, it began to entice cricketers from other States instead of producing them itself.

The depressing truth is that in recent years South Australia has not equalled Western Australia, the new State in the Sheffield Shield. But in membership on the Board, in Test profits, in high posts of office, South Australia equals New South Wales and Victoria. And in general control of Australian cricket it is undoubtedly superior.

In March 1954 I was most interested to read two special articles in the Adelaide *News*. They discussed the question, 'Who will captain Australia?' Neither writer was named but both were introduced as 'knowing the men concerned intimately.' Also it was said: 'Both have the interests of Australian cricket at heart. Both have seen most of the Test matches of the past 25 years and have known all the leading personalities of the game.'

* A South African team played in Australia this year and the States were often without their Test players.

One of the writers, a former Test critic, advocated the cause of Keith Miller as Australian captain because he was imaginative and capable in the field. The other writer, said to be a former Test star, took quite a different view—he was not at all well-disposed towards Miller. Quite the opposite. For one thing, he declared that Miller's temperamental outbursts in the past must tell against him. He alleged that there was a private vendetta against Arthur Morris in New South Wales and this was the reason why Miller had been made captain of the State's team. (Miller, incidentally, was perhaps the most successful New South Wales captain in history; and he was, originally, a Victorian.)

The article further stated that, because Morris had been denied the New South Wales captaincy, Ian Johnson had become the chief candidate for the Australian captaincy, and it was added that he had strong claims for the position. This was very surprising because many people thought—and with substance—that Johnson's Test career had ended. He was dropped from the 1948 Australian Test side in England, returned against Brown's team in Australia (averaging 16 with the bat and taking seven wickets costing 44 apiece), and was not chosen for the 1953 tour of England after being dropped against the touring South Africans.

Furthermore, the article said that some students of cricket believed that the selectors of 1953 had erred in not choosing Johnson for England; and it added that had Bradman, Ryder and Dwyer been the selection committee (it was composed of Bill Brown, Phil Ridings, and Jack Ryder), Johnson might not have been omitted.

The writer identified himself as a South Australian when, in complaining against what he termed 'New South Wales dictation in Australian cricket,' he said, 'We are to be relegated to virtually the role of a minor state.' The writer, whoever he was, took a pretty dim view of how New South Wales ran its cricket—going against Australian opinion, he termed it. Yet New South Wales had won the Sheffield Shield in 1948-49, 1949-50 and 1951-52; and later it did so in 1953-54, 1954-55, 1955-56, 1956-57 and 1957-58.

Not a bad record, that, for a State which, apparently, was hopping along on the wrong foot! Compare it with the one cited earlier for South Australia.

Anyway, even though Johnson was no longer a member of the Australian Eleven, here was a pretty good indication that he stood much higher, in some circles, than did Miller. Accordingly, I gained the impression that, so far as South Australia was concerned, Johnson would not only be restored to the Test team but would be made captain. And so it came to pass, even though Miller far outshone him as a captain in Shield games and as a performer.

Incidentally, I do not say that Sir Donald Bradman wrote the 'informed' article in question—I don't really know who wrote it—but I do know that he and Keith Miller had been operating on different wave-lengths since 1948. There was an immediate clash of outlook, temperament and personality.

Ian Johnson was a perfect captain in some respects. He was a good off-the-field leader, excellent in his public-relations work—I know of no better Test captain in this regard—and was always concerned with the welfare of his team on tour. These are vital assets. But the most valuable quality of all is the ability to lead on the field with inspiration and imagination. It is one thing for a captain to tell his men, 'Do this'; it is another thing for him to go into the field and do it himself, for others to follow. Miller could do that. Perhaps, with bat and ball and in the field, there had been none through the years with the capacity to do it better.

I recall that at Adelaide in January 1955, when England

went in last to get 97 runs to win the Test and the series, Johnson was badly disabled (with one arm hanging limp), so that it was most surprising that he took the field. The vice-captain, Miller, in a last desperate effort to save the series, bundled out Hutton, Edrich and Cowdrey for eight runs. Then he dived brilliantly at cover to catch May. England were 4-49, and there was a long tail. Miller's performance was one of the greatest pieces of offensive bowling I have ever seen.

Under Miller's captaincy, New South Wales defeated Hutton's M.C.C. team during that tour, the first loss suffered by an England team against a State team since New South Wales beat Allen's team in 1936-37. Freddie Brown, Arthur Gilligan, and other Englishmen on that tour were all convinced that Miller was our best captain—and yet he had no more chance of leading Australia than did any schoolboy.

I don't put Miller forward as the paragon of all cricket virtues, but I do think he was badly treated by Australian officialdom, and Australian cricket was therefore the loser. I am sure he would have responded to responsibility and that young players would have responded well to his leadership. They did in the New South Wales team.

When the Australian team was chosen for the West Indies, with Ian Johnson as skipper, Sir Donald Bradman—quickly taking up the pen after helping to choose the team and vote on its captaincy—had this to say of the now-enthroned leader: 'He is a man of wide experience who has already toured South Africa and England, but this will be his first overseas trip as a leader. He is a man of sterling character, with a keen sense of humour, and he makes no secret of his determination that the Australian team will be popular and successful in the West Indies.'

Bradman went on to say: 'During the past season Johnson

suffered from injuries which put him out of one Test and severely handicapped him in two others. I'm afraid his courage in playing under difficulties was misconstrued in some quarters, but, despite his problems and a few unsympathetic critics, Johnson emerged from the series with an enhanced reputation. He headed the batting averages and was second in the bowling. Nobody could possibly accept his responsibilities with a greater desire to vindicate the faith shown in him by the Australian Board.'

And then came this remark: 'It may be as well to point out that the captain and vice-captain of Australian teams are chosen by the Board of Control from the players named by the selectors.' A cynic could have added that the 'grape-vine' from the selectors to the Board was a very strong one.

The emphasis placed on Johnson's averages invites comment. Surely Bradman did not rate Johnson's six innings, four not outs, 116 aggregate for an average of 58, batting at No. 10, anywhere near the merit of Harvey's nine innings, once not out, for 352 runs at an average of 44? Harvey, at No. 3 and No. 4, batted against the full blast of England's pace attack. In point of fact, Bill Johnston shares with Bradman the unusual feat of returning from an English tour with an average exceeding 100—but Johnston was only once out and nobody took that average seriously.

If averages were so important, why was Ron Archer, who had led the Australian Test averages, dropped from the final Test against England? And why wasn't Crawford, who headed the Australian averages, chosen for the West Indies?

Alan Hulls, a sporting writer of the Sydney *Sun*, had these remarks to make on the subject:

'Sir Donald pulled one out of the hat. He made modern cricket history by going into print in defence of the Australian team he had helped to choose for the West Indies. In doing so he had kindly words for captain Ian Johnson, whose cause he is understood to have espoused so well. It has always been accepted that selectors were barred from commenting upon their labours. But perhaps things are changing. If so, a lot of people would like to read Bradman's story of why Miller wasn't chosen for South Africa in 1949.'

Yes, indeed.

Hulls went on to say:

'In addition to being a selector, Bradman is a member of the Board of Control, which keeps upon all its doings a "security" clamp not exceeded in tightness by Service chiefs in war-time. Did other members of the Board know about their fellow member and selector going into print in this fashion? Are fellow selectors Ryder and Seddon happy about the statement?'

The fact (or so it seems) is that Sir Donald Bradman does virtually what he likes in Australian cricket. In 1956 I asked Frank Cush, then chairman of the Board of Control, whether Sir Donald would resign again to work for the Press on the English tour. Mr. Cush was astounded. 'I know nothing about that,' he said. He knew the very next day—from the newspapers which were to take Bradman's service. They saw nothing wrong in a selector and a Board member publicly criticising the team he had helped to choose and pass. Indeed, the Adelaide *News*, which promoted Bradman's service on both the 1953 and 1956 tours of England, expressed disapproval of his having to resign from the Board in order to work for them!

Ian Johnson was again captain for England. Unquestionably, he had done a good job of general captaincy in the West Indies; but, alas, that tour did not discover a single player for the English tour ahead, and so, inevitably, many cricket followers, who had seen our batting crumble badly against Hutton's men, didn't place much reliance upon Johnson's bold claims that the Australians had 'found themselves' again in the West Indies—that they had recovered their lost batting techniques. Anyway, they soon lost it again when faced by Laker and company in England.

I have dealt at some length with this period because the feeling over the captaincy, following so quickly upon the upset to Australian cricket through the much-publicised Barnes case, did a lot of harm to the game at a time when it specially needed support. Personally, like others, I admired various qualities possessed by Ian Johnson but simply could not see how his playing position as an Australian Eleven captain could be justified. Throughout cricket history Australian captains have won their places in national teams as a matter of right—among them Dave Gregory, W. L. Murdoch, Harry Scott, P. S. McDonnell, J. Blackham, George Trott, Joe Darling, M. A. Noble, Syd Gregory, Warwick Armstrong, H. L. Collins, W. M. Woodfull, D. G. Bradman and A. L. Hassett. I could imagine Keith Miller in that band, but not Ian Johnson.

When Hutton's team was in Australia, and when Australia's team was being chosen for the 1956 tour of England, a section of Melbourne writers (one or two of them not distinguished by any special contact with the game) answered every criticism of Johnson's captaincy by claiming that it was merely 'interstate jealousy.' No such feeling had been noted against other Victorian captains—Armstrong, Woodfull and Hassett—but this 'interstate jealousy' is supposedly the answer to a lot of things in Australia.

Being fully entitled to defend himself, Ian Johnson gave some of us a few backhanders during a broadcast he made in Jamaica. He was reported to have laughed 'dryly' when asked whether certain former players, such as O'Reilly and Fingleton, were helping the game in Australia.

'The impression of present-day cricketers in Australia, and I think it is a unanimous opinion,' said Johnson, 'is that Bill O'Reilly and Jack Fingleton are doing more harm than most to the game. They have written it down continuously during the past year. They have made absolutely no effort to be constructive. In fact, they have been entirely destructive. I can safely say they are not doing one bit of good to the game in Australia.'

This calls for a little comment. Bill O'Reilly has always been able to fight his own battles so I can leave him out of it. Johnson says I 'have been entirely destructive.' If it could be shown that my writings and broadcastings over the years on cricket had been calculated to destroy cricket, I would retire from such activities immediately because I love cricket—and owe much to it. In reality, I had always hoped that those who read me or listened to me would, in the result, be more interested in cricket.

That has been my purpose because, as I say, I have a great affection and admiration for the game and want other people to follow it, understand it and feel the same way about it. It would be a tragic thing if cricket's influence faded out of the national character.

However, I agree that I have never aimed at giving indiscriminate praise, any more than I have indiscriminately criticised. The aim of a critic—and especially of one who has been through the Test mill and knows how much easier it is to talk than to do things—is not to take the easy and comfortable path, not to go along with the court claqueur, but to instruct, to interpret happenings, and to so describe the play that those who see it are sufficiently critical to know the best when they see it, and assimilate it.

Had I applauded Johnson's return to Test cricket and his appointment as captain in both Australia, the West Indies and England, and had I not—on the basis of experience—so strongly advocated youth in the team, maybe I would have been doing good for the game. O'Reilly, with years of cricket experience behind him, also could not accept Johnson in the role of a typical Australian Test captain, and (even apart from his tactics, which consisted of a public statement early in the tour that he was not concerned to win county matches but was making the Tests his objective), our fears were confirmed by the English tour. In nine Test innings Johnson averaged seven with the bat and took six wickets, averaging 50·67 per wicket—this on pitches on which Laker, a similar type of bowler, took 46 at an average of 9·60. Johnson, of course, had his supporters in the Press, supporters who clamoured that he had 'answered his critics' when he took 4-151 at Old Trafford—where Jim Laker took 19-90!

Nor were the captain's figures for the whole tour any more uplifting. He finished second-last in the batting (193 runs at an average of 10) and seventh of the regular bowlers (50 wickets at 27).

It was not pleasant to take a firm stand against Johnson's appointment. As I have written, he is a most likeable person and in some respects—unfortunately, the off-field ones—he was the best Australian Eleven captain I have known. But, to my mind, one of the first essentials of a captain is to have his position in the side assured because of his playing ability. The official determination to maintain Johnson as captain and not have Miller, no matter what happened, did Australian cricket more harm than O'Reilly, Fingleton or any other critic could possibly have done.

Eighteen

THE TASKS AHEAD

Ian Craig's remarkable rise to the captaincy is an instance of how Australian officials will try to produce something unorthodox, something that suggests great enterprise. I wish they were as thrustful in other directions.

Some years ago, when Australian cricket was (as I thought) on the verge of a pronounced down-turn, I wrote to Roy Middleton, then chairman of the Board of Control and a South Australian delegate, suggesting that he call a conference between officials and present and past Australian players to plan an extensive campaign to popularise the game. I suggested many things—stimulating the game in the schools and in the country, some guarantees for players who give much time to cricket, and so on. Mr. Middleton sent a pleasant reply, telling me what was being done in his State, but suggesting that the matter generally was one for the States rather than the Board.

Later, when Frank Cush became chairman of the Board, I wrote him a similar letter, adding that I knew that the Australian Press would respond generously to such a campaign, even to searching bush areas for likely internationals. Again, though, I had no luck.

Tennis, in post-war years, has cut the ground from beneath cricket in Australia, and that mainly because of its vigorous organisation. It is fostered in every nook and corner in Australia and is so geared that lads, while still in their teens, can rise to the very top—did not Hoad and Rosewall play in the Davis Cup challenge round at 19? This is to be contrasted with Norman O'Neill, who at the age of 20 became the first New South Welshman in history to make 1,000 runs in a season. But O'Neill was considered to be too young, or too inexperienced, or not good enough to tour South Africa in a team of 15. No wonder the young Australian is so attracted to tennis!

Sir Donald Bradman was only one of a selection committee of three, but it is illogical to suppose that Dudley Seddon, of New South Wales, would not have wished to include O'Neill in the Australian side. O'Neill had created a deep impression on every Australian ground in his first year of big cricket and he was a natural choice for the New Zealand tour, a trial tour for the South African one. He not only topped the first-class averages in New Zealand but scored a brilliant century in the only unofficial Test the Australians won.

Considering the future, O'Neill should have been one of the first batsmen chosen for South Africa. On what ground was he omitted? Immaturity? Of course he was young, but hadn't the young Bradman strewn England's best bowlers all over the countryside when he was only 20? And Archie Jackson—hadn't he played a great innings against England when only 19? Clem Hill—off to England and a success at 19? Stan McCabe—in England at 20 and before he had made a single century score in Australia! Craig—touring England at 17!

After the depressing 1956 tour of England, Australian cricket reached rock-bottom. It was sadly in need of new and young attractions, which it must always have because Australians insist upon new sporting faces. Winning of

Test matches was important and Craig's team in South Africa did a fine job by winning that series by such a clear-cut margin. More important, however, was the necessity to find somebody new, somebody with an appeal that would inspire young boys to play the game and bring it back to popularity in Australia. And Norman O'Neill was the best prospect of the kind produced in years.

Australia's selection committee is strangely conservative. It revealed that attitude with its choice of a team to tour the West Indies, for then it stuck to the Old Brigade and so committed itself in its choice for England, with what results all who are interested vividly remember.

Again, when O'Neill had a season of resounding success in Australia after he had been spurned for South Africa, the frosted outlook of our aged officials became evident when the lad, driving a delivery van in Sydney, was anxious to secure something better for his future. He accepted an offer from Adelaide. Then the president of the New South Wales Cricket Association, Syd Smith (as secretary of the Board of Control he was concerned in the fight with the Big Six in 1912), said that he regretted O'Neill would be lost to New South Wales cricket. 'But,' he added, 'we are not an employment agency and a player is entitled to go where he thinks he can do best.'

Two days before Mr. Smith uttered those sentiments, O'Neill had revived memories of Bradman as he sent a Sydney crowd into rhapsodies through scoring 231 in 244 minutes, and so bringing up his 1,000 for the season. The Victorian captain, Sam Loxton, had attacked the lad with four successive bumpers as he neared the nineties. Crack, crack, crack, crack went O'Neill's bat and all of Loxton's bumpers crashed into the leg-side pickets. He went from 82 to 98 in four strokes and got a two next ball.

Fortunately, certain other men had more drive than the

New South Wales cricket legislators, and so O'Neill gained a sound job which enabled him to stay in New South Wales. Possibly, therefore, he was lucky in not being chosen for South Africa, since he received a 'plum' of a kind which has not come the way of any player who went on that tour, despite all the sacrifices they have made for the game.

During the discussion regarding O'Neill, it was hinted that the selectors had been wise in not choosing him to tour, the suggestion being that he would be all the better for being allowed to mature at home. It was said that had he failed in South Africa he might have lost confidence and his future would have been endangered. That argument was completely unsound. All champions have their failures in moving to the top and Test experience can only be gained in Test matches. Bradman was dropped after one Test but he soon got back again. If O'Neill is chosen against England in 1958-59—as he certainly should be—he has the job of finding his Test feet in the toughest of all circumstances, against England and in a series in Australia. It is far better for a player to get such experience on tour.

Experience is all that O'Neill needs. He is a completely natural cricketer. He has been called in Australia 'Bradman the Second,' but that label, I think, is too big for the lad to carry. In his general attitude, O'Neill reminds me more of Compton than Bradman. He hits off the back foot like Wally Hammond, or perhaps Australia's Johnnie Taylor. In addition, he is a first-class fieldsman and a competent bowler. He headed both the batting and the bowling averages for the 1957-58 Australian season.

Incidentally, when O'Neill was on the verge of leaving Sydney to take a job in Adelaide, tennis-player Lew Hoad made £4,000, in a week-end, by playing two matches against Pancho Gonzales on the White City courts, no more than a mile from where O'Neill hit his brilliant double-century against Victoria. Personally, I don't blame any young fellow for capitalising his sporting ability (though some appear to overdo matters and become old before their time), and, by the same token, I think it unfair that young cricketers, on the threshold of married life and having to safeguard their future, should be asked to make long tours overseas for very little monetary benefit.

Overseas tours are now much too prolonged. Take the case of Richie Benaud. Here is a young man (aged 27), who will be asked to give more years of his life to international cricket. He was married in 1952 and has since been asked to make long tours of England, the West Indies, England again, India, Pakistan and South Africa, in addition to playing throughout the Australian summers. After such service and sacrifice, on the part of his wife as well as himself, Benaud should at least enjoy the certainty of owning his own home. It is the least international cricket can do for him—and also for Davidson, McDonald, Harvey, Burke and others, who are all in much the same financial position.

Of course, Benaud and the others may, some day, receive a Testimonial match. To achieve this, the main thing will be to keep alive. Arthur Mailey and Johnnie Taylor received their benefit 30 years after they had played their last Test; Bill O'Reilly and Stan McCabe 19 years after they had finished with international cricket!

Young amateurs naturally do not worry overmuch about the future when in the flush of international glory. The game's the thing with them. But, no doubt, they are jolted into thinking of it when they note an observation from an official such as Syd Smith: 'It is not our job to act as an employment agency for players.' Where, then, does the responsibility rest?

When I was a Test player, I was somewhat taken aback by

a suggestion from an old-time Test player that we should form ourselves into a Players' Union. But, in fact, that is a necessity nowadays—and it should be stimulated by officials. Moreover, I feel there should be incentive payments for all spectacular or notable feats in Test matches. It would inspire players and would raise appreciably the standard of play and entertainment.

The money lure is one of the chief reasons why tennis has pushed cricket from public favour in Australia. I don't like this lure when overdone but I do know many parents realise the advantages of a well-paid career and encourage their gifted sons to play tennis. Australian cricket simply must take up the challenge. Tennis is better-organised and better-presented. Its officials are live-wires. They send teams and coaches around the Australian countryside, and in this very fact is the reason why tennis has ousted cricket. I doubt whether you would find a tennis turf-court in the Australian countryside. They are hard-courts and permit of play on many dampish occasions when cricket turf-pitches, many of them of indifferent quality, have been declared unfit for play.

Stan McCabe thinks, and I heartily agree with him, that Australian country cricket slipped back when the various city associations demanded the setting-down of country turf-pitches. Turf-pitches must be well-laid and well-maintained to permit of true cricket. They entail a lot of work, whereas the concrete pitches need only a little chipping from time to time and are fit for play half an hour after a downpour.

It is a truism that Australian cricket has made no great gains from country areas since the days of Bradman, McCabe and O'Reilly, all products of the concrete pitch in the country.

Harry Hopman, possibly more than any other man, is

responsible for Australia's pre-eminence in the world of tennis. He has been remarkable in finding young players, leading them on, and then, as Davis Cup captain, guiding them in tactics. Recently I was talking to him and I said, wistfully, 'I wish you would come across to our game for a while and give it a bit of a kick along.' Hopman replied, 'I'd like to do that. I can see plenty of things that need doing.'

Yes, there are plenty of things that need doing, and a start should be made at the top—among officials. No one would disparage Sir Donald Bradman's great ability as a batsman, nor his knowledge of the game, but many of us question his judgment at times, and also his likes and dislikes. We think, too, as I have said earlier, that he has too much dominance in Australian cricket and that he should welcome one or two players of his own generation to discuss and debate affairs and players with him.

It further seems to me that two shrewd English officials, G. O. Allen and Walter Robins (who, incidentally, represents Australia at the Imperial Conference) have 'put it over' Bradman in recent years. Allen, with Robins as his second-in-command, suffered his greatest disappointment in cricket when, in 1936-37 in Australia, he won two Tests straight against Bradman's side but lost the next three. It has been Allen's main ambition in recent years to get his own back against Bradman, and I think he has succeeded to some extent. The English selections have shown much more thought and imagination than some of the Australian ones. After Hutton's captaincy had slowed down the game and our side in Australia in 1954-55, and Tyson and Statham had shot our defences to bits, the Australian selectors—with Tyson and Statham in mind—plumped for solidity for our next tour of England. But Allen and company—and Robins, though not a selector, is a very astute tactician—smartly switched the tactics to spin in England, and again we were left lamenting. It will be pace again in Australia in 1958-59.

By and large, my complaint against Australian officialdom is that it seems so smug about the game. Cricket won't die, officials say, because it has gone on for so long.

That attitude reminds me of some remarks made by Mr. Menzies, the Prime Minister, to the Associated Chambers of Commerce in Sydney a year or two ago. He said: 'One of the chief things standing in the way of increased production is inadequate skill, inadequate effort and inadequate discipline in industry. The cause of these things is the Australian genius for "taking it quietly".' So with our cricket officials—their efforts are inadequate, and they always want to 'take it quietly.'

Actually, the game is much too good to be allowed to stagnate. A million new Australians have entered this country since the war and many of them don't know anything about cricket. They need to be taught. Also, we have big cities growing up away from Sydney and Melbourne—Newcastle with a population of 200,000, Wollongong with 110,000, Geelong with 80,000—and in these days of air-travel it should be possible to bring such cities into the ordinary Saturday afternoon competitions that have been conducted by Sydney and Melbourne throughout the present century.

And the Fijians—how good are they at cricket? We don't know and haven't tried to find out, although they are only a few hours' flight from Australia.

It was a Fijian Rugby Union team which, displaying vigour and enthusiasm rarely seen before on Australian fields, brought financial stability again to its code in Australia; and this suggests that if a good cricketing coach were sent to Fiji for a summer, it might be possible for the islands to produce a team that would give Australian cricket a much-needed impetus. They once beat a West Indian side, en route to New Zealand. Anyway, the experiment is worth trying, and would at least suggest that Australia's officials are awake to their responsibilities.

This next Australian summer will look after itself. Our Test team—thanks largely to Benaud, Davidson, Burke, McDonald, Mackay, and one or two others—has gained esteem in South Africa and so will be doubly anxious to erase the bad showings made in Australia in 1954-55 and in England in 1956. The note of warning is that South Africa is not England. Far from it. The English are our real cricket enemies. The task ahead will be much harder.

The task, also, of getting cricket back to where it was in Australian sport is also difficult. But—it can be done!

Nineteen

THE GAMBLE WITH IAN CRAIG

As with Ian Johnson, the Australian Board of Control drew
another captaincy surprise out of its hat with the appointment
of Ian Craig to lead the national team, firstly in New Zealand
and later in South Africa.

These events had cast their shadows when, on the return
of the Australian team from England in 1956, Craig was made
captain of New South Wales. It was a surprise choice. Richie
Benaud, on several occasions when Keith Miller was absent,
had led New South Wales with distinction and he seemed
certain to become the regular captain upon Miller's retirement. Miller has since written that news came to the Australian team in India that Benaud had been the subject of
favourable reference by a leading Australian authority and
this was taken to mean that he was next in line of succession
for the Australian position. As a result of that information,
Miller says, Benaud became a trifle lofty in manner, and so
did his own cause no service.

Personally, I am inclined to think that Benaud's tactics
at Old Trafford and The Oval in 1956 were detrimental to his
prospects. In my opinion, he sparred too much for time when
Tony Lock was bowling, often not being ready to take strike
and sometimes making Lock wait while he patted down the
pitch in between deliveries. It rather seemed that Benaud was

teasing Lock's patience, just as Bailey had attempted to test that of Miller on many occasions—once, at Leeds in 1953, he stopped the bowler in the middle of his approach. Instances of 'gamesmanship'—they include the pretence that a pad-strap needs adjusting, that a boot-lace needs tying, and that a smut is troubling an eye—are immediately apparent to old campaigners.

But let nobody underestimate Benaud's immense potentialities. I have seen him play three of the greatest innings of modern times—at Bradford, in 1953, at Scarborough, also in 1953, and his Test 97 at Lord's in 1956. He is a shaky beginner. He seems too eager to play forward all the time but, this period over and with Benaud into the twenties, I know of no modern batsman I would sooner watch. He could rise to tremendous heights—Australia's second M. A. Noble and a cricketer superior in all departments to Warwick Armstrong. Benaud has had some lean Test days, some very lean ones, indeed, but there are high hopes now that, having brought himself under control, he will go on to become in the next five years the most outstanding all-rounder in the game. He is frightfully intense, breathing and living cricket, and will do all the better when—as in golf—he learns to relax.

No cricketer in Australia is keener than Benaud to have another 'look' at Laker—on Australian wickets.

If Craig's appointment as captain of New South Wales was interesting, his appointment as Australian captain was a departure from orthodoxy because in two tours abroad he had certainly not made his Test position assured. It surprised many when he was announced leader of the young Australian team to tour New Zealand, and his appointment, coming on the eve of the New South Wales—Victoria match in Sydney, received an immediate jolt when the visitors' leader, Neil Harvey, outwitted him at all captaincy points. Craig won the toss and sent Victoria in. Harvey replied with a typical captain's innings, a double century. Some feeling became manifest during the game, and the indications were that resentment prevailed over Craig's appointment.

Harvey was said not to possess the ability to mix off the field. I sometimes think that so much emphasis is placed upon off-the-field attributes—ability to mix pleasantly, to be able to make nice speeches, to be diplomatic, to sign autographs with a smile—that the real job, that of being able to make runs and take wickets, and of being able to plan tactics and execute them or to change them in a trice, is largely overlooked. A captain who is expected to 'carry' his team both on and off the field is weighed down from the beginning. In my view, off-the-field niceties belong exclusively to the manager. One notable captain of England, Douglas Jardine, was so obsessed with the job he had to do on the field in Australia that he never got around to thinking whether or not people liked his team off the field. Nor did he care.

The appointment for the New Zealand tour of such a young man as Craig was an interesting experiment for the future. Lots of people, however, failed to see why McDonald, Burke, Benaud or Harvey—their Test position assured—should not have been given the job in South Africa. My own choice would have been Lindwall, as an appreciation for services rendered and as an experienced and very capable State captain, ideal for improving young players under his care on a long tour.

It once used to be said by the cynics that it was harder to get out of an Australian Eleven than into it. There is a very natural tendency under these circumstances for the selectors to say, 'We'll show 'em. We'll do the unexpected,' but the unexpected is not good simply because it is the unexpected. I am all for doing something off the beaten track because this is the life of cricket—it makes cricket live—but when it comes to captaincy there are limits to experiments. The limit on the one side is that it never pays to play safe. The limit on the other side is that it is unwise to put a new captain in a position in which he's not sure of his own place. To go to the first extreme produces uninspiring captaincy. To go to the other extreme means that a captain is put in a position where he doesn't quite know whether to play to hold his own playing position or go all out to push his team to victory.

Instead of serving an apprenticeship as vice-captain, Craig has been pushed right to the top. Moreover, as Benaud was denied the State captaincy in favour of Craig, it is apparent that the New South Wales officials were consulted in this long-range captaincy move for the Australian team.

What manner of lad is Craig? At the age of 17 he was the youngest Australian ever to tour England, and such experiences—from the schoolroom to the Savoy, so to speak—must have had a marked psychological effect for the youngster. He had shown great promise when, early in 1953, he made 100 runs in two innings in his first Test against South Africa, but, with his limited experience, the English pitches were far too much for him. He couldn't handle them at all, and so finished third last in the averages, with 429 runs at an average of 16. The further the tour went, the more involved his batting became. At one stage his grip of the bat was so faulty that he believed himself to be playing straight up and down the pitch and yet was being caught on the leg-side.

On returning to Australia Craig dropped out of first-class cricket to study pharmacy. He graduated and returned to cricket again. In the season 1955-56 he played in five Shield matches, making 277 runs at an average of 46, after which he was chosen for England again. Obviously, then, he has not had to work hard in Australia for two trips to England. Opportunities have come looking for him.

This 1956 Australian team was possibly the weakest sent to England since the eighties. In that side, Craig finished fourth in the first-class averages, 872 runs at 36, and eighth in the Test averages, 55 runs at an average of 15. The season, however, was no easy one for batsmen. It produced a lot of rain and some doubtful pitches. Perhaps Craig's best performance was at Old Trafford, where he made 38 at the toughest period of the match. Incidentally, he played Laker as well as anybody. On the way home, however, he didn't distinguish himself in the Pakistani and Indian Tests, making only 100 in five innings.

In South Africa he finished tenth in the Australian Test averages, making 103 runs at an average of 14. For the whole tour he finished ninth—591 runs at an average of 36·9.

In 18 Test innings, therefore, Craig has made 358 runs, at an average of 19. His highest Test score, so far, is the 53 he made against South Africa in Melbourne in his very first Test innings. He made 123 not out against New Zealand but those Tests were not official. On that tour he finished seventh in the first-class averages, 308 runs at 38—behind O'Neill, Benaud, Harvey, Simpson, Favell and Burge, in that order.

Ian Craig, therefore, has a long, long way to go to compensate for all the confidence placed in him. No other Australian in cricket history has had as many chances that have yielded so little.

I can think of many players in my own time who never enjoyed the well-merited experiences of a tour of England. There is good fortune, of course, in coming into a game at a particular period of opportunity but when pondering on the chances given Craig—in addition to a few others—I think of such players as Keith Rigg, Leo O'Brien, Ross Gregory,

Austin Punch, Hughie Chilvers, Andy Ratcliffe, Gordon Morgan, Norman Phillips, Jack Nitschke, Lisle Nagel, Bert Ironmonger, Ronnie Oxenham, Don Blackie, H. S. Love, Laurie Nash, and Lyall Wall—among others. None of these knew a trip to England yet as a combination I think those named would have comprised one of the strongest teams of all time—just as England could name a powerful team of 'Disappointeds' who never toured Australia.

My Australian team of 'Disappointeds' would have had an incredibly strong bowling side—Nash (fast); Nagle, Morgan, Phillips (right medium); Blackie, Oxenham and Lee (off-spinners); Chilvers and Punch (slow leg-breakers) and Wall and Ironmonger (left-hand). Nagle, at 6 ft. 6½ inches (with a twin brother, Vernon, the same height) would have caused a gasp at Lord's as he strolled out, as big a gasp as he caused at Melbourne in 1932 when he took eight English wickets in the first match against Victoria.

I just don't know why Craig doesn't succeed as a Test batsman, although it is well to remember that he has played only two of his 18 Test innings on his native Australian pitches—53 and 47 against Cheetham's South Africans. He has a neat, fluent style, although he bends his knees to a marked extent when playing at the ball, and this, suddenly changing his height of vision, could account for some flaw in defence. It could also account for the fact that he sometimes skies the ball on the drive, not being over the top of it. But, whether it is just sheer bad luck or not, the unfortunate fact is that Craig, for almost five years, has been an enigma, in that he promises so much and produces so little.

He is a very pleasant young man, full of confidence and well-liked by his fellow-players. I think it would have been better for his cricket character had he known some adversity in selections. Further, there is the thought that his background is now possibly more English than Australian. Apart from his two tours of England—he has played 56 first-class innings in England and only 37 Shield innings in Australia—he also made a business trip to England in 1957 and joined the Australian team in South Africa from England. Meanwhile he was made a member of the M.C.C. and a member of the Free Foresters. Both are 'exclusive' cricket clubs and I doubt whether they would provide what Australians would consider a useful background for an Australian Test captain. I myself have been made a member of a number of English clubs since my Test days finished, and have found them to be full of bright and breezy personalities, so that they have given me some of my most delightful moments in cricket. Nevertheless, I don't think a young Australian captain should be linked closely with such bodies. There's plenty of time for that when his Test days are over.

Generally, neither England nor Australia has favoured young Test captains.

For England, Peter May has been the youngest in recent years, being 25. Chapman was 26, MacLaren 27, Douglas 29, Wyatt 29, Gilligan and Jardine 30, Tennyson 31, Yardley 32, Allen and Jackson 34, Hammond 35, and Hutton 36.

The Australians run: W. L. Murdoch 25, Harry Scott, P. S. McDonnell and D. G. Bradman 28, Joe Darling 29, Woodfull and Dave Gregory 33, Collins and Johnson 35, Noble 36, Hassett 37, Blackham 38, Ryder 39, Armstrong 41, and S. E. Gregory 42.

Craig, therefore, ranks as the youngest Australian captain in history. Were some of those I have mentioned asked whether a lad of 23 (as Craig will be on the next English tour of Australia) could lead Australia, I fancy they would snort: 'It's no job for a boy. If you must give it to him, send him out to the Nullarbor for a few years to toughen him up.'

What's more, they would have shuddered at the thought that an Australian captain of 21 should have been already a member of M.C.C. and the Free Foresters.

R. S. Whitington, of the Sydney *Daily Telegraph* (and a former South Australian Shield player), wrote from Salisbury in October 1956 that Craig's Australian team was putting on a very English front in ultra-English Rhodesia. Whitington said further: 'Craig is sporting the orange-and-yellow striped Marylebone Cricket Club tie. His explanation: "Quite. It was the only one I had that would go with my suit."* Commented an Australian now resident in Rhodesia: "What's this—a cricket team or a bow-tie brigade?"'

Whitington also wrote that three hours after the arrival of the manager, J. Norton (who followed the team on from Australia), the team went into camera to form an amenities committee, whose task it would be to impose fines for 'breaches of conduct.'

'These fines,' said Whitington, 'will be imposed at regular weekly or bi-weekly meetings of the team for alleged "misdemeanours"—whimsical and otherwise. Such meetings and penalties have been part and parcel of Marylebone Cricket Club touring teams for many decades. I would be happier if more team members wore their Australian team tie more often. So would several members of the team whose manner of dress remains as it was in Australia. Australia is facing as hard a task as any Australian team faced. I hope it will keep this in mind in the midst of its penchant for ersatz Anglicised fripperies.'

This 'tie' weakness can become a habit. Ian Craig, giving his first impressions of the beautiful Newlands ground at Cape Town, said it reminded him very much of an English ground. 'And it could well be,' he said in an interview to a

---

* It's news to me that the M.C.C. tie goes with any suit!

South African reporter, 'because on all sides one sees M.C.C. and Free Forester ties.' Other times, other ideas. Apart from it beauty and the rearing Table Top mountain that seemingly shot up from the boundary, the main impression Newlands left on the Australian team of which I was a member was the brewery that showed up through the trees! Especially on a hot day.

Craig's team was unbeaten in South Africa. This was a splendid performance because, for one thing, the M.C.C, could do no better than draw the series with the South Africans, and, for another thing, Craig's team was young and under a cloud after the depressing 1956 tour of England. Eric Rowan, the old Springbok player, declared that Benaud was 'the brains of the Australians'; but, whether that was so or not, Craig must be given a great deal of credit.

The regrettable thing was that he didn't do enough with the bat to make his own Test position a certainty. Favell and Burge were on the outside looking in; O'Neill had forged ahead in Australia and there were others pushing in— Stevens (South Australia), McLaughlin (Queensland), Martin (New South Wales), Crompton, Huntington and Shaw (Victoria).

Accordingly, there was much discussion in Australia after the South African tour. Could Craig be chosen against the Englishmen? Sir Donald Bradman was lavish in praising Craig's job in South Africa. Ian Johnson, though he said he would have preferred Lindwall as captain in South Africa, thought Craig should be given the later appointment. Lindsay Hassett had a reservation—he would like, he said cautiously, to see Craig make runs against England before the series started. Arthur Mailey, Bill O'Reilly and Keith Miller were against Craig, as was also Sid Barnes, who, in his blunt way, declared that Craig 'hasn't got what it takes.'

O'Reilly, writing in the Sydney *Sun-Herald*, was quite emphatic. 'Unless,' he said, 'a miraculous run of good form lifts Craig out of the batting mess he has been in for years, his disappearance from the Australian team is a foregone conclusion. I hold out no hope whatever for him after his long string of disappointing failures.'

Mailey and Miller strongly supported Benaud for the captaincy. For my own part, I am inclined to agree with Hassett. Australian cricket is now committed to Craig—provided, of course, that he remains in Australia—and if he scores runs in the early games against the M.C.C. team he must be chosen as the leader. But his task ahead is no easy one. The Australian barracker, if not the selectors, will want runs from him. In addition to the need to make sound scores in Test cricket, he will have the cares of captaincy against England in his own country, and, as he is so young, it will be difficult for older heads to refrain from advising him, so that there is a danger of his becoming confused if the going gets tough.

However, perhaps there will be time enough to cross bridges when we come to them; and meanwhile, of course, Australia can fairly wish Ian Craig the best of luck.

Twenty

A HUTTON, NOT A SURRIDGE

One of the best captains in recent years was Stuart Surridge, of Surrey. He pushed the game along with zest and attack and Surrey's grand list of county championships was tribute to his leadership. Surrey, of course, had many great cricketers in this period but strong links can often function in opposing directions unless they are bound by good leadership.

Jim Laker asked for his sweater one day at The Oval in 1956 after Bill Edrich had given him 'stick.' He didn't play in the next match at Lord's, even though this was just after his record match of 19 wickets against Australia at Old Trafford. Surridge would not stand for any player deciding when he would or would not bowl. As captain, he himself made the decisions.

Now, Peter May has played his county cricket under Surridge's leadership, but, so far as one can judge, he has made little attempt to emulate Surridge's aggressive approach. He is a disciple of Hutton—canny and cautious.

May had the Australians virtually 'sewn up' in the Fifth Test at The Oval in 1956. A draw suited England's pupuses inasmuch as it gave England the rubber, and with the draw assured it could be said that May would have been foolish to have allowed the Australians any chance at all to win the match and so save the rubber.

One had only to watch the Australians in the field around three o'clock on that final afternoon to realise that they didn't want May to close. It was a spinner's pitch but Johnson wouldn't use such bowlers. The Australian fast bowlers sent down 52 overs, against nine by the spinners. As the clock came down from three and began to toil upward to four the Australians showed unmistakable elation as May batted on and on. He closed at 4.10 p.m. At 5.30 p.m. the Australians were four out for 10 runs. At stumps they were five down for 27. May had set them an impossible task—to make 228 to win in 130 minutes.

If the winning of the rubber was the all-important thing, May could scarcely have been blamed for not seeking victory in that final Test. Nevertheless, I thought the foreboding of the Australians that he would make a final thrust was plain to see. A Surridge might have said: 'There's been a lot spoken and written during this series about the pitches at Leeds and Old Trafford. Well, now, I'll sink these Australians well and truly. We'll win this rubber 3-1 or make a pretty good effort at it, and I'll leave no doubt about which is the better side. I'll cut their grumbling from underneath them!'

Nobody seemed to criticise May's tactics and I mention the incident only to suggest that he is a disciple of Hutton, and not of his own county captain of the period, Surridge. After that tour, when May went on to South Africa, it was said there that he had no superior in local experience as a defensive tactician.

It is well to study these defensive tactics because they have been responsible for much dissatisfaction in recent years and it will be a great pity if they are allowed to obtrude again in the next few series between England and Australia. On the other hand, if the game is allowed to gain momentum I think we will see some magnificent cricket in the years immediately ahead. The irrefutable argument against defensive tactics, as we have seen them of late years—carried out more by the English team in Australia than in England—is that the game is never allowed to develop above a certain gait. It must always walk, never run.

Enter Sir Leonard Hutton! As plain Len Hutton he was left with something very indigestible on his plate after Brisbane in 1955. He was the first professional to lead the M.C.C. in Australia and his beginning was not auspicious. He won the toss in the First Test at Brisbane, sent Australia in, and was whipped by an innings and 154 runs. Australia declared at 8-601 and the English bowling made very poor reading:

	O.	M.	R.	W.
Bedser	37	4	131	1
Statham	34	2	123	2
Tyson	29	1	160	1
Bailey	26	1	140	3
Edrich	3	0	28	0

Alec Bedser, who had been suffering from an attack of shingles in the early part of the tour and was not 100 per cent fit in Brisbane, was dropped after that game and never recovered his English position. He was by no means the worst of the English bowlers in Brisbane and, moreover, several chances from his bowling were dropped. The figures show that Tyson didn't bowl as well as Bedser and that Bailey was much more expensive.

If we analyse the Bedser case I think we will find the origin of the defensive tactics which Hutton instituted and which May seems to have copied somewhat closely.

Playing in England in 1953 Bedser established a record in these Tests for the number of wickets taken—39 at an average of 17·51. In this series, Jim Laker (who was to topple Bedser's record in 1956 with 46 wickets at a cost of 9·60 apiece) took nine wickets at an average of 23·77.

Subsequently, in a book published after his retirement, Hutton wrote: 'I am convinced that a pair of quality fast bowlers make a far more potent weapon than one brilliant fast bowler supported by someone of much lesser pace. The absence of a second fast bowler affords a batsman some respite. Indeed, he can be shielded from the fast bowler's attack. If two fast bowlers of real quality had arisen earlier, the problems about Alec Bedser which arose in Australia in 1954-55 might have come to the fore earlier than they did.'

This statement calls for comment. Leaving Tate's great record in English Test cricket out of consideration, the only occasion when the 'problems' (as seen by Hutton) about Bedser could have come to the fore earlier was in 1953 when he took that record number of 39 wickets against Australia. Had England possessed another high-class fast bowler, and had Hutton had his way (he was captaining England for the first time against Australia in 1953), the suggestion is that we might easily have been spared Bedser in that series. What an interesting thought!

Although the senior professional, Bedser was not made a member of Hutton's selection committee in Australia. Nor was Compton, who was vice-captain to Brown on the preceding tour. The selection committee consisted of Hutton, May, Edrich and Evans. Of this set-up Hutton wrote: 'I selected players with forthright views. . . . Others may have seemed just as well qualified to serve through long experience, but I wanted men who were prepared to offer definite opinions.'

Len also wrote in his book about the necessity to 'hate' the opposition. I don't think you should exactly fall upon the neck of the 'enemy' and embrace him; nor do I think it necessary for anybody on the cricket field to use up his gastric juices by steeling himself to 'hate.' Nobody in cricket had more bumpers flung at him than my good friend Len Hutton, nor could anybody ever say that he 'squawked' about it, even though a bad injury and a series of operations left him with a deficient left arm during his post-war career.

Hutton was full of courage. I never ceased to admire him in the days when Miller and Lindwall—never once told by Bradman to 'break it down' or 'cut it out'—plied him with brow-searing deliveries. Under slightly hotter circumstances, a few Australians in 1932-33 yelled to high heaven and the M.C.C. that such tactics were unsporting, were not in the best interest of the game and should be banned—as they were and should have been banned (and with all the 'squawkers' chosen again for a bloodless tour of England in 1934 when Larwood and Voce were not allowed to play!) Yet I never watched Lindwall and Miller against Hutton in post-war years without wondering by which country and under whose instigation the outcry against intimidatory tactics was first raised. Australia has nothing to be proud of in this—the way we indulged in a flood of bumpers when England had no fast bowler to retaliate—and I give Hutton high marks for not retaliating when, later, he had Tyson and Statham at his command.

Accordingly, I don't think Hutton was very serious when he wrote of the need to 'hate' the Australians—although, it is true, he once taxed Bedser with being too friendly with our players. Bedser's reply was to the point. 'I like Australians, Len,' he replied, 'and I'll go on liking them. But it makes no difference to my cricket attitude towards them. Have a look at my figures.'

Later, Hutton obviously had some qualms about Bedser's churlish treatment in Australia. He writes in his book: 'The hardest decision of my cricket career was the dropping of Alec Bedser that tour.' Later he seems to do a little hedging;

'The final decision to omit Alec was taken by the selection committee, of whom I was only one.' That could mean that Hutton wanted Bedser and the others didn't, but it could also mean that the others supported Hutton in not wanting Bedser.

It is never pleasant to see a worthy servant snubbed, but nothing that Hutton has written convinces me as to the real reason why Bedser was put to one side in Australia. My belief is that Bedser was stood down simply because he bowled an over much too quickly.

After that deluge of runs in Brisbane, I think Hutton decided that the game would never again get away from him. He aimed to control it through the simple medium of keeping a brake upon the number of overs bowled in a day. Bedser, always bustling and always attacking the stumps, got through an over in less than half the time taken by Tyson and Statham, who each took a very long run; Appleyard, who took an amazingly long run for a medium-paced man; and Bailey, who once took seven minutes at Leeds in 1953 to bowl a six-ball over, all down the leg-side.

Bedser, in better health than at Brisbane, would have appreciated the Sydney pitch for the Second Test. It had been covered from storms and was a 'green-top.' Bill Bowes, a staunch Hutton man, wrote that Bedser would have been in his element in Sydney. Melbourne was also a bowler's pitch from the start, and Bedser had his hopes raised when Hutton took him out to inspect the pitch before play. Yet, when they returned to the pavilion, Hutton casually said to Bedser, 'You're not playing today, Alec.' Hutton says in his book that he formed the impression during the inspection that Bedser was not in the right mood for a Test.

Hutton's habit of fielding his fast bowlers on the fence also slowed the game down in a marked fashion. Englishmen saw an indication of this in the 1956 Test at Lord's when, under

May's captaincy, Statham and Trueman came up from the fine-leg boundary to bowl. Trueman walked right up to the umpire, gave him his cap, and then walked back to his mark to bowl. While all this was taking place, the fieldsmen amused themselves by throwing catches. It was good that Lord's saw this because, in later matches, England switched to spin. And quick overs, naturally.

The Second Test in Sydney on Hutton's tour gave him the chance, but only by 38 runs, to get things under control in regard to time. In Melbourne he took it too far. He had lengthy conferences with his bowlers and his fieldsmen, often held up an over while he meticulously moved a fieldsman, and his bowlers seemed in no haste at all to get on with the game.

In Adelaide it was worse. On the first day of play, 300 minutes, only 58 overs were bowled by the Englishmen. They averaged $12\frac{1}{2}$ overs an hour for Australia's first innings, slow enough, but in the second innings they slipped down to only 11 overs an hour. In that match, Australia averaged 15 an hour.

Like Hutton, G. O. Allen had three fast bowlers when he toured Australia in 1936-37 but his team averaged 15 overs an hour. Like Hutton's men, again, Allen's fast bowlers could have argued that they didn't like the eight-ball over, nor the heat, but the difference of four overs an hour is highly significant.

In the series between Australia and South Africa in 1952-53, Australia averaged 16 overs an hour and South Africa $16\frac{1}{2}$. (Eight-ball overs are bowled in Australia.)

Mr. S. C. Griffith, Assistant Secretary of the Marylebone Cricket Club, who was a distinguished player for Sussex and England, said at the end of the 1957 season that English cricket was slowing down very noticeably. Highlighting an appeal by his club for captains to cut out time-wasting tactics in the field, Mr. Griffith said: 'What is particularly exercising our minds is the time taken to bowl an over. Now we get only 14 or 15 overs an hour instead of the former average of 18.' Mr. Griffith, of course, was speaking of the English six-ball over.

I don't know how the legislators will jump this hurdle but I do know they must face up to it. Every sport, it seems, has a similar problem. Several professional golfers have unenviable reputations for slow, dawdling play, and I know at least one leading tennis player who is never ready. His opponent is always kept waiting, whether it is for a serve or a mere changing of ends. This is unadulterated 'gamesmanship' and can have a bad effect upon an opponent whose temperament impels him to want to get on with things.

It is not an easy matter to accuse a field-captain of wasting time, but it would be fair enough to place on him the onus of ensuring that time is not wasted. This could be done by setting a firm number of overs to be bowled in an hour, a penalty of runs to be deducted for each over not bowled, or a bonus of runs to be added for extra overs bowled when the fielding side comes to bat. This suggestion might not be easy to implement, but, in any event, there should be some penalty against a field-captain who refuses to keep the game up to his opponents.

A batsman in the middle knows when the opposing captain won't allow the game to flow. Spectators are not usually so well informed. All that most know at a day's end is that they have seen little action, that the game has dragged.

I don't suggest that Trueman was deliberately wasting time when, at Lord's in 1956, he walked from the fine-leg boundary to the umpire to give him his cap and then returned to his mark to begin his bowling. But I am emphasising that this is a practice that has come to be accepted. If it had been necessary, under the penalty of suffering a loss of runs, to bowl a certain number of overs an hour, Trueman's captain would certainly have ensured that the cap got to the umpire through somebody else, and thus Trueman would not have wasted at least 40 walking steps before beginning an over. Assuming that such walking occupies a minute, it would mean that Trueman, himself, could fit another 1½ overs into each hour's play or, if there was a similar wastage at the other end, another 18 overs each English day of play.

I do, therefore, put forward the suggestion that there should be a minimum number of overs bowled each hour. Such a system would make a captain use his wits (and probably every type of bowler) and one can imagine the speed with which the ball would be brought back from the boundary. Furthermore, it would do away with the annoying habit of calling for drinks in every session of a Test.

Other subjects currently under discussion are the l.b.w. rule, Test match wickets and the limitation of the leg-side field behind the wicket. Those who would study the evolution of cricket laws should obtain R. S. Rait Kerr's 'The Laws of Cricket—their History and Growth.' The author traces in detail the history of the l.b.w. rule. He notes that Arthur Shrewsbury, in the last century, developed a new gospel of defensive batsmanship which soon made many converts. From about 1885 this technique involved an increasing use of the pads, which in a year or two was causing deep concern in the cricket world. As a result the reform of the l.b.w. law became the question of the hour and with one interlude has remained so to the present day.

Argument in the matter was very heated in the 1880s. There was a strong attempt made in 1888 to have added to the l.b.w. rule (which ruled a batsman out if he was hit by a ball pitching in a straight line between wicket and wicket and which, in the opinion of the umpire, would have hit the wicket) the words: 'or, should he wilfully cross the wicket to defend it with his person.' This would have reverted to the rule of 1774. It was not accepted because it was thought to be too drastic and difficult for decision, the umpires having to judge the batsman's intent.

In 1888 it was suggested that a batsman should be given out if, with any part of his person between wicket and wicket, he should stop a ball which the umpire considered would have hit the wicket. The M.C.C. would not accept this proposal. Instead, it made a plea to all concerned to put an end to the padding-up disease.

The plea brought results, but only for a short time. Padding-up became as great a nuisance as ever and in 1902 the M.C.C. failed by only a narrow margin to implement the recommendation of 1888 that a batsman should be out if he stopped a ball which the umpire considered would have hit the wicket.

To Robert Lyttleton can be given the distinction of having the l.b.w. rule changed to its present state. He always pressed for the recommendation of 1888 and in 1928 he compromised to the extent that a batsman could be out to a ball pitching *outside* the line of the off-stump if it struck any part of his person between wicket and wicket.

This was introduced as the new law in 1937 and I believe the bodyline season in Australia in 1932-33 eventually brought it about so far as Australian agreement was concerned. At that period, I think, the Australians would have agreed to most suggestions in order to carry their point on the abolition of bodyline. Rait Kerr says that Don Bradman pressed the Australian Board to give a trial to a rule which gave the batsman out from a ball pitching outside the off-stump, and hitting the batsman's person outside of the line

between wicket and wicket. Those who were at the M.C.C·
dinner to the Australians in 1948 say that, on that occasion,
Bradman also suggested l.b.w. should be given to a ball
breaking in from the leg-side, as well as the off.

Obviously, some change in the rule was needed to defeat
the padding-up to a ball pitched outside the off-stump.
O'Reilly once told me that Sutcliffe could never detect his
bosie but overcame it simply by padding-up to anything
pitched outside the off-stump. Nowadays, there is not the
padding-up there once was, but it is doubtful whether the
amended l.b.w. rule has justified itself. It has led to a flood of
in-swing bowling with leg-side fields, and many batsmen—
Cowdrey is one who comes to mind—still pad-up by extending their front foot well down the line to an off-break pitched
outside the stumps. They don't attempt any stroke at all.
Such batsmen work on the assumption that umpires find the
decision too difficult to give if the batsman plays forward and
so they decide in the batsman's favour.

A strong body of opinion in Australia favours a return to
the l.b.w. rule as it was before the off-side amendment. They
argue that strokes would return to the game—that the leg-
break bowler would be more encouraged and the field would
have to be shifted from the leg.

Such a reversion, however, could bring additional padding-
up, and that should be avoided at all costs. I am inclined to
think that the old boys of 1888 had the solution. This was the
recommendation that the batsman should be out l.b.w. if hit
by a ball pitching in a line between wicket and wicket *or should
he wilfully cross the wicket to defend it with his person.*

Pads, I believe, were introduced to guard against injuries
and not to act as a second line of defence. Intent, in such a
case, should clearly be capable of interpretation. A batsman
either offers a stroke at a ball or he doesn't, and I find nothing

more tedious now than the batsman who deliberately pads-up to a ball pitched outside the leg-stump. If the ball trickles away to near the boundary, the game dies until it is recovered because no run can be scored off the pads if the batsman doesn't offer a stroke.

I can see no merit in the l.b.w. rule as it stands, with the benefit being given to off-breakers and in-swingers. To be logical, it should be given to leg-breakers and out-swingers as well, and particularly as such bowlers serve a better purpose than the others in that they allow of the more spectacular off-side strokes and don't crimp a batsman with leg-side field placements. Because they have aided the off-breakers with the l.b.w. rule, the cricket legislators are now searching about to restrict them in field-placement. I don't like a field being restricted. It is not in the spirit of the game at all.

If the l.b.w. rule is to be altered again—and it seems it will be—I think the suggested rule of the 1880s has much to commend it. Why shouldn't a batsman have to play at every ball that is pitched on or near the stumps? Modern batsmen pad-up with impunity to a leg-break bowler, so that such a bowler is at a distinct disadvantage. Bat-play, not pad-play, is the essence of cricket. I think the solution of the l.b.w. rule and pad-play was clearly suggested by our great-great-grandfathers.

Twenty-one

PITCHES, TACTICS, BACK-ROOM BOYS

In all ways, Douglas Jardine is a straight-shooter. As befits a legal man, which he is, he assembles his facts and then delivers a judgment backed by years of experience in cricket. In writing on Test Match wickets in Sir Pelham Warner's *Cricketer*, Jardine says Englishmen feel certain, and rightly certain, that the groundsmen of county grounds are straight and conscientious men.

But, he adds, just as it is important that justice should be done, it is almost as important that justice should be *seen* to be done. Visiting teams to English shores should feel secure from any fear that any groundsman is going to try to produce a wicket favourable to the home bowling strength, or aimed at counteracting the visitors. A visiting captain should be entitled to assume that the wicket upon which his team played a county match will be broadly similar to the wicket upon which his team will play in a Test match on the same ground. Criticism of a pitch, says Jardine, may in fact be no criticism at all of the groundsman. He may have his instructions from the ground committee and carry them out to the letter.

Jardine adds these salient points: 'It is only fair to the groundsmen to remember that for the last three years at least England has fielded a double-edged attack, with both fast and spin bowling more than usually capable of taking advantage of conditions suitable to either type of bowling. If a ground committee on any of our Test match grounds said simply to its groundsman, "Can you produce a wicket for the Test guaranteed to last four days under normal conditions and preferably for five days?" would there be any serious chance of a negative reply if on that simple briefing the groundsman was thereafter left to himself to get on with the job?'

Which brings me to the subject of the Old Trafford pitch at Manchester in July 1956, a pitch that aroused more comment—and from the Australian angle, very bitter comment—than any other Test pitch in modern times.

This was the pitch on which Jim Laker performed his almost incredible bowling feat of 9-37 in the first innings and 10-53 in the second. Statham, Bailey, Lock and Oakman were the other English bowlers. Lock is a devastating spinner when the pitch helps him, yet the staggering thing was that while Laker took 19-90 from 68 overs in the match, Lock took only 1-106 from 69 overs. The astonishing thing is that four other bowlers—and run-outs—could take only one wicket in 20 in two innings on a pitch which, after the first day, favoured spin.

Frankly, there was not a member of the Australian team who didn't think that something particularly 'slick' in pitch preparation had been put over them at Old Trafford.

Here, in this very wet summer of 1956, one didn't expect to see a brown pitch, and that in the north particularly and in Manchester especially. In four trips to England I have not known a brown Old Trafford pitch for the start of a game, other than this one. Old Trafford pitches are particularly green and this brown strip looked incongruous on a field that otherwise was deep green.

The Australians, after encountering and not liking a pitch very responsive to spin at Leeds, were looking forward to a fast pitch at Old Trafford. Indeed, with Miller (whose fast bowling had won the Test at Lord's), Lindwall and Archer the Australians were relying about 80 per cent upon speed at Old Trafford. Their first match there against Lancashire, in late May, when English pitches are not at their fastest, was marked by an all-speed attack from Lindwall, Davidson, Archer and Crawford, and it shot Lancashire out for 108. Miller was captain but didn't bowl in this first innings, the new ball being given to Davidson.

Nor did the Australians do much better. They could make only 160, Statham taking four wickets. Wharton played a brilliant century innings later for Lancashire but this match, on a green-looking pitch, certainly led the Australians to expect a fast pitch at Old Trafford two months later.

There had been grumblings about the Leeds pitch. The ball spun early in the match, and spun sharply, but Leeds had a spinning reputation. Not long before the Test there Tattersall of Lancashire, playing against Yorkshire, took 14 wickets at a cost of 90 runs. I heard at Leeds that the pitches had been moved a few yards and a few hours of play would naturally disturb at one end, on a good length, the bowling and batting marks of other years.

Leeds was understandable but not Old Trafford. The pitch was not only brown with marl. The grass had been shaved to the surface.

The English selectors successfully anticipated the nature of the pitch by dropping Trueman, and that in the face of a remarkable statement by groundsman Flack the night before that the pitch would be fast and well-grassed. Alan Ross, the *Observer* correspondent, in his splendid book *Cape Summer* wrote: 'The pitch, far removed from the fast grassy one predicted the evening before by the groundsman, was shaven bare and marled. The outfield, in contrast to the red-brown, Suez Canal-coloured playing strip, was a rich oasis green.'

After he had bowled an over Miller, to show his disgust at the somnolent pitch and to convey that impression to everybody, bounced the ball hard on the pitch. He had to stoop to recover it on the bounce.

With England 3-307 at stumps that first afternoon, the 'grape-vine' from the Australians' dressing-room had it that the pitch wouldn't last and that they were thoroughly annoyed by it. (And, one imagined, the Australians were already as good as beaten!)

Richardson and Sheppard were in no trouble against pace. May was unlucky because a ball on a length from Benaud jumped nastily and he edged it. This was a very nasty ball to see on the first day of a five-day Test and made one reflect on what an O'Reilly would have done on such a pitch.

Next afternoon, between innings, there was much laughter from Australians in the Press Box as the pitch was being swept. The groundsmen birching it were barely distinguishable in the clouds of swirling marl. Obviously, this was no normal Old Trafford pitch. And the case against it was sewn-up only a fortnight later when Statham, who bowled only six overs in the first innings of the Test, worked up tremendous pace on the usual green-looking pitch to take 6-27 off 12 overs for Lancashire in the return match against Australia. Australia was struggling at 7-86 when rain washed out play.

In arguing the case against the strange preparation of the Old Trafford Test pitch of 1956, one doesn't excuse the Australians. For the most part they played remarkably bad cricket. After being 0-48 in the first innings they were all out 84. In the second innings, when the going was tougher, they made 205 of which McDonald (89), Burke (33) and Craig (38) made 160. As England had made 459 (Godfrey Evans played one of the most spectacular Test innings in years for 47 in 30 minutes), Australia was never in the winning hunt, but the important point was that the Australians failed by only an hour to make a draw of the game and thus take the decision of the series to The Oval.

Benaud, most rashly, hit out immediately and was caught on the boundary before he had scored in the first innings; Archer was easily stumped, and a few of the others didn't fight on. In every way it was a repetition of what happened to Australia at Old Trafford three years before when Hassett's team had an inglorious second innings of 8-32. In two successive Test innings there Australia had made 116 runs for the loss of 18 wickets!

How does one begin to strike a base for values in this match? It is not easy. McDonald's fighting innings of 89 in the second innings suggests that the task was not beyond the Australians. Also, one must give Laker the highest possible praise—to those who say the pitch was made for him the answer is that it was also made for Lock and the two Australian spinners, Johnson and Benaud, had they been good enough.

But the spinning nature of the pitch was only one side of the argument at Old Trafford. Just as important, and possibly more so from the Australian angle, was the fact that the pitch, as made, *was completely against fast bowling.*

More than two days' play was lost in this game because of the weather. Had it remained fine the match could have been over inside three days. This pitch, for a five-day Test, was a complete disgrace. It was an abject snub from those who prepared it—or suggested its preparation—to the spinning dangers of Benaud and Johnson, although had Australia batted first the story might have been different.

What went wrong with this pitch? Under whose directions was it prepared and why did groundsman Flack say the evening before the Test that it would be fast and was well-grassed? Did the groundsman prepare the pitch himself or was it prepared under instructions?

I saw Ernest Tyldesley, the former English international, on the Saturday of the Test and he looked very upset about matters. He told me that his committee of the Lancashire county club would certainly conduct a full inquiry into the matter but, if that was held, nothing further was ever heard about it—despite the great upset and outcry the pitch caused.

Percy G. H. Fender, the old Surrey and English player, wrote a biting letter on the subject to the London *Daily Telegraph*. It ran:

'As an old cricketer, I find it very irritating to read all this nonsense about the Test wickets at Leeds and Old Trafford. Are we to make our Test wickets to suit the likes and dislikes of the visiting side or should they take things as they come, just as our fellows have to do when they go overseas?

'I remember that when Australia had Gregory and McDonald the wickets "down under" were as hard and as fast as human ingenuity could make them. But when they relied almost exclusively on Grimmett and O'Reilly, those wickets were of a totally different character. England then had no complaint and didn't make one. Nor did the Australian Press on England's behalf.

'Would anyone like to tell me what happened, or could have happened, to the Manchester wicket during the lunch interval on Friday to account for the difference between the play before and after lunch? For that day's cricket, only one of two explanations is possible. Either the England spinners, Lock and Laker, are a lot better than their opposite numbers, Ian Johnson and Benaud, or the last seven England batsmen are better than all the Australian batsmen put together. Take your choice!'

Fender's letter didn't do justice to himself or to cricket history. In the first place, he appears to agree that the pitch was specially prepared but condones it because Australia allegedly did the same thing in other years. He instances Gregory and McDonald, and Grimmett and O'Reilly.

What is the evidence? McDonald played in only three Test games against England in Australia, and if the groundsmen suggested to him that they had prepared wickets for Mc-Donald's own particular use, he should have charged them with false pretences. His meagre six English wickets in Australia were got at the enormous cost of 65 runs apiece!

In that same series, in which Fender played, Gregory took 23 wickets at an average of 24, but Armstrong headed the averages with 15 wickets at 21 and Arthur Mailey took 36 wickets. So, then, the two slow bowlers took the honours on wickets which Fender charged were made for Gregory and McDonald—'as hard and as fast as human ingenuity could make them.' Hobbs averaged 50 in this series and Douglas, Russell, Hearne, Makepeace and Hendren all averaged in the thirties, so that it was neither the Australian fast bowling nor spin bowling that carried the side through to five wins. Rather, the fact was that the English bowlers let their side down.

Then Fender claims that with the advent of O'Reilly and Grimmett our wickets became of a totally different character. The evidence, again, lets him down with a jolt. Strange though it may seem, O'Reilly and Grimmett played in only three Tests together against England in Australia, and

Grimmett's five wickets cost an exorbitant 65 runs apiece. If those pitches were prepared to suit our spinners, it was clearly another case of false pretences because Paynter averaged 61, Hammond 55, Sutcliffe 55, Wyatt 46, Pataudi 40 and Leyland 34. England won four Tests against Australia's one, and Larwood's 33 wickets at 19 read much better than O'Reilly's 27 at 26, splendid though they were for a young bowler in his first series and against a very powerful batting side. In the next series in Australia, in which Grimmett did not play, Voce, another fast bowler, had better figures than O'Reilly.

In 1928-29, Grimmett's only complete series of Tests in Australia, he took 23 wickets at 44—so that Grimmett doesn't have any happy dreams of Australian Test pitches.

As far as I am aware, no official explanation was ever given Australia about the Old Trafford pitch and the point, therefore, is that in future officials of both touring teams will be justified in seeking advance information about the preparation of particular Test pitches. There is no reason at all why the groundsman shouldn't tell Peter May in, say, Melbourne in 1959, how his pitch is progressing, how it is likely to play, and what he aims to do in the week before the Test. And there can be no complaint if a manager suddenly leaves his team on an English tour and drops in some days before a Test at Old Trafford or Leeds just to see how things are going and what type of pitch is being planned and produced.

Finally, I agree wholeheartedly with Douglas Jardine's inference—no committee should presume to tell a groundsman how to prepare a Test pitch.

I don't wish to appear unpleasant about this Old Trafford happening, but there was an atmosphere that few liked. Englishmen, naturally, didn't appreciate the suggestion by

Australians that the pitch underwent a special preparation, yet there was the stark evidence of the two fast, green and unmarled pitches for the matches against Lancashire. As I saw Statham bowl on that latter occasion, it was clear that Statham and Trueman would have made the Australians hop on a typical Old Trafford pitch—as Miller and company would have made England hop even though one admits that this English side was much superior to the Australian.

Because of this happening at Old Trafford and because, also, The Oval pitches have had a dubious post-war record, English officials must not be surprised if Australia queries these grounds for future tours. The Oval is not a popular ground—its Press facilities are thoroughly inadequate for a Test match—and many Australians would prefer London's two Tests to be played at Lord's. Nottingham is now to share a Test with Birmingham on alternate visits and though Birmingham deserves recognition, Australians don't think it should be at the expense of Nottingham, a first-class ground run in a first-class manner.

While on the general subject of pitches, one should mention the policy of covered pitches in England. Before 1956, I warmly agreed with the principle of covering and thought that Australians were at a great disadvantage because we no longer have uncovered pitches in this country. The principle of uncovered pitches is a commendable one. It allows luck, in the form of the weather, to enter into the game but in actual practice I think the uncovered pitches as suggested in England nowadays are quite misleading.

No sooner did the weather bring the element of chance into the Tests at Nottingham and Leeds in 1956, than hoardes of attendants rushed out to the middle with brooms, buckets, blankets, towels and mopping-up machines to remove all traces of the rain. Ian Johnson, who stood to gain an advantage from a rain-affected wicket at Leeds, didn't know quite where he stood when attendants put blankets on the pitch and then rolled and re-rolled them to absorb the moisture. This, done under the direction of the umpires in order to get the ground fit for play again, completely robbed the wicket of any hostility. It remained 'dead' for a long time afterwards.

I am amazed that, with such circumstances in mind, the English authorities should still believe that Tests are played on wickets open to the weather. One night during the Nottingham Test the groundsman drained some 80 gallons of water off the surface of the pitch. Technically, I suppose, he had no right to go near the pitch once play had started and without the umpires in attendance, but his action was commendable in that it allowed play to begin earlier next day than would have otherwise been the case.

As the pitches now have the effect, basically, of being covered after the water is drained or absorbed by the roller into blankets, I think it would be much better if they were covered completely from the weather. The present position causes much annoying delay while the effects of rain are removed. Additionally, there would be much more play if covers were used and removed as soon as the rain stopped. One of the saddest sporting sights in England is to see thousands of people strung around the outside of a Test ground in the forlorn hope that there will be play—as there would often be if covers were used. The wearing of the pitch in itself would help bowlers. As it is, while the roller is used over blankets to mop up water, there is not, in essence, a single uncovered Test pitch in England. A pitch cannot be considered open to the weather if the effects of that weather are quickly removed and in a manner that deadens the pitch.

Soon there will be another series of Tests between England

and Australia. Laker, of course, must be chosen at last for the tour, although he has twice been passed over. After Old Trafford, surely no English selection committee would dare omit him. The Australians are eager to settle their score against him on Australian pitches but, though highly confident, they might not succeed because Laker is a better bowler than Appleyard, whose off-breaks upset the Australians in 1954-55. Lock, the greatest offensive fieldsman I have seen, must make the trip, and so must Trueman for he will like Australian pitches and the Australian barrackers will like him. But I repeat that Laker is a 'must' selection for Australia. No English selection committee, surely, would dare deny the Australians their chance of revenge. Never have I known young batsmen so avid as the Australians to tilt again with an executioner. They base their confidence on the assumption that it wasn't Laker who slew them so much as the pitches on which he bowled. They could be very, very wrong, of course.

I do hope that Peter May throws off the restraining shackles of captaincy he learnt under Hutton. He is young enough to do it. Sir Leonard had to fight his way to the top in the intense thirties when competition and life were vastly different and so his outlook can be understood. But May is a Cambridge product of a post-war generation, a generation which has found life much easier. A captain can play the game hard without being relentless, although I readily admit Australia has had its share of characters in the latter category.

If the modern spirit of conceding nothing—so evident in the English—South African Tests of 1956-57 and manifested again by South Africa with disastrous results against Australia in 1957-58—is the spirit in which the 1958-59 Tests are to be played in Australia, then the game will decline again in public favour. Australia could be on the verge of a renais-

sance in cricket interest but, given the tight grip upon
overs an hour, dawdling in the field and too much of 'Slasher'
Mackay and 'Slogger' Bailey, people will stay away from the
matches. The 'Slasher' and the 'Slogger' have received some
odd adulation from critics of their respective countries for
batting behaviour that has sometimes savoured of cricket
sadism. In Durban's Third Test of 1956-57, for instance,
Bailey played nine successive overs from Tayfield, pushing
forward regardless of the length of the ball. Yet, in a Brisbane
Test two years before, Bailey promptly landed one over the
fence the morning after an Englishman said he would give
cash prizes for sixes!

Louis Duffus, who played cricket of a good standard and
sees the game through a pair of capable, critical South African
eyes, had this to say in the Johannesburg *Star* of the Fourth
Test in his country against the Australians of 1957-58:
'By their own modern standards South Africa accomplished
a feat of distinction at the Wanderers yesterday when they
reached 126 for two after five and a half hours. If the match is
saved the end will no doubt justify the means. Yet admiration
for the will-power, concentration and stamina of McGlew,
Endean and Funston was tempered by the horrible thought
that one day a Test innings will be played with no score at all.
In a situation where making runs was as beneficial as con-
suming time there was a suggestion that the inevitable wear
of the pitch was placing South Africa in the position of a
pole-sitter unaware that termites were eating away the base of
his pole.'

This was the Test in which the attendance, over the
corresponding match against the Englishmen the preceding
summer, was cut by half. It followed the 'Dirge of Durban,'
in which McGlew took nine hours five minutes to make a
century and in which the Springboks whittled away their

chances by deplorable tactics. Many people who watched that Test vowed they would never watch another.

Who is responsible for such tactics? Roy McLean, perhaps the most gifted of modern South African batsmen, but who was dropped after the Fourth Test, suggests clearly in his book *Sackcloth without Ashes*, that it wasn't the captain, van Ryneveld, nor the selectors, Nourse, Melville and Ralph.

'Nine times out of ten,' McLean writes of the Cape Town Test, 'I would have moved down the wicket a pace to drive Kline over mid-off's head . . . but here we were, fairly mature players, being told by some influential men in cricket (not the selectors) how to combat the Australian bowlers . . . We tried to argue that to stay in the crease was tantamount to committing suicide, but all to no avail. We were under the whip properly, but the outside world knew nothing of the inward struggle. We pushed and prodded and cut a pretty sorry spectacle. How the Australian spin bowlers must have laughed at the unexpected gift wickets with which they were presented!'

McLean, brilliant batsman that he is, when in full flow, made only 110 runs in seven innings. But he had already played in 20 Tests before this series and should have blocked his ears to anything he was told by the 'professors' in the dressing-room or anywhere else. He had the experience to play his own game and should have had the confidence to stand or fall on his own interpretation and his ability to execute it.

Taking us so far, McLean should have taken us the whole journey. If neither the captain nor the selectors ordered those 'stand-fast' tactics, who did? Was it Ken Viljoen, the former Springbok, who acted as manager of the South African Test team? Was it the home Press critics? Or was it 'back-room boys,' the out-of-sight individuals now common in many walks of life—politics, international affairs, business, sport—who plan the campaign for the actual combatants? They hear all, see all, know all, and are not content until they press their all upon the men who have to do the job.

I believe the back-room boys do exist in modern Test cricket: it is one of the chief reasons why I do not favour young Test captains. An immature player must depend upon outsiders for advice. He has not the necessary background himself, nor has he the inclination—he probably wouldn't last long in his job if he had—to say to well-meaning intruders, 'Thank you very much, but I am the captain of this side in all ways. There's the door.'

There would have been no future for the back-room boys with Jardine, Collins, Woodfull, Bradman, Allen, Vic Richardson, Keith Miller or F. S. Jackson as captain. Nor, in the case of my old club captain, Sammy Carter. They would not have been allowed into the dressing-room, for a beginning, and I am sure Test cricket has become involved mainly because players are loaded down with theories and advice before a match begins.

Clearly enough, once the team is chosen and the captain selected they should be left alone to get on with the job.

There are several other aspects of overseas tours that should be touched upon. In the first place, the tours are now far too long—taxing the home-life of a player and taxing his love of the game. Such experiences become boring, and especially when the captain sets the Tests as his principal objective. Johnson did this in England in 1956, saying that county games were merely subordinate to the Tests—a statement made when he was strongly criticised for batting on and on to make 6-694 against Leicestershire's 298.

Before the last M.C.C. tour of South Africa, Peter May announced publicly that he would play every match to win.

But the bottom soon fell out of the non-Test encounters, and the same has been the case in recent M.C.C. tours of Australia. Hutton's team, although it won the Test series 3-1, with the last Test heavily in its favour, played eight matches against the Sheffield Shield States in 1954-55, winning three, losing one and drawing four.

That record would not have won the Sheffield Shield for England had it been playing in the competition of that year. Nor would Johnson's Australian team of 1956 have won the county championship. On figures, indeed, it would have finished equal fourth with Hampshire, a sad reflection upon a team that went away with its captain proclaiming, 'The job is ahead and for the first time in 20 years we are going to England on the attack. Our batsmen have found and perfected a new technique.'

Both Bradman's team of 1948 and Hassett's of 1953 would have won the English county championship by a wide margin on their results against the counties, and one wonders why the M.C.C. team and the Australian team should not be invited as guests to play in their host's competition.

The present attitude by touring teams towards matches other than Tests is largely one of indifference. The first essential is to provide against defeat, and in many instances no attempt at all is made to push for a win. Far too many of these contests drag on into dull draws. I think a team's reputation should be at stake in all first-class matches on tour, and a competitive flavour would give a touring team the urge to plan and play for victory from the beginning.

Whatever may be wrong with cricket, it is not with the game itself but rather in its interpretation by individuals. Most first-class players are now highly proficient in their knowledge of the game's technicalities. They know all about the game even if they can't execute their thoughts. A delightful element went out of the game when the 'Rabbits' began to take their block with the care of an opening batsman. Much preferable were those who began to hit from the shoulders at the very first ball—Jim Smith, of Middlesex, big, hale and hearty; Arthur Wellard, of Somerset, a gloriously free hitter; Bill O'Reilly, of New South Wales, his ambition to soar one as quickly as possible high over the fence at long-on. These, of course, were definitely not 'Rabbits' but the lower batsmen would do well to copy them.

The last time I saw Eric Hollies bat at Birmingham he was clapped and cheered all the way to the middle at No. 11. Everybody knew there would be no pretty passes at the ball and deft deflections from Eric. They knew that if he could only survive two balls they would see something in batting unknown to any text book. But most No. 11's in first-class cricket nowadays seem anxious to impress that they know the batting technique as well as their No. 1's.

However, I don't want to end this book on the note of Test or first-class cricket. Both could die but cricket would still live because there is no other game like it. An American, Gilbert Highet, wrote of it: 'In the summer comes cricket, which is like baseball, played by men who are either very polite or very ill, and sometimes both; but at its best it is supremely decorative, one of the prettiest of games, combining the charm of a ballet with that of a Wedgwood vase.'

Recently, in Canberra, I met two knights whose eyes lit up as they talked of cricket. One was Sir Hudson Fysh, an air pioneer and chairman of Qantas airlines, who was in his sixties and a few days before had made a cricket comeback with a score of 19. It gave him warm pleasure to know that he could still middle the ball with his bat. Another was Sir Keith Hancock, formerly Professor of Economic History at Oxford and now attached to the Australian National

University. He was slightly apprehensive as his match had yet to come, but there was no doubt as to his love of the game.

I think, too, of my friend Paul Estripeaut, the Frenchman who played cricket, with great vigour and many ejaculations, for Waverley during many years. He was a slow bowler, one who had twirled his wares up at the Sydney Cricket Ground nets against Hobbs, Hendren, Hammond and many other famous batsmen, and one day had knocked back the middle stump of H. L. Collins. Paul had to battle for a long time before he was chosen in a Waverley side, and then (shades of Napoleon!) he was chosen to play at Waterloo Oval! Paul loved cricket, and in clearings in little woods in France now some Frenchmen go off every Sunday to play cricket with exiled Englishmen.

I have seen the Dutch play cricket in Holland, and most enthusiastic and gifted they are too; and there is surely a place for the game in that country of heart-attacks, the United States, for no other game knows the leisurely calm, the peace, the mental relaxation and companionship provided by this game of bat and ball and green grass. The Americans, too, often need something to cool them down.

At the hundredth anniversary dinner of the New South Wales Cricket Association, the Prime Minister, Mr. Menzies, said it was a pity that Russia and the United States didn't play cricket. If they did, he said, there would be no need for Summit talks. Setting aside the fact that 'Summit talks' have sometimes been necessary in cricket, the satisfying thought is that cricket, basically, is good and wholesome. There is no substitute for it. It brings the middle-aged out into the sun, the fresh air, the odour of newly-cut grass; and he can set his own gait, standing his ground and looking inquiringly at his neighbour as the ball goes on its way to the outfield.

And then there is the deep thrill of it when the ball is met sweetly in the middle of the bat. 'Yes, there's two in it. No, only a single. Wait. Go back. Oh, I *am* sorry.'

I think again of my last game in England. It wasn't a Test, nor a county game, but a game of odd bodies—most down from London for the day and one or two home from Singapore, Uganda and America—against Lancing School, high up on a lovely stretch of open ground, a beautiful chapel nearby, and a view that spread for miles across the Sussex Downs—the greenest of trees and fields with the sun caressingly warm in a blue sky. Far up planes droned like overladen bees. The pitch was true, the bowling friendly. And, afterwards, Incog., Arabs, Foresters and the like were all talking at once behind pints of mild in the local.

Great times—great anecdotes—great chaps—a Great Game!

THE PAVILION LIBRARY